Searching CD-ROM and Online Information Sources

G G Chowdhury
Department of Information Science, University of Strathclyde

Sudatta Chowdhury
*formerly Division of Information Studies, School of Applied Science,
Nanyang Technological University, Singapore*

LIBRARY ASSOCIATION PUBLISHING
LONDON

© G G Chowdhury and Sudatta Chowdhury 2001

Published by
Library Association Publishing
7 Ridgmount Street
London WC1E 7AE

Library Association Publishing is wholly owned by The Library Association.

First published 2001

British Library Cataloguing in Publication Data

A catalogue record for this book is available from the British Library.

ISBN 1-85604-388-6

Typeset from author's disk in 11/14pt Garamond and Humanist 521 by Library Association Publishing.
Printed and made in Great Britain by MPG Books Ltd, Bodmin, Cornwall.

Searching CD-ROM and
Online Information Sources

To our parents

Contents

Acknowledgments

Chapter 3

Figs. 3.2 and 3.3: Reprinted with the kind permission of the Library of Congress

Chapter 5

Fig. 5.1: Reprinted with the kind permission of the University of California

Fig. 5.2: Reprinted with the kind permission of the University of Sheffield Library

Fig. 5.3: Reprinted with the kind permission of the University of Glasgow Library

Fig. 5.4: Reprinted with the kind permission of the University of Pittsburgh Library

Fig. 5.5: Reprinted with the kind permission of the City University of Hong Kong Library

Fig. 5.6: Reprinted with the kind permission of the University of Toronto Library

Fig. 5.7: Reprinted with the kind permission of the National Library Board, Singapore

Fig. 5.8: Reprinted with the kind permission of the Nanyang Technological University Library

Fig. 5.9: reprinted with the kind permission of the Library of Congress

Fig. 5.10: Reprinted with the kind permission of the British Library

Chapter 6

Figs. 6.1, 6.2, 6.3, 6.6, and 6.7: Reprinted with the kind permission of R R Bowker, a Division of Reed Elsevier Inc (Copyright 2000, Reed Elsevier Inc. No copyright is claimed as to any part of the original work prepared by a government officer or employee as part of that person's official duties.)

Figs. 6.4, 6.5, and 6.14: Reprinted with the kind permission of the Dialog Corporation

Figs. 6.8, 6.9, 6.10: Reprinted with the kind permission of Waterlow Specialist Information Publishing

Figs. 6.11, 6.12 and 6.13: Reprinted with the kind permission of Bowker-Saur

Fig. 6.15: Reprinted with the kind permission of SilverPlatter Information

Fig. 6.16 and 6.17: Reprinted with the kind permission of MCB University Press

Figs. 6.18 to 6.26: Reprinted with the kind permission of the Microsoft Corporation

Figs. 6.27 to 6.31: Reprinted with the kind permission of Britannica.com Inc.

Chapter 7

Figs. 7.1 to 7.10 and 7.25: Reprinted with the kind permission of the Dialog Corporation

Figs. 7.11 to 7.16: Reprinted with the kind permission of OCLC Online Computer Library Center Inc

Figs. 7.17 to 7.19: Reprinted with the kind permission of CAS, a division of the American Chemical Society

Figs. 7.20 to 7.22: Reprinted with the kind permission of Ovid Technologies Inc

Figs. 7.23 and 7.24: Reprinted with the kind permission of LEXIS-NEXIS. (Copyright 2000, LEXIS-NEXIS, a division of Reed Elsevier Inc. All rights reserved)

Chapter 8

Figs. 8.1 and 8.2: Reprinted with the kind permission of Elsevier Engineering Information, Inc

Figs. 8.3 and 8.4: Reprinted with the kind permission of Ovid Technologies Inc

Figs. 8.5 and 8.6: Reprinted with the kind permission of OCLC Online Computer Library Center Inc

Figs. 8.7 and 8.8: Reprinted with the kind permission of the Dialog Corporation

Chapter 9

Figs. 9.1 to 9.3: Reprinted with the kind permission of SilverPlatter Information

Figs. 9.4, 9.10 and 9.11: Reprinted with the kind permission of Ovid Technologies Inc

Figs. 9.5, 9.6, 9.12 and 9.13: Reprinted with the kind permission of the Dialog Corporation

Figs. 9.7 to 9.9: Reprinted with the kind permission of the ERIC Clearinghouse on Assessment and Evaluation

Chapter 10

Figs. 10.1 to 10.6: Reprinted with the kind permission of Bell & Howell Information and Learning Company

Figs. 10.7 to 10.9: Reprinted with the kind permission of Factiva, a Dow Jones and Reuters Company

Figs. 10.10 to 10.12: Reprinted with the kind permission of LEXIS-NEXIS. (Copyright 2000, LEXIS-NEXIS, a division of Reed Elsevier Inc. All rights reserved)

Figs. 10.13 to 10.16: Reprinted with the kind permission of Euromonitor International

Chapter 11

Figs. 11.1 to 11.4: Reprinted with the kind permission of LEXIS-NEXIS. (Copyright 2000, LEXIS-NEXIS, a division of Reed Elsevier Inc. All rights reserved)

Figs. 11.5 to 11.9: Reprinted with the kind permission of the Dialog Corporation

Chapter 12

Figs. 12.1 to 12.4: Reprinted with the kind permission of the National Library of Medicine

Figs. 12.5 to 12.7: Reprinted with the kind permission of the Dialog Corporation

Figs. 12.8 to 12.11: Reprinted with the kind permision of Ingenta (**www.ingenta.com**)

Figs. 12.12 to 12.16: Reprinted with the kind permission of OCLC Online Computer Library Center Inc

Chapter 13

Figs. 13.1 to 13.4: Reprinted with the kind permission of ISO

Figs. 13.5 to 13.8: Reprinted with the kind permission of BSI under licence number 2000SK/0375

Figs. 13.9 to 13.11: Reprinted with the kind permission of Delphion Inc.

Fig. 13.12: Reprinted with the kind permission of the European Patent Office

Chapter 14

Figs. 14.1 to 14.3: Reprinted with the kind permission of the US Government Printing Office

Figs. 14.4 to 14.5: Crown Copyright

Fig. 14.6: Reprinted with the kind permission of the Stationery Office Limited

Figs. 14.7 to 14.10: Reprinted with the kind permission of Bell & Howell Information and Learning Company

Figs. 14.11 to 14.14: Reprinted with the kind permission of Lonely Planet Publications

Preface

Why this book?

Experience of teaching courses on or related to 'information sources and searching' in library and information science programmes in different parts of the world over the past few years shows that although there are a number of good books on reference sources and services, they do not have good coverage of electronic information sources and searching. Over the years most information sources have appeared in electronic form: on remote online databases that are accessible through online search service providers like Dialog, Ovid, etc; on CD-ROM; and of late on the world wide web. Students and practitioners today need to learn about these electronic sources, as well as the corresponding search and retrieval techniques. There is therefore a need for a book that covers all the different aspects of searching and retrieval of information from various types of electronic information sources, ranging from CD-ROM databases to online information sources, that are accessible through online search service providers and/or through the world wide web.

The audience and the approach

The primary objective of writing this book is to help students of library and information science throughout the world use the wide variety of electronic information sources that are available today. The book will be useful for all students and teachers taking or teaching courses on reference and information sources and services, information retrieval, etc. An effort has been made to cover as many different electronic information sources as possible. The book will also be useful to practitioners wishing to become acquainted with the techniques of searching various electronic information sources.

It may be too ambitious a task to write a book that covers exhaustively all the different varieties of information sources available on all the different disciplines appearing in every possible electronic format. Keeping this, as well as the practical need for such a book, in view, we have tried to cover in this book some general as well as some subject-specific CD-ROM and online information sources.

The book begins by discussing the basics of information services, information searching, the various search aids, and so on. Against this background, we have discussed the basics of CD-ROM and online information searching with appropriate illustrations.

Traditionally, online information searching meant the searching of remote databases through online search service providers or vendors. Nowadays, with the advent and proliferation of the Internet and world wide web, this connotation of online searching has changed. By 'online searching' many people today mean searching for information on the Internet. However, in this book we have also discussed online information searching from the traditional point of view. It is true that most online search services are now accessible through the web, and indeed we have discussed the web versions of various online search services because users mostly need to access the online search services through their web interfaces. However, the search and retrieval features of these systems are different from the tools used for searching information on the WWW, namely search engines, subject directories, virtual libraries, etc. We shall discuss this issue, along with the various information services available on the WWW, in a companion volume.

In this current book we discuss the web versions of various online search services and specific information sources. However, in all the chosen cases the web is used only for accessing the resources and services concerned: each service and/or information product has its own search and retrieval characteristics that are different from typical tools used for searching the web, namely search engines, subject directories, etc.

While the first part of the book discusses the basics of information searching using OPACs, CD-ROMs and online search services, the second part briefly describes the search features of selected subject-specific electronic information sources. To facilitate our discussion, as well as to keep it brief, we have used screen shots of various CD-ROM and online information sources. One may argue that the search interfaces of information sources change from time to time and therefore screen shots may easily become dated. Well, nothing is absolutely static in this electronic information age, as indeed we have noticed during the writing of this book. We have used screen-shots to illustrate the features and techniques of the searching methods of our chosen electronic information sources. We believe that the combination of discussion and illustration offered will help readers to learn some basic techniques that they can use to search information sources, even when the search interface of a specific product is modified or upgraded.

The content

The book opens with an introduction to basic information skills, and the information problem-solving process. It then goes on to discuss the various types of information sources that a user might need to search in order to find a required piece of information. It briefly discusses the different types of information services, viz, information and reference services, current awareness services, and so on, and then highlights some basic tools that can be used to conduct an effective search in a given subject area. The book also briefly discusses the nature and characteristics of various types of reference sources, and gives examples of a range of reference sources available online and on CD-ROM. It goes on to describe, with ample real-life examples, the information retrieval features of OPACs, CD-ROM databases and online search services. In each case, a number of examples and screen-shots have been used to illustrate the discussion. The book also describes the nature and characteristics of selected CD-ROM and online information sources in specific subject fields, viz, science and technology, social sciences and humanities, business, law, medicine, etc. In each case, a number of examples are offered to illustrate the features of the information sources concerned. The book ends with a discussion on trends in the field, followed by appendices listing selected CD-ROM and online information sources on a range of subjects.

Acknowledgments

First of all we would like to express our sincere thanks to all the publishers who have given us permission to use their information products as examples in this book. Descriptions of products often include the words of their suppliers, which are reprinted with our thanks. We would like to thank the people at Library Association Publishing, London, especially Helen, Lin, Beth, Kathryn and June, without whose constant support and help this book would not have seen the light of day.

Thanks are due to Sudatta's mother, who for months took charge of our home, thus freeing us from mundane household tasks, and giving us more time to concentrate on this book. Thanks to our parents and to other relatives, who always encouraged us to accomplish the task. Finally, we would like to thank our two charming sons, Avirup and Anubhav, who have always been our source of inspiration. Despite the fact that we stole time due to them to work on the book, they have never been less than considerate and loving.

G G Chowdhury and Sudatta Chowdhury

Chapter 1
Basic information skills

Introduction

Information, simply speaking, is what we need to know, when we need to know it. It may be just a straightforward answer to a simple question, such as the following:

- what is the capital of France?
- who is currently the President of South Africa?
- what is the chemical formula of benzene?
- what is the venue for the next Olympic Games?, and so on.

Some questions are more complex:

- what causes an earthquake?
- what caused the Second World War?
- how do the web search engines work?
- what is the impact of the web on online information retrieval?, and so on.

While answers to the first set of questions may be found readily in a particular information source, those for the second set may be hidden in a wide range of sources. Now, the question is 'why do we need information?' A simple answer to this would be 'in order to learn, or to solve problems'. Thus, whenever we need to know or learn something, or we want to solve a problem, we need the appropriate information. The next question is: 'how do we know where the information that we need at a given instance is available, and once we can locate it, how can we make the best use of it?' The simple answer is that we need to acquire what are known as information skills, or information literacy/information literacy skills.

Traditionally libraries have played a significant role in helping users find the required information. However, with the introduction of online search services in the 1970s, and more so with the introduction of CD-ROM databases in the 1980s, information searching could be carried out by end-users rather than intermediaries. With the more recent advent of the Internet and world wide web, information sources in digital form are becoming more common, and in many cases people do not need to go to a library to access different types of information sources. There is now an obvious debate on whether we need librarians in a digital library environment, and what will be the nature of reference and information services in such libraries. The need for human-mediated information services is justified by the simple frustration of a user who gets a huge, mostly irrelevant, quantity of information – sometimes millions of 'hits' – in response to a search on the web. However, such mediation need not be a face-to-face communication. Instead, the intermediaries may act from behind the scene by collecting and organizing information sources for target users and adding value to them, as is currently done through many virtual libraries and gateways (see p. 230). Several researchers have discussed the changing role of information professionals in the digital library environment (see, for example, Sutton, 1996; Davenport et al, 1997; Ferguson and Bunge, 1997; Matson and Bonski, 1997; Steele, 1997; Walton and Edwards, 1997; Cronin, 1998; Heckert, 1998; Hutingford, 1998; Tennat, 1998 and Griffin, 1999). These issues, particularly the changing nature of reference and information services in the digital library environment, are discussed in Chapter 15.

Whether it is done by end-users or by intermediaries, the job of information searching is becoming more and more complex. There are several reasons for this, the primary ones being the fast growth of electronic information resources in terms of volume, forms and formats, and also the fast development of the technology governing the information retrieval process. These changes are forcing the information searchers – end-users as well as information professionals as intermediaries – to acquire appropriate information literacy skills. Acquiring such skills will enable information professionals, as well as end-users, to identify and retrieve information from the most appropriate sources in the most appropriate form. As we shall see later in this chapter, and also throughout the book, the two major challenges in the digital information environment are: (1) to select the most appropriate source(s) of information pertaining to a query, and (2) to search and retrieve information from the chosen source(s).

Information literacy

There are several publications that describe information literacy and its various components in detail (see, for example, Marland, 1981; American Library Association, 1989; Eisenberg and Berkowitz, 1990; California Media, 1994; Booker,

1995; Rader, 1995; Bruce, 1997 and Spitzer et al, 1998). A detailed discussion on information literacy is beyond the scope of this book. However, before proceeding, we do need to be aware of the basics of information literacy and of the 'big six' information skills, as proposed by Eisenberg and Berkowitz (1990).

Simply defined, information literacy is the ability to access, evaluate and use information from a variety of sources. An information-literate person is expected to have acquired the necessary skills to retrieve information from a variety of sources, print as well as electronic, to meet his or her information needs at any given point of time. Thus, an information-literate person is able to make informed decisions and solve problems correctly and confidently. The American Library Association Presidential Committee on Information Literacy (1989) recommended that 'to be information literate, a person must be able to recognize when information is needed and have the ability to locate, evaluate and use effectively the needed information'. The report adds that

> ultimately information literate people are those who have learned how to learn. They know how to learn because they know how information is organized, how to find information, and how to use information in such a way that others can learn from them. They are people prepared for life-long learning, because they can always find the information needed for any task or decision at hand.

Information literacy helps us in a number of ways, for example:

- to recognize the need for information and define the information needed for problem-solving and decision-making
- to identify potential sources of information in printed and electronic formats
- to apply appropriate search strategies to retrieve information using the available technologies and tools
- to review, select, interpret and evaluate relevant information critically and to make meaning of this information
- to organize and present information effectively and creatively
- to appraise the process and product of an information search
- to develop a habit of reading for information and for pleasure
- to continually improve and update knowledge
- to demonstrate initiative in information problem-solving and openness to learning
- to collaborate with others for information problem-solving.

In summary, information literacy equips individuals to take advantage of the opportunities inherent in the modern information society.

The 'Big Six' information skills

The 'Big Six Skills' perspective, proposed by Eisenberg and Berkowitz (1990), represents a general approach to information problem-solving consisting of six logical steps or stages. Figure 1.1 shows a simple representation of the major steps in an information problem-solving process, called the big six skills. These steps, although interrelated, do not take place exactly in the same sequence; some of them may take place simultaneously. There are other approaches to information skills too that help in solving information-related problems. For example, Marland's taxonomy (1981) is based on a series of questions. Bruce (1997) presents Marland's questions as follows:

- What do I need to do?
- Where could I go?
- How do I get to the information?
- Which sources shall I use?
- How shall I use the resources?
- What should I make a record of?
- Have I got the information I need?
- How should I present it?
- What have I achieved?

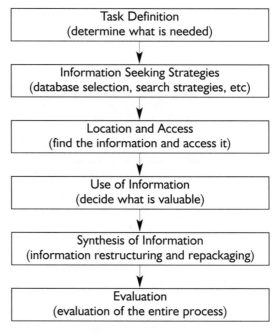

Fig. 1.1 *Six major steps in information problem-solving*

However, in this book we shall limit our discussions to the 'big six' of Eisenberg and Berkowitz (1990), because:

- these skills offer a systematic approach to information problem-solving. It is appropriate and useful to initiate the six logical steps whenever an individual has an information-oriented problem;
- six broad skill areas are necessary for successful information problem-solving. Users need to develop a range of competencies within each skill area.

Task definition

Information problem-solving begins with a clear understanding of the problem at hand from an information point of view. Task definition includes stating the parameters of the problem from an information needs perspective (Eisenberg and Berkowitz, 1990). The various activities involved at the task definition stage are shown in Figure 1.2. These activities are not sequential, and may take place simultaneously. An information professional who is going to conduct an information search for an end-user has to ask the type of questions shown in the figure in order to ascertain the exact information need and to translate that into the appropriate search statement(s). End-users should ask themselves these questions in order to become quite clear about what is required, and to put this down in the form of search statement(s).

Information seeking strategies

Once the problem is clearly articulated, the next step is to look for the possible

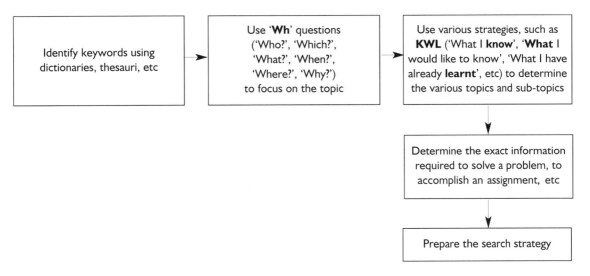

Fig. 1.2 *Processes involved in task definition*

information sources that are available to solve the defined task. This step involves making decisions with regard to the range of information sources that are appropriate to meet that task.

Information sources can be categorized into three major groups: documentary sources (print as well as non-print and electronic media), institutional sources (such as institutions' home pages or special databases – for example, facilities, doctors, treatments, etc, available in a hospital, and so on) and human sources (human experts). In most cases there is not just one right source of information to answer a specific query; instead, there are likely to be a number of possible alternative sources and approaches that can successfully lead to a resolution of the problem. Therefore, one has to find out the best possible strategy at a given instance. Processes involved at this stage are shown in Figure 1.3.

Location and access

This step involves the implementation of the search strategy. After deciding the possible sources, users should use the search strategy to retrieve the required information. It may be noted that different information sources – books, databases, CD-ROMs, online public access catalogues (OPACs), or other online sources – have different ways of organizing information, and consequently one has to follow the appropriate access and retrieval mechanisms.

The output of an information search session may be the bibliographic details of some books (as in the case of an OPAC search), bibliographic details along with abstracts or full texts of journal articles (as in the case of a CD-ROM or online, such as Dialog, database search), or hypermedia documents (containing text, image and sound) on the world wide web. Thus, in some cases, after locating one or more required information sources, one needs to physically access them to get the required information. In electronic information systems – OPACs, CD-ROMs and online databases – some tools are available, such as the Library of Congress Subject Headings (LCSH) List, thesauri, and so on, that can be used to conduct appropriate searches.

The steps involved at the stage of location and access are shown in Figure 1.4. This is sometimes a long and complex process, depending on the information required and the system chosen. One needs to have appropriate training and/or

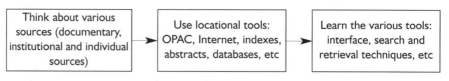

Fig. 1.3 *Processes involved in information seeking strategies*

special software or hardware, and some practice to get the best results. Users should be trained to conduct searches on different types of OPACs, CD-ROM sources, and various other information sources available through online search services, such as Dialog, and the world wide web. Users also need to be familiarized with various information sources, their content, organization, search and retrieval features, and so on.

Use of information

After locating the appropriate information, users need to make use of it. Information may be available in a variety of different forms and formats, and one needs to learn how to use these. For example, some information may be in textual form, some in numerical or tabular form, some in graphical or image form, some in audio or video, and so on. There are also some materials that need some special training to use, for example maps, databases, multimedia information comprising digital audio and video, and so on. Users, at different levels, need to acquire the necessary skills so that they can make appropriate use of all kinds of information.

Synthesis of information

Synthesis in this context is the application of all the retrieved information to the defined task. It may involve the restructuring or repackaging of the retrieved information into new or different formats to meet the requirements of the task defined. For simple tasks – for example, finding out the capital of a country or the date of birth or address of a person – synthesis is just a matter of communi-

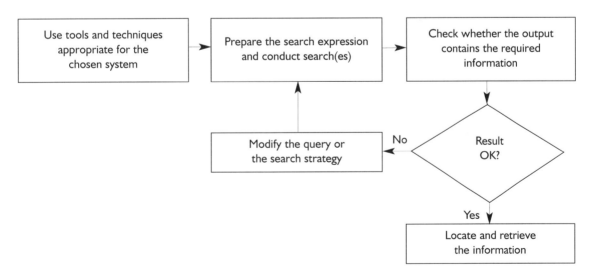

Fig. 1.4   *Processes involved in location and access*

cating or using the information in an appropriate manner. For complex tasks – for example, preparing a report of a project or writing the state-of-the-art report on a research topic – information may have to be collected from a number of different sources, presented in different formats, and therefore synthesis is a major undertaking that usually involves a number of activities. Two categories of activities may be identified: interpreting and evaluating the information, and organizing and presenting the information. However, each set involves a number of processes, as shown in Figure 1.5. These activities are very important because the same information may be available from more than one source, and these may differ in terms of content, currency, form of presentation, and so on.

Evaluation

Evaluation involves the examination of the product of the information search process, as well as the information problem-solving process, in order to know how effectively and efficiently the task was carried out. The following questions may be asked at this stage:

- was the information problem solved?
- was the need met?

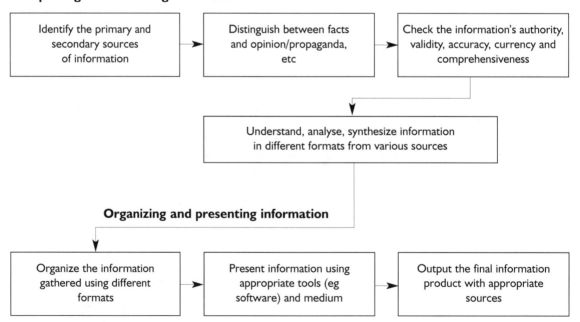

Interpreting and evaluating information

| Identify the primary and secondary sources of information | Distinguish between facts and opinion/propaganda, etc | Check the information's authority, validity, accuracy, currency and comprehensiveness |

Understand, analyse, synthesize information in different formats from various sources

Organizing and presenting information

| Organize the information gathered using different formats | Present information using appropriate tools (eg software) and medium | Output the final information product with appropriate sources |

Fig. 1.5 *Processes involved in synthesis*

- could a decision be made based on the information sought?
- was the situation resolved?
- does the product satisfy the requirements as originally defined?, and so on.

Thus, evaluation also involves an assessment of the efficiency of the entire information problem-solving process.

Recorded information sources

Information sources can be categorized in a number of ways. One simple approach may be to categorize them as natural sources and man- or machine-made sources of information. The former include any kind of information generated by nature, such as the solar system, the oceans, mountains and forests, that is captured and recorded by humans. With the progress of human civilization we have captured a lot of information from natural sources, and have recorded it using appropriate media. Side-by-side human beings and machines have also generated a lot of information that has also been recorded.

Recorded information sources have largely been printed documents – books, monographs, theses, reports, articles, and so on. Even before the invention of printing we had recorded information sources: drawings, paintings, and writings on a variety of media ranging from stone to clay tablets, parchment, cloth, leaves, and paper. Nowadays we have information sources recorded on electronic media ranging from local or home-grown databases to remote (online) databases, CD-ROM databases and, more recently, the Internet and world wide web.

These information sources can be used for a variety of information requirements, from finding an address or telephone number to tracking down an elusive bibliographic citation to identifying and delivering information about a specific research topic. Let's consider the following questions:

1 When was Mr Suharto first sworn in as the President of Indonesia?
2 How many times has Monica Seles won the grand slam?
3 I want to go for a PhD in business management in the US. Where, when and how can I apply?
4 When was the Mir space station first launched, and what has happened since then?
5 What has been the impact of the web on the reading habits of secondary-school children?
6 What will be the impact of digital libraries on commercial publishers?

A closer look at these questions shows that some may have pretty straightforward answers, while others may need detailed study of a number of information sources. Indeed, the first three questions can be answered relatively easily from certain types of sources, while a detailed literature search may be required to get satisfactory answers to the last three.

Information sources can be categorized in a number of ways, in terms of their physical forms, content, and so on. Figure 1.6 shows illustrative examples of various categories of reference and information sources, ranging from natural sources to museum objects, printed sources, analog and digital sources. Printed information sources have been the major type of information sources for centuries; analog and digital information sources are of more recent origin. Electronic information sources are growing at a very rapid rate, and many reference sources are now available in electronic formats. Examples of these – on CD-ROM as well as online – appear in the various chapters of this book.

The first of the electronic information sources to appear was the online database. Online search services appeared in the late sixties and early seventies (Chowdhury, 1999b; Rowley, 1999). Online databases are accessible from remote locations and are usually available through commercial search-service providers or vendors, such as the Dialog Corporation. The appearance of online databases and search services brought about significant improvements in searching because they allowed users from all over the information world to access remote databases, no matter where they are located, through computer and communication facilities. Online search services in the early seventies were relatively expensive but as time passed by, and many search service providers appeared, they became cheaper and formed a significant part of the information industry (Chowdhury, 1999b).

Another major change in electronic information sources took place in the mid-1980s with the appearance of CD-ROM technology. Since then CD-ROM databases containing various types of information – bibliographic and full-text databases, numeric databases, and of late multimedia databases – have become very popular and highly used sources of information. CD-ROM and online databases remained side by side for about a decade, and then came the Internet followed by the world wide web giving online access to millions of electronic information sources. The web, containing a vast wealth of multimedia information from around the world, is now the most highly used medium for access to electronic information sources.

From the point of view of usage or reading, information sources can be divided into two major groups. One includes materials for continuous reading, such as books, journals, reports, conference proceedings, etc. The other group of sources is not meant for continuous reading (though this can be done if

Information sources: types
Natural sources
　　solar system, oceans, rivers, mountains, forests, etc.
Museum objects, relics, etc.
Information sources created before the beginning of the printing era
　　writings, pictures, etc, on stones, clay tablets, parchment, cloth, paper, etc.
Printed sources
　　books, monographs, theses, conference/seminar/workshop/project reports, etc,
　　periodicals, reference sources
Microforms
　　microfilms, microfiches
Analog storage devices
　　audio and video cassettes
Digital sources
　　online sources: Internet and world wide web sources
　　online databases: abstracts and full-text databases available through search services
　　like Dialog, STN, OCLC FirstSearch, etc.
　　CD-ROM databases: LISA, INSPEC, Ei Compendex
Institutional sources
Human sources

Reference sources: types
Dictionaries
　　Oxford English dictionary, New IEEE standard dictionary of electrical and electronic terms,
　　etc.
Encyclopedias
　　Encyclopaedia Britannica, McGraw-Hill encyclopedia of science and technology, McGraw-Hill encyclopedia of electronics and computers, etc.
Almanacs, yearbooks, handbooks and directories
　　The world almanac and book of facts, Information please almanac, etc.
　　Britannica book of the year, Statesman's yearbook, Europa yearbook, etc.
　　CRC handbook of physics and chemistry, Computer engineering handbook, etc.
　　Organizations master index, The world of learning, Commonwealth universities yearbook,
　　etc.
Bibliographical sources
　　Books in print, British national bibliography, Ulrich's international periodicals directory, etc.
Indexes and abstracts
　　Library literature, LISA, INSPEC, ERIC, etc.
Biographical sources
　　Who's who, The international who's who, ASEAN who's who, American men and women of science, etc.
Geographical sources
　　Maps and atlases: eg *The Times atlas of the world, Historical atlas of the United States*
　　Gazetteers: eg *Columbia-Lippincott gazetteer of the world, The national gazetteer of the United States of America*
　　Travel guides: eg the Fodor series, the Lonely Planet series
Government, international and regional information sources
　　United States government manual, Singapore trade connection, United Nations statistical yearbook, etc.

Fig. 1.6　*Reference and information source types*

desired): such information sources are consulted in order to find information on a specific topic to answer a particular question, and they are categorized as reference sources.

Reference sources

According to the ALA glossary of library terms (Heartsill, 1983) a reference book is:

- a book designed by the arrangement and treatment of its subject matter to be consulted for definite items of information rather than to be read consecutively
- a book whose use is restricted to the library building.

Harrod's librarians' glossary (Prytherch, 1995) defines reference books as:

- books such as dictionaries, encyclopedias, gazetteers, yearbooks, directories, concordances, indexes, bibliographies and atlases, which are compiled to supply definite pieces of information of varying extent, and are intended to be referred to rather than read through
- books that are kept for reference only and are not allowed to be used outside the library.

Nowadays, reference sources, sometime called reference tools because they are used as a tool in reference services (see Chapter 4), may be available in printed or in electronic form. There are a number of excellent text- and reference books that describe the nature, content and features of various types of reference sources (see, for example, Bopp and Smith, 1995; Balay, 1996; Katz, 1997; Chalcraft et al, 1998; Wynar, 1998; Mullay and Schlicke, 1999 and Day and Walsh, 2000). Many reference tools are now available on CD-ROMs, and are also available online. There are now over 10,000 databases available on CD-ROM. Information on CD-ROM databases is in the *Multimedia and CD-ROM directory* (1998) and in the *Gale directory of databases* (Kumar, 1999). The number of online databases grew from 301 in 1977 to 10,338 in 1998, and during this period the number of database records grew from 52 million to 11.27 billion (Braun, 1998).

Today the Internet and the world wide web have become the most prominent and highly used vehicles for dissemination and retrieval of information. Through the Internet it is now possible to access and retrieve information sources available all over the world. Such information sources may contain multimedia information comprising text, images, sound and video. Through the web, libraries are now making their OPACs available; institutions, companies, governments, associations and individuals are now publishing information; and online search service providers, such as Dialog, are now offering access to their databases. This has revolutionized the way we think, work, and publish and use information. Many journals are now being published in electronic formats (called e-journals), many institutions are now moving towards a digital library (see Chapter 15), and many commercial transactions are now taking place on the web, giving rise to what is known as e-commerce.

Selection of reference sources

With all the various reference sources around, it is quite difficult for a user to choose the most appropriate source for a particular type of question. While some reference sources cover general information, others contain subject- or document-specific information, such as business information, standards, patents, theses, and so on. Selecting the most appropriate reference source has always been a challenge, and expert information professionals have proposed several guidelines for the selection of such sources (see, for example, Jahoda and Braunagel, 1980). Sometimes it is difficult to distinguish between two reference sources because they may contain the same or a similar type of information. The general guideline shown in Figure 1.7 may be very useful for finding answers to simple or ready-reference type questions. One may follow this guideline to select a particular type of reference tool to answer a particular type of question.

Information retrieval from electronic information sources

There are two major problems related to information searching: the first one relates to the identification of the most appropriate source of information, and the second one relates to the skills to be acquired to find the right information fast. As already discussed in the context of information skills, information related to a particular query may be available in a variety of different sources, ranging from reference sources to textbooks, research monographs, theses, journal articles, conference papers, CD-ROM and online databases, and world wide web resources.

Reference librarians have always played a key role in helping users identify the appropriate information sources and sometimes also to find the required information from those sources. However, with the recent development and growth of electronic information sources and their distribution through different media, including the web, users may not always need to visit libraries to consult information sources, and consequently the possibilities of getting help from library staff become remote. Nowadays many libraries and information service providers make help or guidelines available in the form of a categorized list of information sources – CD-ROM databases, online databases, and web pages – possessed by the library or the organization concerned. Such guidelines may be used to select the appropriate source of information. However, the problem multiplies when the user does not know where to start and often gets lost among the various types of electronic information resources provided.

The second issue, ie the need to acquire the skills necessary for finding the right information fast, is much more critical. Although finding information

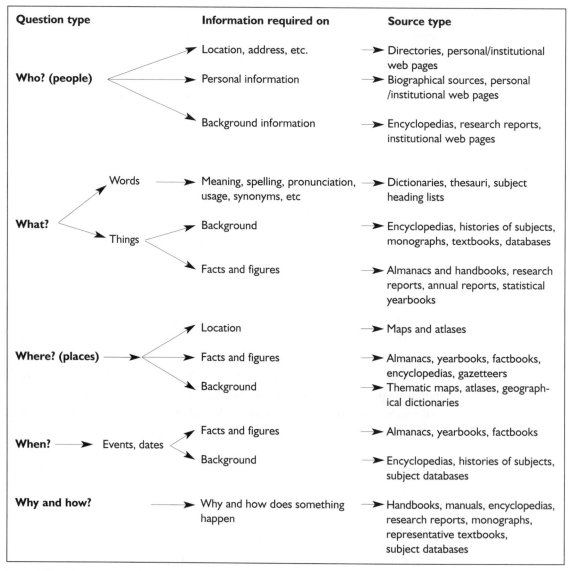

Fig. 1.7 *A general guideline for the selection of general reference sources*

from reference sources has not always been easy because of the specific style followed for organizing information in these sources, people can use their basic reading skills and find the required information from printed sources, though it may take some time. The same basic reading skills cannot help in the case of electronic information sources unless the appropriate technologies and techniques are used. In such a situation the user has first to learn the basic skills of using computers and the related technologies. Then the user has to learn the nature and structure of the chosen CD-ROM database, online search service, web search engines (tools used to search information on the web) or the website (the address of a particular information source on a computer on the Internet) containing the required information. Acquiring such skills may often take a long time, and unfortunately doing so once and for all is not possible because, as we shall see, the organization, structure, user interface, search and retrieval facilities, etc, differ significantly from one electronic information source to the other. Hence, a user has to acquire appropriate skills every time he or she wants to use a new electronic information source, and sometimes even with an updated version of the same source.

About this book

This is not a book on information sources per se: as already mentioned earlier in this chapter, a large volume of literature is available on information sources and services (see for example, Jahoda and Braunagel, 1980; Walker and Janes, 1993; Bopp and Smith, 1995; Balay, 1996; Lea and Day, 1996; Katz, 1997; Chalcraft et al, 1998; *Multimedia and CD-ROM directory*, 1998; Wynar, 1998; Forrester and Rowlands, 1999; Mullay and Schlicke, 1999 and Day and Walsh, 2000). The major objective of this book is to discuss the various information search and retrieval techniques that one has to learn in order to retrieve information from various electronic information sources. It particularly focuses on CD-ROM and online sources available through service providers (such as Dialog) as well as through the world wide web. However, it does not cover information retrieval issues pertaining to Internet search engines and the like, mainly because this is a huge area beyond the scope of the present work. A number of good books covering the Internet and the world wide web, written especially for library and information professionals, have appeared on the market (see, for example, Diaz, 1997; Kennedy, 1998; Bradley, 1999 and Poulter et al, 1999).

Basic features of OPAC, CD-ROM and online database searching are outlined, followed by descriptions of some selected CD-ROM and online databases. For each chapter describing the features of electronic information sources in specific subjects or types of documents there is an appendix that lists some relevant CD-ROM and online information sources. The list of such databases is not exhaustive, for obvious reasons of space limitations. Nevertheless, in order to show the variety of information search and retrieval techniques required for using digital information sources, appropriate illustrations have been drawn from over 50 electronic information sources ranging from simple reference sources to subject- and document-specific sources. Also discussed are various types of information services, the bibliographic tools that are used in the process of information searching, and trends in the electronic information sources and searching environment.

Chapter 2
Information services and subject study

Information systems

An information system is designed to create a link between two sets: the sources of information and the users. The linking mechanism between these two sets can be a user interface linking them electronically, or human intermediaries who are engaged in collecting, organizing and retrieving information in response to (or in anticipation of) user queries. According to Vickery and Vickery (1987), an information system is an organization of staff, materials and equipment that is concerned with the functions of linking the sources and recipients of informative communication. According to a definition provided in a UNESCO report by Neelameghan and Tocatlian (1987), information systems and services include:

- information and data in textual, factual, numerical and geographical representations, recorded in conventional or non-conventional media
- information and data sources, systems, networks and services of different types, including data banks, databases, library systems and services, documentation centres and services, information clearing facilities, referral centres, information analysis, consolidation and repackaging centres and services, and
- information and data handling in conventional ways as well as through the application of modern information technologies.

Figure 2.1 gives a conceptual representation of a simple information system, showing that information can come from a number of different sources. In Chapter 1 (p. 9) we saw that recorded information sources can be categorized in a number of ways. One way is to divide them into three categories, viz:

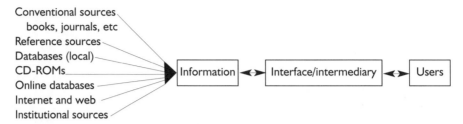

Conventional sources
    books, journals, etc
Reference sources
Databases (local)
CD-ROMs
Online databases
Internet and web
Institutional sources

Information ← → Interface/intermediary ← → Users

Fig. 2.1   *A simple diagram of an information system*

1   Primary sources: a primary source of information is one that contains first-hand information from its originator. Examples of primary sources include research monographs, theses and dissertations, research/seminar/conference papers, journal articles, and so on.

2   Secondary sources: a secondary source of information is one that contains information collected from primary sources, often presented and/or packaged for a particular audience, from a particular viewpoint, and so on. Examples of secondary sources include textbooks, abstracting journals, etc.

3   Tertiary sources: these are information sources that do not give information per se, rather they contain 'information about information'. Examples of tertiary sources include bibliographies, indexes, etc.

Another approach to categorize information sources is based on the medium of presentation, such as:

1   printed materials, such as books, journals, reports
2   microforms, such as microfilms, microfiche
3   databases – locally produced databases, CD-ROM, and online databases
4   Internet and web resources, and
5   human as well as institutional resources.

Electronic information sources, such as local databases, CD-ROM and online databases, and Internet resources, may often contain meta information, or information about information, such as bibliographic details of documents (as in OPACs), abstracts (as in many CD-ROM as well as in local and online databases) or full text/documents. The nature of information contained in these electronic sources may be textual, numeric, or multimedia – text, image, audio and video.

Information services

The primary job of an information professional is to link the user with the appropriate information. An information service aims to provide the answer(s) to a user's question or information need, regardless of its complexity or the length of time it takes to find the information. Bopp (1995) suggests that information services can take a variety of forms, from the simple provision of an address or telephone number to the tracking down of an elusive bibliographic citation to the identification and delivery of documents about a specific topic. An information service may take the form of a retrospective search service conducted in response to a user's query, or it can be a current awareness or SDI (selective dissemination of information) service, proactive services that are provided in anticipation of users' requirements.

Retrospective search services

Most information retrieval systems are designed to provide retrospective search services. In a retrospective search, a user may want to retrieve all the relevant materials, on a given topic, by a given author, etc, published within a certain period of time. The period may be limited through the search expression, or it may be limited by the coverage of the information source – the CD-ROM or the online database concerned. Thus, usually when users search on a CD-ROM or an online database or on the Internet, they basically conduct what is called a retrospective search. A retrospective search service is a reactive service, because it is provided on demand. This is in contrast to current awareness and selective dissemination of information (SDI) services, which are proactive.

Current awareness and SDI services

The major objective of these services is to let the user know about recently added materials to a collection, in a database, say. *Harrod's librarians' glossary* (Prytherch, 1995) defines 'current awareness' as a system, and often a publication, for notifying current documents to users of libraries and information services. This is a proactive rather than a reactive service, because here the users do not approach an information system, rather the information system makes all the newly acquired information available to the users.

The nature and scale of a current awareness service may vary from commercial services provided by large companies, like Dialog, with a huge volume of current literature, to small information units serving a small user community with a small collection. Traditionally current awareness services have been provided by libraries and information centres simply by sending photocopies of the contents pages of all newly acquired materials – books, journal articles, conference papers, reports, etc – to all the users of a library, or by informing the users about recently added records in a library or in a database through in-house publications called current awareness bulletins. Current awareness services have also been available commercially, for example, through *Current Contents*, from the Institute of Scientific Information (ISI). Nowadays, current awareness services are provided free by a number of journal publishers through their 'contents page' service, whereby a registered user can regularly get a list of all the articles published, often along with abstracts, through e-mail. Libraries and information centres also provide this kind of service by automatically providing a list of newly acquired materials through the users' e-mail or by publishing the information on their web pages.

While this can help users keep abreast of the latest developments in various subjects, the number of documents produced by a current awareness service – the contents pages, or the database records, for example – at times may be too much to read/manage. This is more so in the case of a large collection. In order to alleviate this problem, information professionals have introduced the selective dissemination of information (SDI). This, as the name suggests, is a tailor-made information service. It is also a current awareness service because it is designed to let users know about the new additions to a collection. However, it does not send everything to the user. Instead, the newly added materials are sifted, based on user requirements, and a selected set of materials is sent to the user. Katz (1997) defines SDI as a term commonly employed in computer-assisted searches, which is a way of saying that once a day, once a week, or once a month, the librarian searches the new literature and prepares a bibliography of materials likely to be of interest to a particular person.

An SDI programme basically matches user profiles against all the newly acquired information, and identifies those items that match a given user's interests. According to *Harrod's librarians' glossary* (Prytherch, 1995) SDI is a system, usually automated, whereby literature items are matched against the interest profiles of individual or corporate users of an information service, and relevant documents or abstracts are supplied to the user immediately. Figure 2.2 shows the conceptual representation of a simple SDI programme.

Much text retrieval software has built-in SDI service features that allow information professionals to develop user profiles. Each user profile specifies the user's areas of interest, and every time the program is run, all newly added records are selected for each user based on his or her profile. Thus, users get newly added/acquired information that is in their areas of interest.

Rowley (1998, 1999) suggests that current awareness services can be divided broadly into those managed by an organization on behalf of its user community, or corporate current awareness, and external services that may be acquired to meet the needs of specific users. Features of some software for providing current awareness services at the corporate level, such as *Personal agent*, *I3 daily briefing*, *I3 live alert*, etc, have been briefly reviewed by Rowley (1998, 1999). External current awareness services are available from journal publishers, through their

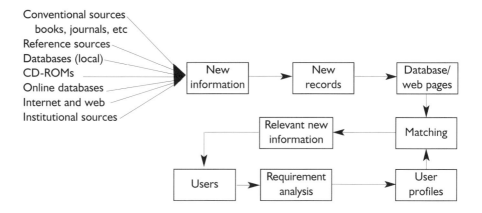

Fig. 2.2 *SDI programme: a simple representation*

contents page services; online service providers like Dialog, through the alert service now available on the web (**http://www.dialog.com/info/products/alert/**); and through the products and services of specific institutions, such as the Institute of Scientific Information's *Current Contents* service, available in print, on diskettes, on CD-ROM, and now on the web (**http://connect.isihost.com**), and so on.

SDI programs can also be run in the web environment to retrieve materials newly added to the web after a particular time. Intelligent agent technology can play a significant role in providing current awareness services. An agent can be trained to pick new information from the web on a given topic. Such new information can be packaged, as necessary, and can be presented to user(s) as the latest additions to a given field of interest. Intelligent agents can also be used for providing SDI services in one of the two following ways:

1 A given agent can be trained according to a single user's interest, and it can then pick up only the recent and relevant information from the web. The collected information can again be filtered by using certain predetermined criteria, and the resulting output can serve the purpose of an SDI service.
2 A given agent can be trained for multiple users within a subject area, and the output can be filtered by applying various criteria according to the interest of various users in the chosen subject field, thereby producing an SDI service for more than one user.

The Dialog Alert Service is an agent-based current awareness service. It automatically sends users notice of sources of knowledge that are likely to be of interest. The service allows users to create personalized intelligent agents to notify them of new additions or changes in the information collection. Agents can be trained to identify and deliver related topics that may be of interest. Users may review and update the agent profile to include the new topics. The agent learns from the user and will refine suggested additional topics based on this training. At any point, a user may manually intervene to accept or reject new suggestions.

Current awareness and SDI services are also considered in Chapter 15 (pp. 228–30).

Reference services

A reference service, simply speaking, involves referring a user to an appropriate source of information. *Harrod's librarians' glossary* (Prytherch, 1995) defines a reference service as 'the provision and organization by a library of reference work', and it defines reference work as 'that branch of library services which includes the assistance given to readers in their search for information on various subjects'. Rothstein (1953) defined reference work as 'the personal assistance given by the librarian to individual readers in pursuit of information; reference service I hold to imply further the definite recognition on the part of the library of its responsibility for such work and a specific organization for that purpose'.

Although the nature of reference services has changed over the years, their essence, ie the provision of assistance to individuals seeking information, has remained the same. Traditionally, reference services were limited to the boundary of library walls, but over the past few years users have become increasingly involved in using information sources that are not limited within the library buildings and search services not necessarily intermediated by human beings, such as CD-ROM and remote online databases, and more recently the virtual and digital libraries available through the web.

Reference services can be divided into two major categories: short-range, or ready reference, services and long-range reference services. The former deals with reference questions that are rather straightforward, directional or of a fact-finding type. Answers to such questions may be found easily from one or more reference sources. However, at times one may receive questions whose answers may not be found from one particular source; instead one may have to go from one source to another, and the process of finding the answer may take a long time. In providing this type of long-range reference service one may have to use a combination of various reference and other sources that can be identified through OPACs, CD-ROM and online databases, websites, and so on.

Referral services

Sometimes answers to a given question may not be found easily from documentary sources, and the user may have to be referred to human experts and/or to specific institutions that can provide the information sought. This is called a referral service. In the late 1960s and 1970s, the concept of an information and referral service developed in a number of public libraries in the US (Bopp, 1995). Childers (1983) comments that the goal of a referral service is to facilitate the link between a person with a need and the resource or resources outside the library that can meet the need. Referral services have become more common, and perhaps more convenient, with the introduction of the web, whereby a user can easily refer to individual and institutional web pages to find answers to specific queries.

The information search process

In Chapter 1, while describing information problem-solving skills, we discussed the various steps that a user goes through in solving an information-related problem. An information search process has a number of steps, as shown below:

- understanding the query
- analysis and representation of the query such that it can be used to search a particular type of source
- selection of the appropriate source of information
- understanding the organization of information within the source, the interface and the access points
- selection and use of tools (index/dictionary, thesaurus, subject headings list, etc.)
- submission of the query (search statement) to the source
- retrieval of information
- review of the retrieved information
- modification of the query, changes in the databases, etc, if necessary, and
- saving/printing, etc, of the retrieved information in a desirable format.

These steps may not follow exactly the same order in which they are presented here, but usually one has to go through all of them. They may apparently look very simple, but depending on the nature and complexity of the query and the information sources, sometimes they may be quite complex and time-consuming activities.

The reference interview

Traditionally library users have approached human intermediaries with reference questions. While some questions are straightforward, others may need more clarification and discussion. To understand the queries and requirements of users, library professionals follow a process called a reference interview, through which a human intermediary tries to understand a user's query, the exact requirements, constraints, etc. This is necessary because in many cases users may not be able to clearly state what they want (and also what he or she does not want). Sutton and Holt (1995) define the reference interview as a conversation between a member of the library staff and a library user for the purpose of clarifying the user's needs and aiding the user in meeting those needs. Grogan (1979) mentioned that there are two major groups of information users: 'the first comprises those who know what they need but have not put it into quite the right words; the second group is made up of those who are not certain what is needed'. Therefore the reference interview is needed for both groups of information users. Jahoda and Braunagel (1980) have divided the reference process into a series of decision-making steps, the second of which, called negotiation, is actually the reference interview; it involves a 'discussion with the user about the request in order to gain a more complete understanding of the actual information need'.

Katz (1997) mentions that 'when it comes to explaining how to conduct the reference interview or, in fact, when not to engage in conversation, there are no specific rules, no well-beaten paths, no completely sound responses. Almost everything depends on the situation, the individuals, and the particular time and place'. However, descriptions of the various aspects of the reference interview process appear in several publications: see, for example, Sutton and Holt (1995); Hoskisson (1997); Jennerich and Jennerich (1997); Katz (1997). A reference interview is conducted in order to address the following points.

- **What kind of information is needed?** This helps the intermediary understand exactly what is required by a user. The intermediary may need to know several points at this stage, such as whether the user needs brief or detailed information, and in which form and format it is required (books, reports, full-text documents, images, multimedia information and so on). It may also be important to know at this stage what is the user's background, how much the user knows about the given topic, whether the user needs an exhaustive information search on the topic, and so on.
- **How much is needed?** This is a very critical question because it not only helps the intermediary to choose the most appropriate information sources, but it also helps in filtering the retrieved information. It is important to know whether the user needs everything available on the given topic, or wants just something 'rough and ready'.
- **How is the information going to be used?** It may be necessary to know the user's purpose: is the information required simply to satisfy curiosity, or is it

needed for serious work such as writing an essay, paper, thesis or a report, preparing an experiment, giving a lecture, and so on. This is influenced by the user's education, status, age, subject background, profession, work environment, and so on.

- **What degree of sophistication is needed?** This helps the intermediary choose the appropriate information source(s), the search strategy, as well as to decide how much time has to be allocated, and to estimate how much would be the cost, no matter whether this is paid by the user or any other agency, including the parent organization of the intermediary and/or the user.

- **How much time does the user wish to spend?** Some information search processes may take just a few moments, while others may take hours, days, or even weeks. Therefore it is important to know how much time the user would like to devote, either directly or through an intermediary, for the information search process. This relates directly to the user's and/or intermediary's time, as well as to cost – direct, such as searching cost, as well as staff time.

- **What are the constraints?** There may be several constraints related to a given information search process. For example, the user may want to restrict the search to one or more specific languages, time periods, geographical areas, type and/or format of information sources, and so on. Each of these will have an impact on the selection of the information sources as well as the search and retrieval process.

Answers to all these questions will facilitate the information search activities. Although the points mentioned above form part of a reference interview process, they are equally important when the user conducts the search directly without going through any human intermediary. Users who have considered these points will be more able to conduct a successful information search session.

Subject study

An information professional may often come across queries from a wide variety of disciplines, many of which will be unfamiliar. However, before going to search for information on a completely unknown topic one must first acquaint oneself with the subject/topic, and only then can one go ahead with conducting an information search for the user. Given that the information professional has easy access to a wide variety of information sources, it may not be very difficult to get some knowledge about the connotations, scope, coverage, etc, of a new subject. A simple and successful methodology has been developed to find out about a new subject/topic, before going on to conduct an information search. This involves asking some simple questions as shown below, with indications of where the answers may be found.

1 **What is the definition and meaning of the new term/phrase?** Whenever we come across a new subject or topic, we need to know the meaning and connotations of the term/phrase. Definition of a new term/phrase can be obtained from general dictionaries, subject dictionaries, handbooks and encyclopedias. We may consult any general language or subject dictionary. In order to identify the appropriate subject dictionaries etc on the given subject, we may consult guides to reference books (for example, Balay, 1996; Chalcraft et al, 1998; Wynar, 1998; Mullay and Schlicke, 1999 and Day and Walsh, 2000). If the subject is very new, we may not find it in a dictionary or encyclopedia. In such a case, we need to consult recent journals, conference proceedings or research reports on the subject. We may also search the web to find the meaning or connotations of new subjects/topics.

2 **What is the scope of the subject?** Having learnt the definition and connotations of a new subject/topic, we may proceed to find out about its scope so that we can decide on the information sources to search, as well the areas or sub-topics to include in the search. We may learn about the scope of a subject by consulting subject handbooks, general and subject encyclopedias and representative textbooks. We can consult OPACs to locate these items in a library. We may get a brief idea about the scope of a subject from the 'scope note' given under terms/phrases in vocabulary control tools, such as the Library of Congress Subject Headings (LCSH).

3 **What are the major divisions and subdivisions of the subject?** Once we know the definition of a new subject/topic, we need to know its various divisions or branches. This will help us focus on the search topic. We can find out the various broader and narrower topics that may be useful in formulating or refining a search. For this we may consult classification schemes, such as Dewey Decimal Classification. This will give us an idea about the broader subject/discipline as well as the various subdivisions of the subject concerned. We may also consult thesauri and subject headings lists, such as LCSH.

4 **What is the period of development of the subject?** This information will help us decide the time frame for our search. Information on the origin and historical development of a subject can be obtained from subject encyclopedias, textbooks or any book on the history of the subject concerned.

5 **What are the educational and research trends in the subject?** This information may be useful to understand the scope and status of the subject. If the subject is taught as a course in a degree or diploma programme, it is likely

that it has been in existence for quite some time, and consequently a significant number of publications may be available in different forms and formats. Such information can be found by browsing through the index of educational resources such as the *World of learning*, *Commonwealth universities yearbook* and so on. We can also consult indexes and abstracts on the subject to identify the major areas of research, and browse the web to locate important research institutions/groups.

6   **What are the major sources of information on the subject?** Information sources on the given subject may come in different forms and formats, such as printed and electronic books, printed and electronic journals, microforms, CD-ROM and online databases, etc. To identify these information sources we may consult *Books in print*, guides to reference materials (Balay, 1996; Chalcraft et al, 1998; Wynar, 1998; Mullay and Schlicke, 1999; Day and Walsh, 2000), *Ulrich's international periodicals directory*, *Gale directory of databases* (Kumar, 1999), *Multimedia and CD-ROM directory* (1998), and so on. We may consult biographical dictionaries and directories to locate human and institutional resources on the subject. We may conduct a search on the Internet to identify the electronic discussion groups, important persons and their home pages, important institutions and their home pages, etc, relevant to the subject.

7   **What are the various standard terms/keywords used in the subject?** Identification of the appropriate keywords and phrases is very useful because this will help us formulate the search statement. We may consult LCSH and thesauri. We may also consult abstracting journals/databases on the subject and take note of the keywords appended to the records.

Consolidation of the information gathered on all the above points can help us develop a reasonably good idea of the subject, and with this we can go ahead to select the appropriate sources and conduct searches to retrieve the required information.

Summary

In this chapter we introduced the basic concepts of an information system. We then briefly discussed the various types of information services, viz retrospective search services, current awareness service, SDI, and reference and referral services. We described the process of subject study, a simple process that helps an information professional gather essential information about any new subject or topic through a brief but systematic study of a set of information sources. All these issues have been discussed at an elementary level in order to help readers develop a general idea of reference and information services. However, with the recent developments in the information field caused by the web, virtual and digital libraries, and so on, the nature of information services is changing dramatically. Several recent publications discuss the changing nature of reference and information services in this changing environment (see, for example, Sutton, 1996; Davenport et al, 1997; Diaz, 1997; Ferguson and Bunge, 1997; Anderson, C R, 1998; Heckert, 1998; Rowley, 1998). We shall discuss some of these issues in Chapter 15.

Chapter 3
Basic search techniques and tools

Introduction

As already mentioned in Chapter 1 (p. 5), the first step in an information search process involves a clear understanding of user requirements. Once this exact information requirement is understood, and is represented by appropriate terms/phrases, the user, or information intermediary, proceeds to select the search system – OPAC, CD-ROM and/or online databases. The selection of an appropriate search system is dictated by the nature of the query, the nature of information required through the search process, and so on. If the user wants to locate some books, journals, reports, etc, from a library, then he or she searches the OPAC of the library concerned. The user can search CD-ROM or online databases in order to get some bibliographic items with abstracts, full texts or multimedia information. Choice of the appropriate source will depend on the nature of the query and requirements of the user.

Whichever source is selected – OPAC, CD-ROM or online database – an information searcher has to know how to use basic search techniques, and depending on the nature of the search system, he or she may then use search tools that are designed to facilitate the search process. In this chapter we shall discuss the basic search techniques and tools that one needs to know to be able to conduct searches on any system. Exact search techniques, the corresponding search operators, and the tools will depend on the search system chosen, and these will be discussed in the subsequent chapters.

Basic search techniques

The enquirer looking for information in a database may use search keys to do so. For a bibliographic database, these can be author name, title, ISBN, subject keywords, etc; other keys may be used in a non-bibliographic database. In a bibliographic information retrieval environment, searches can be divided into two main classes: known item search and unknown item search. A **known item**

search is what is conducted when the user knows something about the item being sought. This may be any key, such as author, title, publisher, ISBN, and so on. In such a case, the user can enter the appropriate key, say, the author's name, and thus retrieve full details of the item concerned. However, if, as is often the case, the user does not know the author, title, etc of the item that he or she might need at a given instance, most searches are for unknown items. An **unknown item search** is conducted when users are not aware of the existence of any document that may solve their problems. In other words, users do not know whether or not any such item exists that can meet their information requirements.

Keyword and phrase search

A search can be conducted by entering a single search term or a phrase comprising more than one term. The keyword search is the simplest form of search facility offered by a search system. In keyword search mode, the system searches the inverted file (the index) for each keyword/term forming the search expression. The search terms can be entered through the keyboard or can be selected from an index or vocabulary control tool, such as subject headings lists or thesauri. Search expressions containing more than one keyword may require the use of Boolean or proximity operators (discussed below).

In a phrase search, the system searches for the entire phrase rather than each individual keyword forming the phrase. Phrase searches can be conducted only on those fields that are phrase indexed. If the index file comprises only single terms, then phrase searches cannot be conducted, unless proximity operators (discussed later in this chapter) are used, whereby the system searches for each constituent keyword in the search expression separately, and retrieves only those records where the keywords occur consecutively (as prescribed by the proximity operator), as in a phrase. Usually only a few fields in a database are phrase indexed, and phrase searches can be conducted only on those fields. A search phrase can simply be entered through the keyboard, or selected from an index file or vocabulary control tools like subject headings lists and thesauri.

Different search systems provide different facilities for conducting keyword and phrase searches. For example, in a Dialog search one can simply enter a keyword or a phrase preceded by the search command (**s**, or select or find) and can click on the search button to conduct the search. The user can restrict the search to one or more fields (for further details on Dialog searching, see Chapter 7, pp. 133–45). Some Internet search engines, for example, *AltaVista*, *HotBot* and *InfoSeek*, conduct a phrase search when a search expression is entered within double quotes.

Many bibliographic information retrieval systems provide two types of search facilities for conducting an unknown item search: keyword search and subject search. A **keyword search** allows users to enter one or more keywords pertaining to their query. These keywords can be chosen by the user in any combination depending on requirements, and there are several search operators that can be used to combine several keywords to formulate a search expression. The search keywords can appear anywhere, or in one or more chosen fields, in the database records. A **subject search** allows the user to submit a subject expression that reflects his or her information requirement. Such a search is conducted on the subject field that contains the subject headings assigned by the indexer when the database record was created. Thus, a record will be retrieved only when the user's subject search expression exactly matches the subject heading assigned by the indexer. In order to standardize the process, and also to help the user identify the appropriate subject heading, information retrieval systems use certain tools, called vocabulary control tools. Later in this chapter we shall see how these are used in information searching.

Boolean search

This is a very common search technique that combines search terms according to Boolean logic (Chowdhury, 1999b). Three types of Boolean search are possible: AND search, OR search and NOT search.

The **AND** search allows the user to combine two or more search terms using the Boolean AND operator. The search will then retrieve all those items that contain all the constituent terms. For example, the search expression 'Internet AND computer' will retrieve all those records where both the terms occur. The search is restricted by adding more search terms. The more search terms are ANDed, the more restricted, or specific, will be the search, and as a result the smaller will be the search output. Sometimes, a search may produce a blank result if too many search terms are ANDed.

The **OR** search allows the user to combine two or more search terms such that the system retrieves all those items that contain either one or all of the constituent terms. Thus, the search expression 'Internet OR computer' will retrieve all those records (1) where the term 'Internet' occurs and (2) where the term 'computer' occurs, and includes those where both the terms occur. Note that this is contrary to the use of the term 'or' in normal English. The Boolean OR search, though it adds more terms to a search expression, broadens rather than restricts a given search expression, because the search is conducted for occurrence of each single ORed term irrespective of whether the other term(s) occurs or not. Consequently, the output of OR searches will be greater. When too many search terms are ORed, the search output may be too big to handle.

The **NOT** search allows users to specify those terms that they do not want to occur in the retrieved records. For example, the search expression 'search engines NOT HotBot' will retrieve all the records on search engines except those where the term 'HotBot' occurs. Boolean NOT searches restrict a search by causing the search system to discard those items containing the NOT term(s). Hence the search output will decrease with an increase in the NOT terms. Boolean AND, OR and NOT searches can be conceptually represented by Venn diagrams, as shown in Figure 3.1. The operators used for conducting a Boolean search vary from one search system to another. Techniques and operators for Boolean searching in various CD-ROM and online databases are described in Chapters 6–14.

In some search engines there are two approaches to conduct a Boolean search. The usual approach is by combining the search terms using the Boolean AND, OR, NOT, or any corresponding operators. For example, in *AltaVista* and *HotBot,* searches can be conducted using Boolean AND (&), OR (|) and NOT (!), and combining terms and operators using parentheses. However, most search engines use the plus and minus operators for Boolean searching. For example, the plus operator (+) placed before a word or phrase means that all returned pages should contain that search term, and thus if the '+' symbol is used before two search terms, then the result will in effect be a Boolean AND search. Similarly, the minus operator (–) can be placed before a word or phrase to exclude all documents containing that search term, and this implies the Boolean NOT search.

Truncation

Truncation is a facility that enables a search to be conducted for all the different forms of a word having the same common root. As an example, the truncated word COMPUT* will retrieve items on COMPUTER, COMPUTING, COMPUTATION, COMPUTE, etc. A number of different options are available for truncation, viz, right-truncation (as in the COMPUT* example), left-trunca-

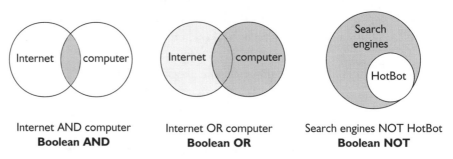

| Internet AND computer | Internet OR computer | Search engines NOT HotBot |
| **Boolean AND** | **Boolean OR** | **Boolean NOT** |

Fig. 3.1   *Boolean searches*

tion, and masking of letters in the middle of the word. Left-truncation retrieves all words having the same characters at the right-hand part: eg *HYL will retrieve words like METHYL, ETHYL, etc. Similarly, middle-truncation retrieves all words having the same characters at the left- and right-hand parts. For example, a middle-truncated search term COL*R will retrieve both the terms COLOUR and COLOR. A 'wild card' is used to allow any letter to appear in a specific location within a word.

Right-truncation and character masking or wild cards are the most common truncation search facilities available in search systems. Various types of these search facilities, and the corresponding operators are available in many CD-ROM databases and online search services, and are described in Chapters 6 and 7 respectively.

Proximity search

This search facility allows the user to specify (1) whether two search terms should occur adjacent to each other, (2) whether one or more words occur in between the search terms, (3) whether the search terms should occur in the same paragraph irrespective of the intervening words, and so on. The operators used for proximity searching and their meanings differ from one search system to another. The various types of proximity search facilities, and the corresponding operators, available in some CD-ROM and online databases are discussed in Chapters 6–14.

Field-specific search

A search can be conducted on all the fields in a database, or it may be restricted to one or more chosen fields to produce more specific results. Specific fields and codes vary according to the search systems and database. The following examples show some valid Dialog searches that have been restricted to specific fields. The general format for using suffix codes is 'SELECT <term>/xx,xx', where xx is a basic index field code:

```
SELECT computer?/TI
```

searches for records containing the term 'computer' in the title (/TI) field only.

```
S (information OR communication)/DE,ID
```

searches for records containing 'information' or 'communication' in either the descriptor (/DE) or identifier (/ID) fields only.

```
S S12/TI,AB
```

restricts a previous results set S12 to either the title (/TI) or abstract (/AB) field.

In some cases one can use prefix codes to restrict a search in a specific field. For example, in Dialog one can enter the following search expressions to restrict the search in the author or corporate source field:

```
SELECT AU= Chowdhury, G
```

Limiting search

Sometimes the user may want to limit a given search by using certain criteria, such as language, year of publication, type of information source, and so on. These are called limiting searches. Parameters that can be used to limit a search are decided by the database concerned. Below are two examples of limiting searches in Dialog:

Limit	Qualifier	Example
English-language documents only	/ENG	SELECT URBAN(S)CRIME?/ENG
Patents only	/PAT	S TRANSISTOR?/PAT

Range search

The range search is very useful with numerical information. It is important in selecting records within certain data ranges. The following options are usually available for range searching, though the exact number of operators, their meaning, etc, differ from one search system to another:

- greater than ($>$)
- less than ($<$)
- equal to ($=$)
- not equal to ($|=$ or $<>$)
- greater than or equal to ($>=$)
- less than or equal to ($<=$)

The following are two examples of Dialog range searches limited by publication year:

```
/yyyy                    S Internet/1994
/yyyy:yyyy               S Internet/1993:1994
```

Search tools

Library and information professionals have been using four types of tools for organizing information for some time. They are:

1 **classification schemes**, such as Dewey Decimal Classification (DDC), Universal Decimal Classification (UDC), Library of Congress Classification (LC), and so on, for classifying documents for their physical organization in libraries
2 **catalogue codes**, such as Anglo-American Cataloguing Rules (second edition, known as AACR2), used to prepare catalogue records of documents, which tell a user what a given library/information centre possesses
3 **standard bibliographic formats**, such as MARC (MAchine-Readable Cataloguing), used to prepare machine-readable forms of bibliographic and other types of records
4 **vocabulary control tools**, such as thesauri and subject headings lists, used to standardize the terminology at the time of indexing and searching records.

While all these tools are used for organizing information in various types of information systems, including digital library systems, here we shall concentrate on vocabulary control tools, which are used for searching information.

Subject headings lists

Both subject headings lists and thesauri contain alphabetically arranged terms with necessary cross-references and notes that can be used for indexing or searching in an information retrieval environment. However, there is a difference between the two. Subject headings lists were initially developed to prepare entries/headings in a subject catalogue that could replicate the classified arrangement of document records. Therefore, they include rather broader subject terms or headings. On the other hand, thesauri have been developed on specific subject fields with a view to bringing together the various representations of terms (synonyms, spelling variants, homonyms, etc) along with an indication of a mapping of that term in the universe of knowledge – by indicating the broader (superordinate), narrower (subordinate) and related (coordinate and collateral) terms.

The Library of Congress Subject Headings (**LCSH**) list contains a complete entry vocabulary of the Library of Congress catalogues. It is available in various formats including hard copy, CD-ROM, microfiche, and so on. LCSH is the most widely used tool for assigning subject headings to manual and machine-readable catalogues. It is also now being used to control the vocabulary in a virtual library environment (see, for example, *Infomine* (**http://infomine.ucr.edu/**), an academic virtual library located at the University of California, Riverside). The approved subject headings, in LCSH, are set in bold face while those in the entry vocabulary only, eg synonyms, appear in normal typeface. Each entry may accompany all or some of the following (see Figure 3.2):

1   a scope note showing how the term may be used
2   a list of headings to which *see also* references may be made
3   a list of headings from which *see* references may be made, and
4   a list of headings from which *see also* references may be made.

LCSH provides all the reciprocal entries for USE/UF ('use for'), NT/BT (narrower/broader term), BT/NT and RT/RT (related term) relations. For example, the heading **Computer software** has 'Computer programs' as one of the narrower terms. Now if we look at the entry under **Computer programs**, we shall find the heading 'Computer software' shown as the broader term (Figure 3.3).

Thesauri

Thesauri appeared in the late 1950s. They were designed for use with the emerging post-coordinate indexing systems of that time, which needed simple terms with low pre-coordination, not provided by the existing indexing languages (Aitchison, 1992; Aitchison and Gilchrist, 1997). A post-coordinate indexing system is the one where each search term/phrase is indexed separately (in isolation without referring to the context in which it appears in a given document); it is the user who coordinates the search terms at the time of searching in order to formulate a search expression. A pre-coordinate indexing system, on the other hand, coordinates the search terms in a specific order at the time of indexing, and thus shows the context in which a search term has appeared. A user, at the time of searching, has to enter the search terms in the same order in which they occurred in the index entry, in order to retrieve the concerned document(s). A thesaurus is a compilation of words and phrases showing synonym, hierarchical, and other relationships and dependencies, the function of which is to provide a standardized vocabulary for information storage and retrieval systems (Rowley, 1992). The major objective of a thesaurus is to exert terminological control in indexing, and to aid in searching by alerting the searcher to the index terms that have been applied (Aitchison and Gilchrist, 1997). Entries in a thesaurus contain terms and phrase arranged alphabetically. Under each term/phrase, there may be several entries with scope notes, and various other terms that are broader, narrower or related to the given term. Figure 3.4 shows an entry from the LISA thesaurus.

Computer software (*May Subd Geog*)
   [QA76.755]
   Here are entered general works on computer programs along with documentation such as manuals, diagrams and operating instructions, etc. Works limited to computer programs are entered under Computer programs
      UF   Software, Computer
      RT   Computer software industry
            Computers
            Programming (Electronic computers)
      SA   *subdivisions* Software *under subjects*
      NT   Acquisition of computer software
            Application software
            Bachman software
            Children's software
            CLEMMA (Computer system)
            Communications software
            Computer programs
            Computer viruses
            Electronic data processing documentation
            Free computer software
            Groupware (Computer software)
            Integrated software
            Interactive media
            Master graphics software
            Microsoft software
            Middleware
            Novell software
            PFS software
            SCO software
            Shareware (Computer software)
            Systems software
 – **Accounting**
      [HF5681.C57]
 – – **Law and legislation**
      (*May Subd Geog*)
 – **Catalogs**
      UF   Computer programs—Catalogs
 – **Development**
      [QA76.76D47]
         UF   Development of computer software
               Software development
         RT   Computer programming management
         NT   Cross-platform software development
               POLYP (Computer system)
               UML (Computer science)
 – **Failures**
         USE Software failures
 – **Human factors** (*May Subd Geog*)
      [QA76.76.H85]
         UF Computer software ergonomics
               Human factors in computer software
               Software ergonomics
         BT Human engineering
 – **Law and legislation** (*May Subd Geog*)
 ....
 ....

Fig. 3.2   *Sample entries from LCSH (Library of Congress, 1998)*

Computer programs
    Here are entered works limited to computer programs.
    General works on computer programs along with documentation
    such as manuals, diagrams and operating instructions, etc are entered
    under Computer software.
    UF   Computer program files
            Files, Computer program
            Program files, Computer
            Programs, Computer
    BT   Computer files
            Computer software
SA   *subdivision* Computer programs *under subjects.*

    ....

Fig. 3.3   *The entry for 'Computer Programs' in LCSH*

Information retrieval
  NT Computerized information retrieval
        Online information retrieval
        Searching
  UF Retrieval
  BT Information storage and retrieval

Fig. 3.4   *An entry from the LISA thesaurus from the LISA Plus database*

Recognition of the thesaurus as a widely-used form of indexing language came with the first international standard for the construction of monolingual thesauri in 1974 (Aitchison, 1992). Since then the processes of developing and maintaining thesauri have been standardized, and there are several national and international standards. For example, there are British Standards, BS 6723:1985 and BS 5723:1987, international standards, ISO 5964:1985 and ISO 2788:1986, and UNISIST standards (*UNISIST guidelines*, 1980, 1981).

Use of vocabulary control tools

Subject headings lists and thesauri are used both for indexing and for retrieving information from OPACs and other information retrieval systems. In OPACs, subject headings lists are used to select the most appropriate heading(s) to represent a given record in the database. Hence, to retrieve that record, the user must use the same tool to select the appropriate heading. For example, while preparing the record of a book on the legal aspects of computer software, the indexer would use the subject heading **Computer software – Law and legislation**, according to LCSH. Similarly, according to LCSH a book on software development would be indexed as **Computer software – Development**. The user therefore, unaware of what terms the library has used to index the book, has to consult LCSH to choose the appropriate heading to retrieve the records. The OPAC software then, after a search has been entered, displays a block of the index file that shows the subject headings according to LCSH. For example, a search on the NTU (Nanyang Technological University, Singapore) OPAC on **computer software** would produce the result shown in Figure 3.5.

In the same way a thesaurus can be used for indexing records as well as for searching in an information retrieval system. A thesaurus is also used by a searcher to narrow down, by selecting NT (narrower term), or to broaden a search, by selecting BT (broader term), with respect to a given search term. For example, if a search on the term **information retrieval** produces too many records, the user can narrow down the search by selecting an NT, viz **online information retrieval** (see Figure 3.4). Conversely, if a search on **online information retrieval** produces too few records, the user can broaden the search by selecting the BT, viz **information retrieval.**

Figure 3.6 gives an example of the use of an online thesaurus along with the web version of the LISA database, called LISANET (http://www.lisanet.co.uk). In LISANET the user can enter a search term or phrase in a search box, or can go to the right side of the search window to display a thesaurus. There again the user can enter a search term to find the term in the thesaurus. If the search term appears in the thesaurus, the corresponding thesaurus block will appear for the user to select a term. Here the user can select a search term/phrase to conduct a search, in which case the term/phrase will be automatically typed in the search box and the user then clicks on the search button to conduct the search. Alternatively, user can select a term/phrase to view other parts of the thesaurus. Sup-

Computer software. (LC) (159 titles)
    Computer software – Abstracts – Periodicals. (LC) (1 title)
    Computer software – Accounting. (LC) (4 titles)
    Computer software – Auditing. (LC) (1 title)
    Computer software – Bibliography. (LC) (1 title)
    Computer software – Bibliography – Databases. (LC) (1 title)
    Computer software – Canada – Purchasing. (LC) (1 title)
    Computer software – Catalogs. (LC) (26 titles)
    Computer software – Catalogs – Periodicals. (LC) (2 titles)
    Computer software – Certification – Congresses. (LC) (1 title)
    Computer software – Congresses. (LC) (25 titles)
    Computer software – Costs. (LC) (1 title)
    Computer software – Databases. (LC) (1 title)
    Computer software – Development. (LC) (254 titles)
    Computer software – Development – Auditing. (LC) (1 title)

Fig. 3.5 *Sample output from NTU Library OPAC*

```
VIRTUAL LIBRARY CONCEPT
        Digital libraries
        Electronic library concept
        Library technology
Virtual museums
Virtual reality
...
....
```

Fig. 3.6   *A thesaurus block from LISANET (http://www.lisanet.co.uk)*

pose we want to conduct a search on **virtual library**. Upon entering this phrase, we shall get the thesaurus block shown in Figure 3.6. The underlined phrases are hyperlinked: if you click on them, you'll get the corresponding portion of the thesaurus. Now we can choose the phrase **virtual library concept** to conduct a search or can select any other phrase, such as **digital libraries**, **electronic library concept**, etc, to display the corresponding thesaurus blocks.

Summary

In this chapter we discussed the basic techniques used for conducting an information search. The specific search techniques and search operators vary from one search system, and database, to another. We have also discussed why and how vocabulary control tools are used in information searching. Simple examples of subject headings lists and thesauri have been given in the context of information searching. However, we have been concerned with only basic search techniques, and there are many more search techniques available in specific information retrieval systems. Some of these will be discussed in the context of OPAC, CD-ROM and online searching, discussed in Chapters 5, 6 and 7 respectively, and some will be used as examples when we discuss information searching on specific subjects later in the book.

Chapter 4
Common reference sources

Introduction

This book is about searching information from CD-ROM and online information sources. Later, we shall discuss how to search different types of information sources, ranging from OPACs to CD-ROM and online databases. First, however, as reference sources form a significant part of information sources, it is therefore important that we learn about the nature, characteristics, etc, of reference sources, no matter in which form they appear – print, CD-ROM or online databases. In this chapter we shall briefly discuss the features of some common reference sources. Details of these are available in a number of publications (see, for example, Bopp and Smith, 1995; Balay, 1996; Lea and Day, 1996; Katz, 1997; Chalcraft et al, 1998; Wynar, 1998; Mullay and Schlicke, 1999; Day and Walsh, 2000). In describing the different types of reference sources, we take a simple approach. Beginning with a simple definition and meaning, we address issues such as why and how particular reference sources are used, and how we can evaluate them. For each category of reference source, we give some examples. However, the list of examples is far from exhaustive: only some CD-ROM and online reference sources, in each category, are shown here. Some more examples of these reference sources will appear in Chapters 8–14. When evaluating specific types of reference sources, the points made here about evaluating reference sources generally should be borne in mind.

Evaluation of reference sources

Increased costs of reference sources and the variety of formats and titles mean we must systematically evaluate reference sources. Smith (1995) suggests that in building the reference collection, one must evaluate the quality of particular sources and their suitability for inclusion in a collection. There are several approaches to the evaluation of reference sources, as discussed by Katz (1997), Smith (1995), and so on. Here we shall discuss some simple points, abbreviated as APPARATUS (**A**uthority, **P**urpose, **P**hysical production, **A**rrangement, **R**ecency, **A**ccuracy, **T**reatment, **U**sers, and **S**cope), that can be used to evaluate all kinds of reference sources. Although these were originally developed for printed sources, they can equally be used for the evaluation of electronic sources. However, for the latter some additional points need to be considered; these are discussed at the end of this section.

Authority

This relates to the authority of the author or the compiler of the reference book. We can ask the following questions:

- what are the author's (or compiler's or editor's) qualifications or expertise with respect to the publication?
- how well known (and reliable) is the publisher?
- does the author or the publisher have any bias towards religion, politics, sex, region, and so on?

Purpose

The purpose of a reference book should be evident from its title or type of publication it is. We should consider whether the author (or compiler or editor) has fulfilled this purpose. The clues may be found in the contents, the introduction or preface, the index, and so forth.

Physical production

This relates to a number of questions, such as:

- in what form and format is it published?
- what is the cost of the publication and how does it compare with equivalent products in the market?

Arrangement

This is a very important quality. Reference books have adopted various, and often complicated, techniques for arranging information, and users have to learn these to find the required information. Whatever the arrangement is, it should be clearly mentioned at the beginning of the book with sufficient illustrations.

Recency

This is extremely important, particularly for those areas where information dates quickly or where the user wants the latest information in a given field.

Accuracy

Information must be accurate, and care should be taken to ensure that a reference tool is reliable. In some cases information from one tool may be cross-checked with another. However, a general and safe guideline is to go for a reputed publication rather than an unknown one.

Treatment

Treatment of the subject in a given reference work is influenced by a number of factors, mainly by the editorial policy and the target audience. Treatment may vary from the very general to the much more detailed.

Users

Reference works are targeted to a specific type of audience: for children, novice users, the general public, experts and professionals, and so on. Hence, the selection of a reference tool should take into account the user being served.

Scope

The scope of a reference work is an important criterion for its selection. Whether it would be a real addition to the collection, and what exactly it would add, should be carefully considered. The scope of a book, for example, is usually mentioned in the preface, in the blurb, and in the publicity material. Aspects of scope include: subject and geographical coverage, time coverage, language coverage, and so forth.

Evaluation of electronic reference sources

All the above factors are to be considered when choosing an electronic reference source. However, there are some additional issues to be considered:

- hardware and operating system requirements
- user interface
- search fields
- search options and query formulation facilities
- display and print options
- index and/or thesaurus support
- facilities for interfacing with other software
- multiple database search facilities
- online help facilities, and
- user group and support services.

Dictionaries

A dictionary is an alphabetical list of words with their definition, meaning, usage, etc. The derivation of a word, the part of speech, syllabification and hyphenation, variant spellings, and pronunciation are also indicated. Entries may also include inflected forms, run-on or derivative entries, etymologies or word histories, synonyms and antonyms, usage or status labels, usage notes, illustrative quotations and examples, and pictorial illustrations.

Types

Katz (1997) identified eight general categories of dictionaries:

1 general English language dictionaries which include unabridged titles and desk or collegiate dictionaries
2 paperback dictionaries
3 historical dictionaries, which show the history of a word from date of introduction to the present
4 period or scholarly specialized titles which focus on a given time period or place, such as a dictionary of Old English
5 etymological dictionaries, which are like historical dictionaries but tend to put more emphasis on analysis of components and cognates in other languages
6 foreign language titles, which are bilingual in that they give the meanings of words in one language in another language
7 subject works, which concentrate on the definition of words in a given area, such as science and technology, and
8 'other' dictionaries, which include almost everything from abbreviations to slang and proper usage.

Why use dictionaries?

Usually dictionaries are used to:

- find the definition of words
- verify spelling, syllabification, or pronunciation
- check the usage, or
- determine the etymological history of a word.

To some extent dictionaries also help us standardize a language based on the current usage of words. However, there are some special types of dictionaries that are used to find specific types of information, full forms of abbreviations, authors or origins of quotations, and so on. One of the most common uses of electronic dictionaries is as a spell-checker in word processing software: for example, MS Word automatically checks each word with its internal dictionary as it is keyed in. Dictionaries of special terms and vocabulary control tools, like subject headings lists and thesauri, are used along with OPACs and various other bibliographic databases available on CD-ROM as well as online.

How to search dictionaries

As with all areas of reference work, the strategy of answering dictionary-related questions is dictated by the nature of the question itself. An interesting problem might arise with regard to the date of the dictionary being used in relation to the information being sought. A representative selection of dictionaries should answer most of the general lexicographical questions that are commonly asked. Specialized vocabulary questions may require the use of specialized (subject) dictionaries or encyclopedias.

The following examples indicate how the various dictionaries may be used:

- for questions relating to definition, etc the *Oxford English Dictionary* (p. 47) could be the first stop, followed by the *New World dictionary*, and so on
- for questions relating to a quotation, turn to whatever dictionary of quotations is available, for example the *Quotations database* (p. 48); the time frame may be important
- general desk dictionaries and thesauri can used as writing aids (to check a spelling, find a synonym, and so on)
- questions relating to foreign languages, slang, usage, and abbreviations may require more specialized dictionaries.

How to evaluate dictionaries

Katz (1997) suggests the following general points to be considered when evaluating a dictionary. In addition, for electronic versions of dictionaries, the user interface and the ease of use are the most important features to be considered.

Authority

There are only a limited number of publishers of dictionaries. However, the name of the publisher is an important consideration.

Vocabulary

This can be evaluated in terms of

- the period of the language covered and
- the number of words or entries.

Special vocabulary features may include slang, dialect, obsolete forms, and scientific or technical terms.

Recency

Up-to-dateness is an important criterion for evaluating a reference tool, and this is true for dictionaries too. However, certain dictionaries need not be up to date, particularly those that cover a specific period in the past, quotations of some specific authors/statesmen, and so on.

Format

Electronic dictionaries are available in CD-ROM and online database formats and on the web; ease of use and up-to-dateness are considerations.

Encyclopedic material

Some dictionaries also include encyclopedic features. Katz (1997) suggests that an exception to the rule against buying a combination of a dictionary and an encyclopedia is when one turns to a CD-ROM, because in this form it is easy to use and update.

Spelling

Where there are variant forms of spelling, these should be clearly indicated; for example, differing British and American spellings should be clearly indicated.

Etymologies

All large dictionaries should indicate the etymology of a word by a shorthand system in brackets, the normal procedure being to show the root word in Latin, Greek, French, German, Old English, or some other language.

Definitions

Modern meanings of words should be given first. Separate and distinct meanings of words should be indicated clearly. A clear and precise definition is always expected.

Pronunciation

There are several different methods of indicating pronunciation, though a diacritical one is commonly used. Dictionaries should provide familiar examples to indicate phonetics. Electronic dictionaries may enable the user to hear the sound of the word.

Syllabification

Some dictionaries indicate, with a hyphen or other symbol, how a word is to be divided into syllables.

Synonyms

Inclusion of synonyms is a desirable feature because this helps the user differentiate between similar words.

Grammatical information

Grammatical information, such as parts of speech, is essential.

Bias

Dictionaries of English, for example, may have a UK, US or other geographical bias.

Usage

Dictionaries may indicate words that are acceptable in formal/informal usage, or are considered vulgar or offensive. Dictionaries can be prescriptive or descriptive. Prescriptive dictionaries categorically indicate what is or is not good or approved usage, while descriptive dictionaries simply describe the language as it is spoken and written without any critical judgment. Dictionaries vary as to how they handle usage. Many people believe that dictionaries should be prescriptive in setting down the right and wrong usage of terms.

Examples

CD-ROM

There are 1652 entries for dictionaries in the *Multimedia and CD-ROM directory* (1998). Some examples of language and subject and/or special dictionaries on CD-ROM include the following;

Language dictionaries

Oxford advanced learner's dictionary (Oxford University Press, Electronic Publishing Department) contains spoken headwords, 500 interactive photographs and colour illustrations, 800 visual references, educational games, and maps, and allows fast and flexible searching.

The Oxford English dictionary (2nd edn, Oxford University Press, Electronic Publishing Department, £250): contents are as the paper edition of the *OED* with some modifications. It is possible to search for every occurrence of one or more specific words, phrases or abbreviations appearing anywhere in the database. Users can also search for definitions, etymology and quotations.

French dictionary of business, commerce and finance (Routledge) contains some 50,000 entries in both French and English, including 4000 abbreviations. Terms are drawn from the whole range of business, commerce and finance terminology.

German–English/English–German talking dictionary (Softsource Inc) contains several thousand everyday and technical words.

Subject/special dictionaries

American Heritage talking dictionary 5.0 (The Learning Company Inc) includes photographic images, spoken pronunciations, and more than 200,000 definitions.

Dictionary of science and technology (Academic Press Inc) covers 124 fields, from acoustics to zoology. It offers 130,000 entries, 350 illustrations, 3500 spoken pronunciations, bookmarking and annotating, sophisticated Boolean search options, custom spelling dictionaries, which can be loaded into the user's word processor. Essays by scientists introduce each field of science.

Elsevier's dictionaries of chemistry (Elsevier Science Ltd). This CD-ROM dictionary contains over 9000 scientific terms in chemistry.

Online

Allwords.com (**http://www.allwords.com/**) is an English language dictionary with multilingual search facilities.

Cambridge international dictionaries online (**http://www.cup.cam.ac.uk/elt/dictionary/**) offers a choice of the *Cambridge international dictionary of English*, *Cambridge dictionary of American English*, *Cambridge international dictionary of phrasal verbs*, or *Cambridge international dictionary of idioms*.

The quotations database (Dialog file 175) is an omnibus file of literary, political and other quotations of note. The file consists of material from the *Oxford dictionary of quotations* (*ODQ*), published by Oxford University Press. The *ODQ* was originally compiled in the 1930s; the third edition was published in 1979. The database presents relatively brief quotations accompanied by the author's name, birth and death dates, and the source of the quote. Material is drawn from poets, novelists, playwrights, politicians, public figures, the Bible, the Vulgate, the Book of Common Prayer, the Latin mass, ballads, Greek and Latin classics, modern European language classics, and famous historical *mots*, dicta, quips, and utterances.

Gale's quotations: who said what? (Gale Research Inc). This CD-ROM is a collection of over 100,000 quotations from ancient times to the present.

Roget's thesaurus (**http://www.thesaurus.com/**) is the online version of *Roget's thesaurus of English words and phrases*, made available by Lexico LLC, a company based in Los Angeles, California.

Webster's New World dictionary and thesuaurs (**http://work.uesd.edu.5141/cgi-bin/http_webster**). (Macmillan Digital Publishing). This CD-ROM dictionary provides the meaning of common English words. It also includes 15,000 most common misspellings of words, and thus enables users to search for words even if they cannot spell them correctly.

The worldwideweb acronym and abbreviation server (**http://www.ucc.ie/info/net/acronyms/index.html**). This is a list of acronyms and abbreviations in the Network Acronym and Abbreviation Server. Users can simply enter an abbreviation and get its full form.

Encyclopedias

An encyclopedia is a repository of information in an interdisciplinary or a subject-specific field, and it gives a systematic overview and summary of human knowledge. An encyclopedia aims to provide authoritative information either on all branches of knowledge or in a single subject area, and to arrange it, in alphabetical or topical order, for ready reference.

Why use encyclopedias?

A good encyclopedia will usually include detailed survey articles, often with bibliographies, in certain fields or areas; explanatory materials (normally shorter); and brief informational data, such as the birth and death dates of famous people, geographical locations or historical events. Typical questions that can be answered through encyclopedias include:

1   Fact finding:
    When did World War I start and what was its background?
    Where can I find information on the Eurotunnel?
2   General background information:
    What causes an earthquake?
    How does a generator work?
3   Pre-research information:
    At the novice level, encyclopedias teach research skills – they provide an overview and a systematic approach to gathering information on an area of study; eg when did research on space exploration begin? When did man first land on the moon?

How to search encyclopedias

Finding information in encyclopedias requires firstly an understanding of the various access points, secondly an acquaintance with the particular encyclopedia being used, and, thirdly, some practice in searching for information. Understanding the structural arrangement of an individual title is the first step. Some common questions raised at this stage might be as follows:

- How many indexes are there – only one index or a separate index for each field?
- Is there a separate subject index?
- How is the information organized – under various broad heading/topics?
- How can the user search for images, video, sound, etc?
- Are the related documents hyperlinked so that users can navigate from one document to the other?

A crucial aspect of developing search strategies for encyclopedias lies in understanding their place within a larger framework. Encyclopedias are often used as intermediate tools: a search strategy may start with an encyclopedia and then move on to other tools and sources.

How to evaluate encyclopedias

There are several published sources that provide good comparative studies on encyclopedias, such as Kister (1994) and *Encyclopedias, atlases and dictionaries* (1995). A decision regarding the choice of an encyclopedia is primarily based on daily use. Katz (1997) suggests the following general points for the evaluation of encyclopedias; the points given in the section on evaluation of electronic reference sources (p. 43) should also be considered.

Scope

The scope of the specialized encyclopedia is evident in its title. The scope of general encyclopedias is indicated by target audience (for example, children) and emphasis (of the editorial board, for example; on science, humanities or social sciences, etc; or on certain topics).

Authority

Authority is evident from the names of the scholars and experts who sign the articles or who are listed as contributors. It is also associated with the name(s) of the publisher.

Writing style

Usually encyclopedia articles are meant for the general public rather than specialists. The usual editorial practice is as follows:

- contributors are given certain topics and outlines of what is needed and expected
- articles are then submitted to the editors, who revise as necessary to make them suitable for the target reader.

Recency

Most large encyclopedias issue revised individual volumes each year (year-books) containing updates. Electronic publication facilities have made this process easier: editors are able to enter new materials or delete or correct existing materials without completely resetting the whole article or section.

Viewpoint and objectivity

Although editorial policies are governed largely by the market and the audience, one should check how topics and various related issues are handled, if any particular viewpoint is emphasized, and so on.

Arrangement and entry

As this is the key to the resources in the encyclopedia, one should check how systematically the information is organized and how easily one can find the information. In the electronic versions, user interface, search and retrieval facilities, etc, are of key concern.

Index

Systematic and easy-to-use indexes are very important. Some encyclopedias provide cross-reference entries – *see* and *see also* references. Nevertheless, a detailed index is absolutely necessary in both the printed and electronic versions.

Format

There are several relevant issues here, such as the organization and format of the text, image and sound files, and the links within the text.

Cost

Prices do vary from set to set. Usually library discounts are available for hard copies: this may not be the case with CD-ROMs, but could perhaps be negotiated with the supplier. Replacement and updates are an important issue here. Prices vary from single user to multi-user and site licences.

Examples

CD-ROM

A search on the *Multimedia and CD-ROM directory* (1998) retrieved 576 entries on encyclopedia. Some examples are shown below.

General

The 1998 Grolier multimedia encyclopedia (deluxe edn, Grolier Interactive Inc) includes over 35,000 articles (with over 1100 new and 4200 updated articles); twice as many video clips; over 15,000 images (with over 3700 new pictures); 31 'guided tours'; 1200 maps with 400 points of interest; 10 custom interfaces; and over 15 hours of sound.

American Concise encyclopedia with Webster's New World dictionary (Zane Publishing Inc) contains 150,000 entries, including 11,000 words and phrases, up-to-date spellings, definitions, etymologies and development, pronunciations and a pronunciation key.

Bookshelf 97 (Microsoft Corporation) contains over 80,000 spoken pronunciations, over 170 audio clips, and over 80 video clips and animations of ideas. It includes *World almanac and book of facts, Longman original Roget's thesaurus, The people's chronology, Hammond atlas of the world, Concise Columbia encyclopedia, Columbia dictionary of quotations*, and the *American heritage dictionary*.

British multimedia encyclopedia (Global Software Publishing Ltd) is a multipurpose world information reference tool, with a total of 30,000 articles, 30 minutes of video, 3500 illustrations, 14,000 dictionary entries, 3000 quotes and 180 sound clips. It also includes a world atlas, search functions, quizzes, a timeline and 'on this day' information.

Canadian and world encyclopedia 1998 (Image Media Services) includes the *Canadian encyclopedia, Columbia encyclopedia*, and a thesaurus.

Encarta 98 deluxe encyclopedia (Microsoft Corporation) includes 30,000 articles, 1400 maps, charts and tables, 12,000 photographs, plus 8000 illustrations.

Grolier encyclopedia Americana (AND-USA Inc) contains all the 30 volumes of the 1995 print version and all the charts, fact boxes, information highlight boxes, glossaries, and bibliographies. The multi-platform CD-ROM contains material commissioned exclusively for the electronic edition.

The Grolier multimedia encyclopedia 1998 (Grolier Interactive (UK) Ltd) is a multimedia encyclopedia which has over 50,000 articles and images, and 15 hours of sound. Also includes an activity book and a 1996–97 yearbook.

Oxford children's encyclopedia (Oxford University Press, Electronic Publishing Department): this encyclopedia, aimed at children aged 8–13 years old, includes the complete text of the printed edition and includes articles, photographs, videos, animation, maps, and sound clips for information discovery purposes.

Webster's world encyclopedia 1998 (Webster Publishing) features nearly 12,000 photographs, 10 million words, over 50,000 articles including 20,000 biographies, over 100 video clips, and over 1200 sounds.

Subject/special

The American Indians: a multimedia encyclopedia (D C Heath and Company): this encyclopedia on North American Indians is divided into four manuals – *Voices of the wind*, *Encyclopedia of Native American tribes*, *Atlas of the North American Indian*, and *Who was who in Native American history*. Contains over 1100 photographs, maps, original recordings, and 1000 biographies of relevant people.

Arms and weapons encyclopedia (Dimenziya Publishing) includes information about weapons and arms from the Stone Age to the present.

Barbados tourism encyclopedia (Axes Inc) presents an ecological atlas of Barbados and information for tourists, including where to eat, stay and shop, and things to do.

Encyclopedia of associations CD-ROM (SilverPlatter Information Ltd, UK) provides complete descriptions of over 110,000 non-profit-making membership organizations worldwide, including details on activities, purpose, membership, budget, staff and affiliation sizes, services provided, publishing activities, conventions and meetings. Names, addresses, phone numbers and other contact information are also provided. Entries are arranged by subject and subject keywords.

Encyclopedia of inorganic chemistry (John Wiley & Sons Inc) contains the text of all eight printed volumes, including 260 encyclopedic chapters and over 850 definitions.

The encyclopedia of molecular biology on CD-ROM (Blackwell Science Ltd) includes the full text of all the entries and definitions found in the printed edition. The search facility works on words and phrases. The bookmark feature allows the user to return to any place within any entry, and the annotate feature contains an on-screen notepad.

Encyclopedia of music (Helicon Publishing Ltd) is a collection of data and images and includes sections on early music, opera and women composers and performers, and other material such as summaries of stage and concert works.

Encyclopedia of religion – network (Macmillan Reference US) presents 2734 articles on all religions in the world.

Online

Encarta online deluxe encyclopedia (**http://encarta.msn.com/EncartaHome.asp**). This multimedia encyclopedia, available through the Internet, contains 42,000 articles including text, images, digital audio and video, atlases and web links to various other information sources.

Encyclopedia Britannica online (**http://www.eb.com**). This includes the complete *Encyclopedia Britannica*, as well as *Merriam-Webster's collegiate dictionary* and the *Britannica book of the year*. It contains more than 72,000 articles, including photographs, drawings, maps and flags; and more than 75,000 definitions from *Merriam-Webster's collegiate dictionary*.

Encyclopedia of associations (Dialog file 114) is a comprehensive source of detailed information on over 81,000 non-profit-making membership organizations worldwide. It provides addresses and descriptions of professional societies, trade associations, labour unions, cultural and religious organizations, fan clubs, and other groups of all types.

Grolier multimedia encyclopedia online (**http://gi.grolier.com/gi/products/reference/gmeol/docs/gmeol.html**). This contains over 36,000 articles, 6000 pictures and line art, 150 sound files, and so on.

McGraw-Hill encyclopedia of science and technology (**http://www.books.mcgraw-hill.com/reference/est/intro.html**). This gives information about the current (eighth) version of the *Encyclopedia*, including a list of over 7500 articles that can be downloaded.

Almanacs, yearbooks, handbooks and directories

These are called ready-reference sources because they provide quick, concise factual information about many things, such as:

* current and historical events
* organizations, people and things
* countries and governments, and
* statistical trends.

The information available in these sources is not unique – it is available elsewhere. However, it has been collected and extracted from several sources and presented in a handy way so that it can be used to answer many common questions.

How to search almanacs, yearbooks, handbooks and directories

The first step in developing a search strategy is to determine the exact nature of the question. Decisions depend upon knowledge gained from previous use and continual re-examination of the reference tools. As more and more ready-reference sources appear in electronic formats, choice of format must also be considered. If current information is required, frequently updated databases are preferable. Reference sources with a national or regional bias/slant may be better for questions related to those areas. The effective use of yearbooks, almanacs and handbooks requires an understanding of the nature and coverage of the sources.

How to evaluate almanacs

The general points for evaluation mentioned earlier in this chapter also apply to ready-reference sources. Katz (1997) suggests that the following three points are of particular concern:

1   **Arrangement:** is the work easy to consult for quick facts? Is it indexed? Can Boolean logic be employed?; are there subject terms?; can keywords be used?
2   **Current information**: printed almanacs, yearbooks, and other titles are updated once each year. Some sources are updated twice a year, for example the *Gale directory of databases*. Electronic information sources are often a better choice for their up-to-date nature.
3   **Illustrations:** these may be an important consideration. Electronic versions, with multimedia capabilities, may be able to illustrate things better with moving images and sounds.

Handbooks

A handbook or a manual is a reference work that serves as a handy guide to a particular subject or topic. Emphasis is normally placed on established knowledge rather than on recent advances. The information provided in these sources is presented in such a way that users can obtain what is required promptly. The content and treatment of the subjects/topics, as well as the organization of the information, vary widely. Examples and illustrations are often included.

Why use handbooks?

The primary purpose of a handbook or manual is to serve as a ready-reference source for a particular field of knowledge. Some handbooks presuppose a basic knowledge of the subject field. A good part of the information may be given in shorthand form or in a concise manner, freely employing tables, graphs, symbols, equations, formulas and jargon. Handbooks and manuals help users find answers to questions of the following type:

- how does a nuclear reactor work?
- does aspirin have any side-effects?

- what is the chemical formula of benzene?

Examples
CD-ROM

1997 SAE handbook on CD-ROM (SAE International Electronic Publishing): this handbook from the Society of Automotive Engineers provides facilities for locating reports and accessing cross-referenced standards, and includes over 1400 ground vehicle standards.

Atomic, molecular and optical physics handbook (American Institute of Physics) contains the complete text of the *AMOP handbook*, including all the illustrated material, with hypertext links connecting the cross-references, and an encyclopedic compendium of basic AMOP terms, formulae, techniques and data.

Butterworths corporate finance and banking 'books on screen' (Butterworths) provides instant access to legislation, rules and regulations in corporate finance. Includes *Listing rules of the London Stock Exchange*, *Rules of the London Stock Exchange*, *Butterworths company law handbook*, *City code on take-overs and mergers*, *Bank of England materials*, *Securities and futures authority regulations*, and *Butterworths banking law handbook*.

The complete reference collection (The Learning Company Inc) is a collection of ten reference works that includes 5000 photographs, 50 video clips and animations, 7 hours of sound and over 300 maps. It includes *Webster's New World dictionary*, *Compton's concise encyclopedia*, *1997 world almanac and book of facts*, *Compton's Internet directory*, *Merriam-Webster's concise handbook for writers* and others.

The electronic mark's handbook for mechanical engineers (McGraw-Hill Publishing Company): the core textual material is surrounded by mathematical formulae, graphs, tables and illustrations. User can access information through several paths including textual table of contents, full-text searching, and browse mode with linked cross-references.

Gardening multimedia handbook (CD Titles) covers a variety of plants, including fruits, vegetables, flowers and more. Explore the Boboli Gardens of Italy, Gardens of Versailles, Japanese Rock Gardens and more.

Handbook of optics on CD-ROM (2nd edn, Optical Society of America) contains all 3500 pages of the two-volume *Handbook of optics*, fully indexed and hyperlinked. Written by over 200 of the top names in optics and including illustrations and data, this handbook provides not only reference materials but also tutorial guidance in every topic area.

Water treatment chemicals electronic handbook (Gower Publishing) is an international guide to over 2500 trade name products and generic chemicals that are used throughout the water treatment industry. The information gathered from over 300 manufacturers worldwide is fully indexed and cross-referenced.

The world factbook (**www.odci.gov/cia/publications/factbook/**). *The world factbook* is produced by CIA's Directorate of Intelligence. It is a comprehensive resource of facts and statistics on more than 250 countries and other entities.

The world factbook on CD-ROM (CQ Staff Directories Inc) contains background information on 265 countries, including current leader, total area, capital, constitution, birth and death rates, diplomatic representation, economic aid, disputes, GDP, GNP, legal system, money, population and more.

Online

Chemical economics handbook (Dialog file 359), produced by SRI International, is the full-text database of the *Chemical economics handbook* (*CEH*), the world's leading chemical marketing research service. The handbook has been a primary provider of comprehensive supply and demand information describing international chemical markets since 1950.

Flight surgeon handbook, US Navy (**http://www.vnh.org/FSHandbook/FSH97. html**) has been designed to be a useful tool in the day-to-day practice of aerospace medicine. It is presented in a more or less 'bulletized' format to help users find the information fast and get the job done. It provides references and points of contact where possible to aid users dealing with difficult problems. It is meant to be a combination of pocket memory and checklist to help users wade through issues that they don't have time to fully research.

Military standards and handbooks (**http://www.enre.umd.edu/s&h.htm**): *Military standards* (MIL-STDs) generally impose requirements and are what-to-do documents; *Military handbooks* (MIL-HDBKs) are generally how-to-do-it documents.

Almanacs

Almanacs appeared first as calendars containing days, weeks and months, and astronomical data such as the phases of the sun and moon. Currently, an almanac is seen as a compendium of useful data and statistics relating to countries, personalities, events, subjects and the like. Almanacs often play the role of yearbooks and factbooks, and are usually published on an annual basis.

Why use almanacs?

Almanacs can be broad in their coverage. In addition to the astronomical data, they may contain information on last year's events, as well as information on politics, the economy, sports, personalities, and so on. There are now almanacs covering specific subject fields, for example, sports, cinema, and so on. Some almanacs give more coverage to a particular country than others. An almanac can be used to find answers to questions of the following type:

- what is a hurricane?
- how many calories are there in a tablespoon of butter?
- where was George Washington born?
- what is the population of Australia?
- which country won the most gold medals in the last Olympic Games?

Examples

CD-ROM

Time almanac of the 20th century (The Learning Company Inc). This CD-ROM provides information on the major events and important personalities of the 20th century combined with historic videos, photographs, maps and charts.

The bankers' almanac bankbase (Bowker) contains information on finance, banking and economics.

Canadian almanac and directory (William Snyder Publishing Associates) contains information on library catalogues and directories.

Sports illustrated almanac (Memorex-N-TK, Entertainment Technology, Inc) contains information on sports.

World trade almanac 1996–97 (McGraw-Hill Publishing Company) contains business and company information.

World War II almanac (BeachWare) contains information on the second World War.

Online

1999 farmers' almanac (**http://www.farmersalmanac.com**): this site is packed full of weather forecasts, recipes, humour, helpful hints, gardening advice, and entertaining stories.

Almanac of disasters (**http://disasterium.com/**): find out what disaster(s) happened on a particular day with categories for fires, earthquakes, and transportation.

Baseball almanac (**http://baseball-almanac.com/**) contains information on baseball awards, records, quotes, feats and facts, and on the game's history.

The celebrity almanac (**http://celebrityalmanac.com/**) contains over 300 celebrity profiles, birth and death dates, and original autographs and photos.

Computer almanac (**http://www.cs.cmu.edu/afs/cs.cmu.edu/user/bam/www/numbers.html**) is a collection of numbers relevant to computers, along with references.

Information please (**http://www.infoplease.com/**) is the world's largest free reference site. Here you can find facts on thousands of subjects including sports, entertainment, technology, business, education and health.

MyTravelGuide.com (**http://www.mytravelguide.com**) contains almanac and factual information categorized by country.

Olympic almanac (**http://www98.pair.com/msmonaco/Almanac/**) contains information on all aspects of the Olympic Games, including logos, mascots, venues and bid candidates.

StarDate (**http://stardate.utexas.edu/**) contains celestial information.

Whatweather (**http://www.whatweather.com/**) provides information on weather. This database has thousands of climate summaries that span the globe.

Yearbooks

A yearbook is an annual compendium of data and statistics of a given year, usually the year preceding the publication date, and often of a given country. Yearbooks are often published by institutions to provide different types of information on various countries for the previous year.

Why use yearbooks?

A yearbook's fundamental purpose is to record the year's activities by country, subject or specialized area. A general yearbook can be searched for answers to the following type of questions:

- what happened in an earthquake in Afghanistan last year?
- who won the French Open Tennis in 1996?
- how many votes did Tony Blair get to win the last election?
- which actors won Oscars in 1995?
- what was the GDP of Thailand last year?

Examples

There are some excellent printed yearbooks, such as the *Europa world yearbook* and the *Statesman's yearbook*. These cover all the countries in the world and publish all sorts of information about events that took place in the previous year. However, some countries are better covered than others. As well as commercial publishers, national and international organizations, such as the United Nations, produce yearbooks giving information on the past year's incidents in relation to a particular country, or to countries within the jurisdiction of the international organization concerned. While there are a large number of printed yearbooks available, the number of yearbooks in CD-ROM and/or online format is very small.

CD-ROM

The complete year book collection CD (SilverPlatter Information Ltd, UK) combines the contents of 39 individual volumes published by Mosby Yearbook, giving physicians access to expert information on every field of medicine. Over 50,000 articles of relevance to practitioners in most medical, surgical, dental and other health specialities are summarized with abstracts and expert commentary.

Eurostat yearbook 1996 (Statistical Office of the European Communities, Eurostat) contains the main socio-economic statistics of each EU member state from 1983 to 1994, and a comparison with their principal economic trading partners such as EFTA, the USA and Japan. It offers 500 tables, 200 charts, 50 maps and 70 methodological texts.

International statistical yearbook (DSI Data Service & Information GmbH) provides databases from official institutions such as Eurostat, the OECD, IMF, UNIDO, FAME, Deutsche Bundesbank, Statistical Office of the German Government and the German Institute of Economic Research.

United Nations statistical yearbook (DSI Data Service & Information GmbH) contains about 1 million entries relating to data for countries and areas worldwide, and describes the world economy, its structure, major trends and recent performance. It includes 140 table systems, covering world and regional summaries, population and social statistics, economic activity and international economic relations.

Yearbook of international organizations plus (K G Saur Verlag GmbH) combines the *Yearbook of international organizations* and *Who's who in international organizations*, including information about range, activities and key personnel in more than 32,000 international organizations active in over 225 countries.

Online

Malaysia Homep@ge (**http://www.mymalaysia.net.my/**) provides all-round information on Malaysia, including history, geography, culture, travel, education, sports, business and so on.

Singapore statistical office site (**http://www.singstat.gov.sg/**) is the official site of the Department of Statistics, Singapore. Contains a list of statistical publications, a description of the Singapore statistical system and key statistics.

WWW virtual library-Burma (**http://iias.leidenuniv.nl/wwwvl/southeas/burma.html**) includes general information, news, business, government and politics and more.

WWW virtual library-Indonesia (**http://coombs.anu.edu.au/WWWVLPages/IndonPages/WWWVL-Indonesia.html**) is an attractive and detailed site of information on Indonesia, covering art, architecture, literature, media, business, education, travel, statistics and databases.

WWW virtual library–Singapore (**http://library.berkeley.edu/SSEAL/SouthAsia/ WWWVL/singapore.html**) is an excellent source for information about many aspects of Singaporean society, including the mass media, politics, business and economics, culture and academic institutions.

WWW virtual library–Thailand (**http://www.nectec.or.th/WWW-VL-Thailand.html**), sponsored by the National Electronics and Computer Technology Center, Royal Thai Government, covers news, culture, travel, education, health care, social sciences, economics, science and technology.

Directories

A directory is a list of persons or organizations, systematically arranged, usually in alphabetical or classified order, giving addresses, affiliations, and so forth for individuals, and addresses, officers, functions, and similar data for organizations. The simplest example of a directory is a telephone directory or the *Yellow pages*. Other types of directories include local, government, institutional, investment, professional, trade and business directories, and so on.

Why use directories?

Directories can be used to find out:

- an individual's or firm's address
- the full name of an individual, a firm or an organization
- a description of a particular manufacturer's product or service
- the name of the president of a particular firm, or head of a school, and so on.

Directories can also be used to obtain:

- limited but up-to-date biographical information on an individual, a firm or an organization
- historical and current data about an institution, a firm or a political group, such as when it was founded, how many members it has, and so on
- data for commercial use, such as selecting a list of individuals, companies or organizations for a mailing in a particular area
- random or selective samplings in a social or commercial survey, and so on.

Examples
CD-ROM

American library directory/American book trade directory (SilverPlatter Information Ltd, UK) includes profiles of over 36,000 public, academic, government, medical, armed forces and law libraries in the US, Canada and Mexico; each entry includes over 40 areas of library information.

Moody's global company data (Moody's Investors Service) provides comprehensive information on over 15,500 public companies across the USA and in over 100 countries worldwide.

The multimedia and CD-ROM directory (Waterlow New Media Information) provides comprehensive details on over 16,000 companies, 30,000 commercially available DVD, CD-ROM and other multimedia titles, their publishers and distributors worldwide. It also extensively covers multimedia software and hardware producers, production services, and other service providers. It contains information on conferences, books and journals aimed at multimedia professionals, and a glossary.

Software directories (DataPro Information Services Group) includes a directory of software and directory of microcomputer software; the former covers all varieties of commercially available mid-range and mainframe software. More than 11,000 packages are profiled on the basis of features, price, compatibility, date of introduction, installed base and other characteristics.

World guide to libraries plus (K G Saur Verlag GmbH) provides the user with a worldwide network of resources, spanning 70,000 libraries in 189 countries. One disc contains three major databases: *World guide to libraries*, *World guide to special libraries* and *American library directory*.

Online

American business directory (Dialog file 531), produced by InfoUSA, contains company addresses, current addresses, telephone numbers, employment data, key contacts and title, primary Standard Industrial Classification (SIC) codes, yellow pages and brand/trade name information, actual and estimated financial data, and corporate linkages on over 10 million US business establishments.

The American library directory (*ALD*) (Dialog file 460) is compiled annually with information on over 39,000 public, academic, special and government libraries, and more than 75,000 library personnel. The database contains three subfiles: (1) library records containing complete descriptions of libraries in the US, Canada, and Mexico; (2) consortia/network records; and (3) library school records. Listings may include the following types of information: name and address, branch locations, holdings, budgets, programmes, special collections, automation systems, telephone and fax numbers, library school entrance requirements and tuition details.

The Asia/Pacific directory (Dialog file 758) is derived from general company, industry and product databases from the Asia/Pacific region. Currently it includes the following directories:

- *China business directory*, a directory of large industrial, wholesale, retail and supply companies located in China
- The China External Trade Development Council, covers imports and exports of the Republic of China and Taiwan. It provides all data necessary to locate Republic of China importers and exporters of virtually any product
- *Chinese major enterprises database*, produced by Wanfang Data Corporation, Beijing, China, includes approximately 25,000 records of profile information on top manufacturers and trading companies in China
- *CMIE*, produced by the Centre for Monitoring Indian Economy Pvt Ltd, contains company information on the largest and most important public and private companies in India
- *CMIE: survey of investment projects*, provides information on the latest projects announced, proposed, and under implementation in India
- *CRISIL: banks*, produced by Credit Rating Information Services of India Ltd, provides analysed information on banks in India
- *CRISIL: ratings review* provides information on Indian company financial instruments
- *CRISIL: view records* provides in-depth profiles on Indian companies
- *Korea trade directory* contains contact information and product lists for 19,000 Korean manufacturers and exporters.

Canadian business directory (Dialog file 533), produced by American Business Information, Inc, contains company name, current address, telephone number, employment data, key contact and title, SIC code, yellow pages and trade name information, and actual and estimated financial data on over 1.1 million Canadian business establishments.

Companies online (**http://www.companiesonline.com**) provides free information on over 900,000 public and private companies in the USA. Information on companies can be obtained by browsing through 14 major categories, or can be searched by company name, city, URL, number of employees, annual sales, etc.

CorpTech directory of technology companies (Dialog file 559), produced by Corporate Technology Information Services, Inc, contains company address, telephone number, employment data, key contact and title, primary SIC code, a detailed business description, and annual sales data for over 48,000 US technology companies. Data for each company are updated annually with senior level executives and verified in writing.

D&B-Dun's electronic business directory (Dialog file 515), produced by Dun & Bradstreet, provides online directory information for over 9.7 million businesses and professionals throughout the United States. A full directory listing is provided for each entry, including address, telephone number, SIC codes and descriptions, and employee numbers. Data for Dun's EBD are drawn from D&B's global database of 52 million businesses. Their staff of 1200 business analysts actively interviews millions of entrepreneurs each year. This information is supplemented with data from large-volume telemarketing, direct mail campaigns, government filings and a variety of other sources.

Directory of chemical producers – companies (Dialog file 364), produced by SRI Consulting, a subsidiary of SRI International, is a database of international manufacturers of commercial chemical products. The data correspond to the companies section of SRI's printed *Directory of chemical producers* (*DCP*) with the important advantage of full multi-region searchability. Published continuously since 1961, the *DCP* programme is considered the pre-eminent source for timely and accurate coverage of the international chemical industry. *DCP – companies*, in combination with *DCP – products* (file 363) contains the entire contents from the more than 6000 pages published in the directories. The regional directories are each updated annually, based on data developed from comprehensive surveys sent to every producing company. Data are researched and analysed by a team of professional researchers dedicated to maintaining the accuracy and timeliness of information in the DCP by constantly monitoring information through direct company contact as well as literature review. The programme also benefits from information developed for other SRI marketing research studies.

Directory of corporate affiliations (Dialog file 513) covers over 101,000 US and non-US companies in the manufacturing, distribution and service areas. This includes private as well as public companies, both parents and affiliates (divisions and subsidiaries). Corporations and their affiliates are included as follows:

- American Stock Exchange (all companies and affiliates)
- New York Stock Exchange (all companies and affiliates)
- OTC Exchange (all companies and affiliates)
- top privately held companies and affiliates.

Foundation directory (Dialog file 26) is a comprehensive directory providing descriptions of more than 41,000 grant makers, including private grant-making foundations, community foundations, operating foundations, and corporate grant makers. Records include entries from the following Foundation Center print publications: *The foundation directory*, *New York State foundations*, *Guide to U.S. foundations*, and *National directory of corporate giving*. The centre defines a foundation as a non-governmental, nonprofit organization with its own funds (usually from a single source, either an individual, family or corporation) and programme managed by its own trustees and directors. Principal sources of information are voluntary reports by many grant makers directly to the Foundation Center and public information returns filed each year with the Internal Revenue Service by private foundations.

The ICC British company directory (Dialog file 561) is a comprehensive reference source for 3.35 million registered companies in the UK. The file contains a record for each company included on the Index of Companies maintained by the official Companies Registration Offices in the UK. The database also indexes companies that have been dissolved since 1968.

IMSworld drug market – companies (Dialog file 943) provides full coverage of the IMSworld publication, *World drug market manual – companies*. There are three types of records in the database: company–sales data combined, company details only and sales profile only. Each company has only one type of record.

IMSworld pharmaceutical company directory (Dialog file 443) profiles the most significant pharmaceutical companies, including subsidiaries of multinationals, operating within the world's main health-care markets. As of January 1999 the database covers more than 5300 pharmaceutical organizations in more than 60 countries. Details provided include name, address, e-mail and web sites together with IMS Health MIDAS sales data and more than 7700 senior executives' names.

The research centers and services directory (Dialog file 115) is a comprehensive source of detailed information on over 27,500 organizations conducting research worldwide. It corresponds to the print *Research centers directory* family of publications: the *Research centers directory*, which covers over 14,000 university-based and other nonprofit research facilities in the USA and Canada; *International research centers directory*, which covers over 8200 non-US research organizations in approximately 145 countries; *Government research directory*, which covers more than 4300 research units of the US and Canadian federal governments, and *New research centers*, an inter-edition update covering some 800 newly identified research centers. The *Research centers and services directory* database provides full contact information and descriptions of university, independent nonprofit, government, and commercial research and development centres, institutes, laboratories, bureaus, test facilities, experiment stations, research parks, foundations, councils, and other organizations that support and conduct research worldwide.

General fact books

These titles are considered basic reference tools. They are often published on an annual basis and may be thought of as yearbooks, though they may also contain information on previous years. A common, and very highly used, example is the *Guinness book of records*.

Examples

The world factbook (**http://www.odci.gov/cia/publications/pubs.html**): this is produced by the CIA's Directorate of Intelligence. It is a comprehensive resource of facts and statistics on more than 250 countries and other entities.

The world factbook on CD-ROM (CQ Staff Directories Inc) contains background information on 265 countries, including current leader, total area, capital, constitution, birth and death rates, diplomatic representation, economic aid, disputes, GDP, GNP, leaders, legal system, money, population and more.

Biographical sources

Biographical sources provide information about individual persons, such as date of birth, profession, major contributions, etc. Some may offer brief and basic biographical data, as does *Who's who*, while others provide lengthy biographical essays, as do *Current biography* and the *Dictionary of American biography*. The former are generally referred to as *biographical directories*, while those that offer more detailed information are called biographical dictionaries. Some biographical sources also direct users to further sources. For example, *Contemporary authors* provides fairly extensive information about the individuals it includes, and it also often lists other sources where further information can be found.

Biographical sources can be divided into three major groups depending on their coverage: *current,* providing information about the living; *retrospective*, providing information about the dead; and those that cover both. Some biographical sources also cover specific subject fields, with titles like *Who's who in . . .* . There are some sources that are national in scope (for example, *American men and women of science*), and others that are international (for example, *McGraw-Hill encyclopedia of world biography*).

Why use biographical sources?

As well as being used to find basic information on known persons, these sources can be used to find:

- information on people who are famous in a given occupation or profession
- supporting material about an individual for any number of reasons, from research on the fall of the Roman Empire to a study of the modern automobile's braking system.

How to search biographical sources

Two basic points should be established before deciding which biographical source to search:

- what type of data are required, and
- how much of the history of an individual's life is required.

A person's full name, place or date of birth, address, etc, may be easy to find out from biographical directories, but these will not provide detailed information or more critical information, such as details of published correspondence. The level of depth and sophistication required of the search will depend on the educational background and needs of the individual user, as well as on his or her prior knowledge about the person/subject.

How to evaluate biographical sources

General guidelines for evaluation, discussed earlier in this chapter, are applicable to biographical sources. Ease of use, accuracy of information, and the degree to which the source is comprehensive within its stated scope are of particular importance. For current biographical sources, the information should be as up-to-date as possible, while retrospective biographies should be considered in terms of their scope and coverage (subject, period, etc).

Examples

CD-ROM

The American presidency (Grolier Interactive Inc) is a historical view of the presidency, presidential politics and the executive branch. It contains text from three encyclopedias, presidential flip cards, biographies of each president, first lady and vice-president; election results from 1789 to 1992, a presidential quiz and access to online sites.

Biography index (H W Wilson) contains biographical citations from more than 2700 books and periodicals. It offers access to biographical material appearing in biographies, autobiographies, obituaries, memoirs, journals, diaries, reviews, letters, interviews, bibliographies, novels, drama, poetry and juvenile literature.

Chambers biographies (Liris Interactive, UK) combines eight different books including the *Chambers biographical dictionary*. It allows the user to access information on 24,000 famous people and their lives.

Cricket (Mirror Group Newspapers) features 2000 player biographies, over 500,000 statistics, score cards for all England test matches, audio footage from prominent commentators, video footage and a cricket quiz.

Current biography: 1940–present (H W Wilson) contains full-text biographies from 1940 to today, covering 15,000 international personalities from business, education, film, government, politics, journalism, law, music, literature, science, social science, sport and TV. The database is searchable by name, profession, place of origin, ethnicity, gender and more.

Profiles in business and management: an international directory of scholars and their research (Harvard Business School Publishing) contains profiles of more than 5300 international scholars, researchers and practitioners engaged in business and management research from 63 countries. There are 15 indexes available for browsing.

Sports illustrated for kids awesome athletes! (The Learning Company Inc, HQ) is an interactive sport encyclopedia complete with slides, video clips, 3-D animation and facts and figures. It covers 50 sports, over 250 athletes' biographies, more than 700 photos of highlights and over 45 minutes of video footage.

USA presidents: head honchos of America (Rom-Man Technology) includes pictures and biographies of the first ladies of America as well as information on the presidents and their deputies.

UXL biographies (Gale Research Inc) offers a collection of over 1500 biographies of famous people from artists to world leaders, with 1500 illustrations.

Wilson biographies (H W Wilson): more than 38,000 full-text profiles in this database provide complete information on each subject's life and career. Many of the profiles include autobiographical statements written exclusively for Wilson. Profiles also feature lists of books and articles by and about each figure.

World authors 1900–present (H W Wilson) combines the full text of *World authors 1900–1950* and *World authors 1950–present*, including 5300 biographies of authors.

Yearbook plus – international organizations and biographies (K G Saur Verlag GmbH) contains descriptions in English of 35,222 organizations, as well as 13,000 biographies published in *Who's who in international organizations*.

Online

Biography: index of USA athletes (**http://www.usa-gymnastics.org/athletes/**). USA Gymnastics official athletes biography.

Biography master index (*BMI*) (Dialog file 287) is a master key to biographical information on approximately 4 million persons who have distinguished themselves in all fields of endeavour. *BMI* indexes some 700 biographical dictionaries and directories, including current works such as *Who's who in America* and *The writers directory*, as well as such retrospective sources as *Great lives from history* and *Medieval women writers*. Each *BMI* record provides the complete name of the person, the years of birth and death (when known), and complete bibliographic citations of the source publications that contain a biographical sketch on the person. The database corresponds to Gale Research's eight-volume *Biography and genealogy master index* (2nd edn, 1980), updated annually since 1982, and a similar microfiche product known as *Bio-base*.

The Bowker biographical directory (Dialog file 236) is an authoritative collection of biographical directories, each of which is indexed as a separate subfile. The database corresponds to the following printed publications:

- *American men and women of science* (*AMWS*): covers leading US and Canadian scientists and engineers in the physical, biological and related sciences
- *Who's who in American politics* (*WWAP*): covers American political decision-makers at all levels, from federal to local government
- *Who's who in American art* (*WWAA*): covers North American artists, critics, curators, administrators, librarians, historians, collectors and dealers.

Colonial Hall: biographies of America's founders (**http://www.colonialhall.com/index.asp**) includes the biographies of 103 'founding fathers' of the United States of America.

Classical composer biographies (**http://www.cl.cam.ac.uk/users/mn200/music/composers.html**) is a list of biographical information about a variety of classical composers. Includes information about selected pieces.

D&B – who owns whom (Dialog file 522) is a worldwide company directory file that links a company to its corporate family, showing the size of the corporate structure, family hierarchy and key information (including D-U-N-S® numbers) on the parent company, headquarters, branches and subsidiaries worldwide. Corporate family structure information is provided in one easy-to-read online record. *The D&B – who owns whom* database has been developed from interviews conducted by Dun & Bradstreet business analysts located around the world, as well as government sources, large-volume mailings, and third-party sources.

Marquis who's who (Dialog file 234) contains detailed biographical information on outstanding achievers worldwide in a wide variety of professions and virtually every important field of endeavour. The file contains over 790,000 profiles drawn from the entire 19-volume *Marquis who's who* library since 1985, including active, retired and deceased listees. Approximately 90% of the file consists of fielded biographies; approximately 10% consists of free-text biographies. Volumes included in the file are:

Who's Who Among Human Services Professionals®; Who's Who in Advertising®; Who's Who in America®; Who's Who in American Education®; Who's Who in American Law®; Who's Who in American Nursing®; Who's Who in Entertainment®; Who's Who in Finance and Industry®; Who's Who in Medicine and Healthcare®; Who's Who in Religion®; Who's Who in Science and Engineering®; Who's Who in the East®; Who's Who in the Midwest®; Who's Who in the South and Southwest®; Who's Who in the West®; Who's Who in the World®; Who's Who of American Women®; Who's Who of Emerging Leaders in America®; Who's Who Was Who®; Who's Who Was Who in America®.

NASA astronaut biographies (**http://www.jsc.nasa.gov/Bios/**): these biographies are prepared by the Astronaut Office of the Johnson Space Center and are provided through the Internet as a public service to the world wide web community.

The publishers, distributors and wholesalers of the US database (Dialog file 450), produced by R R Bowker, a division of Reed Elsevier Inc, contains over 116,000 publishers, distributors, wholesalers, and publisher-related imprints in the electronic and print publishing business. The file includes address and ordering information and makes it easy to identify distributors. Publishers include museums and associations, books in print publishers, audiocassette publishers and software producers; distributors include hardware and peripheral wholesalers, CD-ROM manufacturers and remainder book dealers. This database can be used to find publisher information for items found in *Books in print*, file 470.

Standard & Poor's register – biographical (Dialog file 526) provides extensive personal and professional data on approximately 70,000 key business executives. Most officers and directors included in the file are affiliated with public or private, U.S. or non-U.S. companies with sales of $1 million or more. After an individual is identified, the *Standard & Poor's register – corporate* (file 527) can be searched for company information. The biographical file is derived from the printed publication *Standard & Poor's register of corporations, directors, and executives, volume 2*. Information is gathered from annual questionnaires completed by individuals, company press releases, and other Standard & Poor publications.

Geographical sources

Maps and atlases

Generally speaking a map is, among other things, a flat representation of certain boundaries of the earth. Maps may be divided into flat maps, charts, collections of maps, atlases, globes, and so forth. These are *general maps*, ie, they are used for general reference purposes. There are various types:

- a *physical map* traces the various features of the land, from the rivers and valleys to the mountains and hills
- a *route map* shows roads, railroads, bridges, and the like
- a *political map* normally limits itself to political boundaries (eg cities, towns, countries, states, etc), but may also include topographical and route features
- a *thematic map* focuses on a particular aspect of geographical interest: history, economics, industry, mining, agriculture, climate, and so on.

Gazetteers

Gazetteers are geographical dictionaries. Each entry refers to the name of a city, town, or smaller place, with information such as its location (latitude and longitude), history, population, climate, and so on, and there are also entries on names of rivers, mountains, and other geographical features.

Guidebooks

These furnish information on everything from the price of a motel room in Paris or Kansas to the primary sights of interest in New York or London.

Why use geographical sources?

Geographical sources may be used either at a basic level (where is it?), or in a more sophisticated way to help clarify linkages among human societies. The first and the most common need is the typical question about where this or that town is located, the distance between points X and Y, or what type of clothing will be needed for travel in, say, Australia in December. Moving away from the ready reference query, the user may want to investigate relationships between climate, environments, commodities, political boundaries, history and virtually everything related to a place, a country or a region.

How to search geographical sources

Geographical sources should be used when the question asked involves location. A 'sliding-scale' concept should be used when answering geographic reference questions (Katz, 1997). The reference interview process can help define the appropriate type of map to answer the question. It should be remembered that the user may not know what is available, and may not be able to define his or her exact needs in the first instance.

How to evaluate geographical sources

Although the criteria applicable to other reference sources may be used, there are criteria unique to the evaluation of maps and atlases, such as: scale and projection, colour and symbols, publisher/authority, indexing and currency (Katz, 1997).

Scale and projection

These are the two most common characteristics that make cartographic materials different from all other reference sources. Scale is the most important element in a map; it shows actual distance between places. It also defines the amount of information that can be shown as well as the size of the geographical area. Map projection is one of the most complicated areas. When a spherical globe is drawn on a flat surface (projected), there will be some distortion and unavoidable error. Certain projections are better suited to large-scale maps and others to the small-scale.

Colour and symbols

Colour is used on maps in many different ways. The simplest of maps use colours to show political boundaries. Colour is also used to show standard types of information: for example, brown is used to show contours (altitude lines); blue shows rivers, canals, lakes; black indicates roads, buildings, railroads; green indicates vegetation, and so on. Sometimes red is used to indicate road classification for major highways, some administrative boundaries, and built-up areas in the centre of many cities. Colour may also be used to show land heights, ocean depths, or gradients on a thematic map. Many atlases use colours to portray the varying land heights in a country; deeper colours may be used to represent the highest land, with pastel shades used for low land and coastal plains, for example. Another subtle use of colour is shading that creates shadows along the eastern sides of mountains, assuming a light source from the northwest. The results produce an easy-to-read relief map.

Publisher/authority

With few exceptions, national mapping agencies produce high quality, current and authoritative maps for their nations. These agencies, such as the US Geological Survey, the Ordnance Survey of Great Britain and the Institut Géographique National in France, are a source of good-quality mapping products. Commercial map products can be difficult to evaluate, though only a few commercial publishers produce large maps, atlases and gazetteers. It is prudent to purchase materials from established and reputed publishers.

Index

The key to a map is its index, which is therefore an essential component. The following should be considered:

- how is the index to be used?
- does the index locate the features on the map with the necessary coordinates?
- does the index include all the place names on the map?
- does the index include not only cities and towns but also national parks, administrative divisions, mountains, etc.?

Currency

Because the world is prone to change, it is imperative that geographical sources are regularly updated to provide current information. Recent events have seen changes in political boundaries (in Eastern Europe, the former Soviet Union, and so on), and more subtle changes have taken place in terms of the environment, forestry, mining, agriculture, industries, trade, and so on.

Scope

Some atlases are universal while others are limited to a single country or region. However, even those with a broader scope may pay more attention to a certain country or part of the world. Geographical sources should be carefully compared to ascertain their suitability to meet the requirements of a target user group.

Examples

CD-ROM

Antique maps of the continents and regions (Image Club Graphics Inc) is a collection of 24 images of maps of Europe, Asia, Africa and America. It offers drum scanned, retouched maps in uncompressed (unzipped) TIFF format, with a choice of three resolutions for each image (high, medium and low quality).

Atlas of the ancient world (Maris Multimedia Ltd) is a resource for human cultural origins and includes 44 key cultures from the first human settlements to the end of the Roman era, and 8 regional overviews, 52 documentaries, 7 reconstructions, 2000 illustrations, and 274 maps.

Digital vision – globes and maps (Image Club Graphics Inc) is a collection of photos of relief images that document the earth's geographic features. It offers 100 CMYK TIFF (JPEG compressed) images (a process for colour images), three resolution sizes per image, and *Kudo image database*, with no usage restrictions or additional licence fees.

Discover series – geography (Arc Media Inc) enables children aged nine and over to learn about geography, with graphics and animations, quizzes and printed certificate of accomplishment.

The earth and its geography (Zigzag Multimedia): CD Factfinders are educational CD-ROMs which offer speedy navigation control, informative text and a narrator to encourage reading and pronunciation skills. The content has been graded according to the National Curriculum key stages in England and Wales and is designed for children aged five to eleven.

Encarta virtual globe 98 (Microsoft Corporation): contains 3D representation of the world map.

Exploring geography (Anglia Multimedia) includes *World of weather*, *World population atlasfile* and *British Isles from the air*. The aerial photography is linked to an interactive map, and there is a factual database, with explanation of the world's weather systems. An educational tool developed for the National Curriculum in England and Wales, this is aimed at those aged seven to sixteen.

Exploring maps (Yorkshire International Thomson Multimedia Ltd) gives an introduction to the concepts of maps and mapping. Users can work in three section: 'What is a map?', 'Working with maps' and 'Map skills'. Each map is featured with three case studies, each presenting information using pictures, text, audio and video.

Geography (SilverPlatter Information Ltd, UK) is a bibliographic database for physical and human geography, including international development issues. It includes abstracts, and provides coverage from over 2000 primary journals in addition to books, monographs, reports and theses.

Geography – comparing places, comparing lives (CD-i. New Media) allows pupils to explore two locations in different parts of the world – a small town in southern France, and a suburb of Dhaka in Bangladesh.

Geography – physical world (Mentorom Multimedia, a division of BFS Entertainment and Multimedia Limited): this is divided into three parts: features and processes, natural hazards, and people and their environment.

Geography search (Tom Snyder Productions Inc): in the context of an ocean voyage, the user learns geography skills and lessons of history. The student learns how to use the stars and sun to navigate, and about trade winds, rotation of the earth, and more.

Globes and maps (Digital Vision) offers a collection of 100 relief images created by cartographers.

The image of the world – an interactive exploration of ten historic world maps (British Library Publishing) offers a view of how images of the world have changed over 2000 years, through the Middle Ages to today's satellite views, with ten maps revealing close-up details.

Interactive geography – geodome landforms (Attica Interactive Ltd) is an interactive, virtual geography museum, which gives the choice of entering four different rooms, each dedicated to a syllabus subject of coast, rivers, earthquakes or volcanoes. It has been produced in association with BBC Education and complements the National Curriculum geography syllabus at key stages 3 and 4.

Maps (Expert Software Inc) is an electronic atlas that includes 120 flags, topographic maps of over 120 countries, statistical and text data for each country, MDI (Multiple Document Interface) and graph data for various topics.

Maps & globes (PhotoSphere Images Ltd) is a collection of 100 images of the world and its continents; it is suitable for annual reports and presentations.

Nigel's world – adventures in world geography (Lawrence Productions) is a fun learning activity for elementary social studies classes, and provides hours of travel, adventure and challenge at home. The game motivates children to learn about the continents, and the names, shapes and locations of a variety of countries on each continent, and to recognize cultural similarities.

Nigel's world geography (ABLAC Learning Works Ltd) is a geography-based adventure game based on collecting digitized real-life colour photographs of people, places and animals from different continents, countries, regions and cities. Includes maps, photographs, sound effects and native folksongs.

An odyssey of discovery: geography of earth (Pierian Spring Software) is an interactive tutorial for children aged 8 and above covering planet earth, environment, directions, continents and oceans.

Science and geography education (*SAGE*) (Commonwealth Scientific and Industrial Research Organisation Publishing) indexes Australian journals in the areas of science and geography. Coverage is from 1986 onwards for some titles, with the remainder covered from 1989. A broad range of subjects is covered – from agriculture and ecology to geology and astronomy – with particular reference to Australia and the Asian-Pacific areas.

US geography – an overview (CLEARVUE/eav) is an in-depth introduction to the study of the US and its people. Many facets of the American character are explored, along with six important regions of the country, their cultures, unique characteristics and major cities.

US geography – the land and its people (Zane Publishing Inc) explores America's diverse regions, which are grouped according to commonality of landforms, climate and resources. It offers 45 minutes of multimedia presentations, 1000 images, 100 interactive questions, a customized glossary, *American concise encyclopedia*, the *Merriam-Webster dictionary*.

World geography (Beijing Winmedia Computer Co Ltd) combines using geographical knowledge with playing games.

Worldview geography (John Wiley & Sons Inc) is a rich collection of sources to design multimedia projects. Location videos, photographs and captions of life within Southeast Asia, North Africa/Southwest Asia, South Asia, and New Zealand/Australia are included, with 65 interactive maps.

Online

Baltic Sea region GIS, maps and statistical database (**http://www.grida.no/baltic/**) is a database of maps and GIS (Geographical Information System) datasets of the Baltic Sea drainage basin.

Cartographic images (**http://www.iag.net/~jsiebold/carto.html**) contains pictures and descriptions of maps from the ancient and medieval worlds.

Crossroads of empire (**http://www.humanities-interactive.org/Crossroads/**) contains images of early printed maps of New Spain, Texas, and the Southwest.

Historical atlas of the twentieth century (**http://users.erols.com/mwhite28/20century.htm**) includes information on socioeconomic trends, systems of government, wars and religion.

Library of Congress railroad maps 1828–1900 collection (**http://memory.loc.gov/ammem/gmdhtml/rrhtml/rrhome.html**): the maps contained here illustrate the growth of travel and settlement as well as the development of industry and agriculture in the United States.

The map case (**http://www.rsl.ox.ac.uk**) is a selection of worldwide historical maps from the University of Oxford's Bodleian Library Map Room.

Map collections: 1597–1988 (**http://memory.loc.gov/ammem/gmdhtml/gmdhome.html**) contains information from the Geography and Map Division, Library of Congress.

Maps of Asia (**http://www.lib.utexas.edu/Libs/PCL/Map_collection/asia.html**) covers the continent and regions and countries within it, and is taken from the Perry-Castañeda Library Map Collection.

Maps of Europe (**http://ns.itc-cluj.ro/Euromaps.htm**) contains political maps of Europe at various points in history.

Maps of the Pimeria (**http://dizzy.library.arizona.edu/branches/spc/set/pimeria/intro.html**) covers rare and historic maps portraying a region of New Spain from the 16th to the 19th century.

National Geographic map machine (http://**plasma.nationalgeographic.com/map-machine/**) offers political and physical maps, country facts, and other geographical resources.

One degree land cover map derived from AVHRR (Advanced Very High Resolution Radiometer) data (**http://www.geog.umd.edu/landcover/1d-map.html**): phenological differences among vegetation types, reflected in temporal variations in NDVI (Normalized Difference Vegetation Index) derived from satellite data, have been used to classify land cover at continental scales.

Paleomap project (**http://www.scotese.com/**) enables the user to view the earth in paleogeographic maps as it has changed through time as a result of plate tectonics and continental drift.

Peters projection: an area accurate map (**http://www.webcom.com/~bright/petermap.html**): this projection improves the accuracy of how we see the earth, eliminating some of the distortions and biases of traditional maps.

Quick maps of the world (**http://www.theodora.com/maps/abc_world_maps.html**) offers small GIF-formatted maps of the countries of the world.

ReliefWeb map centre (**http://www.reliefweb.int/mapc/index.html**) includes unique maps reflecting humanitarian emergency situations, agencies, and resources worldwide.

This dynamic planet (**http://pubs.usgs.gov/pdf/planet.html**) shows the earth's physiographic features, the current movements of its major tectonic plates, and the locations of its volcanoes, earthquakes and impact craters. The information is delivered in PDF format.

United Nations cartographic section (**http://www.un.org/Depts/Cartographic/english/htmain.htm**): digitally prepared, current maps are available for reference and download, including general world and peacekeeping mission maps.

USGS atlas of Antarctic research (**http://usarc.usgs.gov/antarctic_atlas/**) provides a common base for displaying research results and data collected, as well as descriptions of ongoing and past projects.

US states (**http://dir.yahoo.com/Science/Geography/Cartography/Maps/By_Region/U_S_States/**) contains maps of all the US states.

Worldtime (**http://www.worldtime.com/**) contains information on local time and sunrise and sunset times in several hundred cities, and a database of public holidays worldwide.

Bibliographic sources

Simply speaking, a bibliography is a list of books. The information contained in bibliographies and catalogues is used to answer a wide variety of questions and to further research by identifying sources on various topics.

Types of bibliographies

There are different types of bibliographies:

- *current bibliographies* list books and/or other items around the time they are being published
- *retrospective bibliographies* cover materials published during an earlier period
- *national bibliographies* list the materials published in and on a particular country; usually published by that country's national library, they indicate the country's bibliographic output
- *trade bibliographies* are commercial publications that exist to provide the information necessary to select and acquire recently published materials; usually these include books that are intended for sale to the general public and are available for sale in bookstores. *Global books in print, British books in print*, etc are common examples of trade bibliographies
- *subject bibliographies* are lists of materials on a particular subject or topic
- *author bibliographies* list materials written by or on a particular author
- *library catalogues* list the materials held in the collection of a particular library. Many library catalogues (online public access catalogues) are now accessible to users via the Internet and thus can partly serve the purpose of a bibliography of international coverage
- *union catalogues* list materials held in the collection of more than one library in a group or region. Such shared cataloguing networks as RLIN (Research Libraries Information Network), OCLC (Online Computer Library Center) (often referred to as bibliographic utilities) serve as union catalogues for their members
- *bibliographies of bibliographies* are lists of bibliographies that have been created as a means of bibliographic control. They are usually general in scope and offer a good starting place when trying to locate lists of works on a particular subject.

Why use bibliographic sources?

Bibliographic sources are used for a variety of reasons, such as:

- to know what has been published in a given subject, by a given author, in a given country, over a given period of time, etc
- to verify the missing details of a bibliographic citation that may be useful to order the item
- as an essential aid in research to help the researcher chart the development of knowledge in a given subject field.

Other uses of bibliographic sources, such as union catalogues, might be:

- to prepare local library catalogues
- to know what materials libraries in a given region have in stock
- to make plans for cooperative acquisition for cost saving
- to make arrangements for interlibrary loan

and so on.

How to search bibliographical sources

Techniques for searching bibliographic sources depend on the nature of the query as well as the nature of the source concerned. Searches may be conducted by author, keyword/phrases, subjects or topics, title, publisher, ISBN or ISSN, and so on. A given search may be restricted by type of source (eg books, journals, conference proceedings, etc), time, language, country of publication, price, and so on.

How to evaluate bibliographies

In addition to the general criteria used for evaluating any reference tool, one should take into account the following points for evaluation of bibliographies (Katz, 1997):

- Purpose: it is important to ascertain that the bibliography is worth consulting; make sure that the subject is stated clearly in the title and well defined in the preface.
- Scope: the bibliography should be as complete as possible within its stated purpose.
- Methodology: the method of compiling the bibliography should be straightforward and should make clear that the compiler has examined all the material listed. The items should be described in a standard bibliographical style.
- Organization: the bibliography should be organized in a clear, easy-to-use fashion, and indexes (both subject and author) should be included where multiple access is desirable. There should be a clear explanation as to how to use the work, as well as a key to abbreviations, definitions, and the like.
- Annotations and abstracts: where descriptive and critical notes are used for entries, these should be clear, succinct and informative.
- Bibliographical form: this is a standard entry with the information one needs to identify and locate the item.
- Currency: the material should be current, where this is required.
- Accuracy: the information provided must be accurate.

- Format: is the bibliography available in print, online, CD-ROM, on the web, and so on? If available in electronic form, is it easy to retrieve the required information?

Though it has become easier to prepare bibliographies, the job still needs expertise in information sources and searching. As more and more information is published, one has not only to know where to search for the relevant information, but also to learn how best to search and retrieve that information. Sometimes items retrieved from various sources may need some reprocessing to make the product more useful and easily accessible. A large number of subject, author and special bibliographies are now available on the web: when using these one should consider the authority of the compiler, as well as the scope, coverage – geographical, language and time period – updating frequencies, and so on.

Examples

CD-ROM

African studies on CD-ROM (National Information Services Corporation) is an anthology of five CD-ROM databases providing access to multidisciplinary information on Africa. These include information supplied by the Africa Institute, *The Southern African database*, the School of Oriental and African Studies, *Bibliography on contemporary African politics and development* and the *International library of African music*.

Agriculture and natural resources (RMIT Publishing) contains *ABOA* (*Australian bibliography of agriculture*), *Streamline* and *ARRIP* (*Australian rural research in progress*). The databases contain coverage of bibliographic and research information relating to all aspects of Australia's natural resources, including pasture and animal production, fisheries, horticulture, soil sciences, water resources, conservation and the rural environment.

Annotated bibliography for English studies (Swets & Zeitlinger Publishers) contains over 25,000 records and is prepared and reviewed by a network of international scholars. Records on books, essays or journal articles in English studies are annotated with the approach adopted and its value described. This publication is available online since 1999, and about 4000 records are added every year.

Annual bibliography of English language and literature (Chadwyck-Healey Ltd) is compiled under the auspices of the Modern Humanities Research Association by an international team of editors, contributors and academic advisors. The bibliography lists monographs, periodical articles, critical editions of literary works, book reviews, collections of essays and doctoral dissertations published internationally.

Bibliografia de la literatura Española (Chadwyck-Healey Ltd) is a resource for scholars of Spanish literature. It includes a bibliography of all related documentation published in any language. It covers monographs, periodical articles, critical editions of literary works, book reviews, bibliographies, congresses and other miscellaneous material.

Bibliografia nazionale Italiana su CD-ROM (Chadwyck-Healey Ltd) contains over 450,000 records of the Italian national bibliography, from 1958 to the present day.

Bibliography of native North Americans (SilverPlatter Information Ltd. UK) provides bibliographic access to monographs, essays, journal articles and dissertations on Native North American history, life and culture, with over 80,000 records. Alternative name forms are given to facilitate the search process.

A bibliography of nineteenth-century legal literature (Chadwyck-Healey Ltd) is an author/subject catalogue of law treatises and law-related literature held in 12 legal collections in Britain, Ireland and the USA. It contains 40,000 records and 250,000 items in a subject classification scheme with 1000 headings. Only purchasers of the print version can receive the CD-ROM.

Bibliography of the history of art (Getty Information Institute) provides access to the literature of Western art published since 1990, covering late antiquity to the present. The 1996 edition includes more than 100,000 citations.

Biological & agricultural index (Ovid Technologies Inc) is a bibliography of periodicals in the biological and agricultural sciences, and related disciplines. Among the areas covered are animal husbandry, biochemistry, biotechnology, botany, ecology, entomology, environmental science, genetics, nutrition, physiology, veterinary medicine and zoology.

British national bibliography on CD-ROM (British Library Publishing) contains the Library's complete bibliography on three CD-ROMs: the two backfiles cover the years 1950 to 1985, and the current file covers the years from 1986 to the present.

Chinese national bibliography (Chinese MARC Data Center) includes information on all the books in the National Library of China published after 1975.

Czech national bibliography (Albertina Icome Praha) includes the *Bibliography of Czech books* database since 1983 (more than 120,000 records), *Czech magazine articles abstracts* database covering 1991–92 (over 300,000 records), *Database of Czech periodicals* (4800 records), and the *Czech dissertations database*. The databases are in Czech; however, the bibliographic information follows international standards.

Elsevier's electronic bibliography: analytical separations (Elsevier Science Ltd) is a database of 85,000 records of bibliographic details of all articles in analytical separations published between 1989 and 1997.

English bibliography 1901 to 1945 (K G Saur Verlag GmbH) is an index of over

2.4 million titles printed between 1901 and 1945. It covers classical and modern authors, as well as books by famous statesmen.

MLA international bibliography (SilverPlatter Information Ltd, UK): indexes materials on modern languages, literature, linguistics and folklore, covering literary and language scholarship from 1963 to the present, with access to 3000 journals and series published worldwide, monographs, working papers, proceedings, bibliographies, etc. Covers subjects from prose to poetry, genres to literary forms, national literatures to regional dialects.

Russian national bibliography plus (K G Saur Verlag GmbH): contains bibliographic information on 800,000 titles published between 1980 and 1995 in the Soviet Union and Russia. Features numerous search criteria – by individual or corporate author, title, publisher and publication year.

Springer complete catalogue 1842–1996 (Springer-Verlag GmbH) presents a bibliography of all the books published by Springer-Verlag (approximately 50,000 entries), a complete journals bibliography, as well as an overview of Springer's electronic media products. Users can follow the history of a book from its first printing up to the present edition.

The world of Shakespeare bibliography on CD-ROM, 1990–1993 (Cambridge University Press) contains over 12,000 bibliographic records and abstracts on the life and work of William Shakespeare edited between 1990 and 1993.

Ulrich's international periodicals plus (R R Bowker, a division of Reed Elsevier Inc) features about 215,000 regularly and irregularly issued serials and newspapers from over 200 countries worldwide, over 67,000 revisions and over 47,000 cessations, addresses for 99,000 publishers from 200 countries, 2500 title changes in the last year, nearly 63,000 titles and descriptive annotations. This title is also available from other vendors, such as SilverPlatter.

Online

Bibliography of the history of art (BHA) (Dialog file 190) abstracts and indexes current publications in the history of art. *BHA* is the successor to *RILA* (*International repertory of the literature of art*, file 191) and *RAA* (*Repertoire d'Art et d'Archeologie*). The database is a joint effort of the Art History Information Program (AHIP) of the J. Paul Getty Trust and the Institut de l'Information Scientifique et Technique (INIST) of the Centre National de la Recherche Scientifique. The database corresponds to the print bibliography of the same name.

Books in print (Dialog file 470), produced by the R R Bowker Company, is the most comprehensive source of information on books published in the U.S. The database contains bibliographic records from over 44,000 publishers. These records cover books currently in print and titles about to be published (as far as six months in advance), as well as information on titles declared out of print or out of stock indefinitely since 1979. Reviews from *Publishers weekly*, *Library journal*, and *School library journal* have been included since the mid-1980s.

British books in print (Dialog file 430) provides comprehensive indexing of books published in the United Kingdom, plus those books published throughout the world that are printed in the English language and are available within the U.K. from an exclusive stockholding agent. Information on forthcoming titles is provided up to nine months in advance of publication.

Collection of computer science bibliographies (**http://liinwww.ira.uka.de/bibliography/index.html**) is a highly searchable database of references to scientific literature in *Computer science* (journal articles, conference papers, technical reports, etc) with more than 400,000 entries.

Environmental bibliography (Dialog file 68) provides access to the contents of periodicals dealing with the environment. Coverage includes periodicals on water, air, soil and noise pollution, solid waste management, health hazards, urban planning, global warming and many other specialized subjects of environmental consequence. The print equivalent is *Environmental periodicals bibliography*. More than 400 journals are covered including those from the world's major publishers in science and technology as well as from smaller publishers from many parts of the world; many university press, society and private publications are covered as well, some of which are available only on the Internet. (Availability of the web publications is noted in the Notes field, along with the relevant URL.)

Ulrich's international periodicals directory (Dialog file 480) is a unique, current, comprehensive and continuously updated source of information on over 200,000 periodicals and serials from 80,000 publishers in 200 countries. Annuals, continuations and conference proceedings are included, as well as academic/scholarly publications, trade publications, consumer magazines, newsletters and bulletins, and titles that have ceased publication since 1974.

Online bookshop and publishers' catalogues can be used to find bibliographical information: for example, Amazon (**http://www.Amazon.com**), Addison-Wesley (**http://www.awlonline.com/search/index.html**) and Prentice Hall (**http://www.prenhall.com/search.html**).

Indexes and abstracts

An **index** is used to get easy access to a document or particular portion of a document. An index represents an analysis, usually by name and by subject, of a document. A good index provides enough access points to allow the user to find precisely what is needed.

Abstracts present a brief summary of the content of a document. Abstracts can be indicative or informative; some are evaluative too (Chowdhury, 1999b). Although professional abstractors do exist, most abstracting services rely on authors to provide their own abstracts.

An *informative abstract* is intended to provide the reader with quantitative and qualitative information presented in the parent document. Informative abstracts may include information on purpose, scope and methods, as well as results and findings. An *indicative abstract* simply indicates what the document is all about. Indicative abstracts may contain information on purpose, scope or methodology, but not on results, conclusions or recommendations. An *evaluative abstract* contains some kind of critical comment or review by the abstractor. For indicative and informative abstracts, abstractors usually function as objective reporters, whereas in an evaluative abstract, the abstractor inputs his or her own opinion and interpretations.

Why use indexes and abstracts?

Both indexes and abstracts are used to locate a document. However, abstracts also serve as an aid in assessing the content of a document and its potential relevance. Indexes and abstracts are often thought of as value-added services because a human indexer or abstractor has analysed the document content and developed a document surrogate including assigned indexing terms and an abstract. Indexes and abstracts are believed to benefit the user by improving retrieval performance, enabling the identification of the best set of items for the user's purposes.

How to evaluate indexes and abstracts

An index should be current and should be capable of being accessed in such a way that it does not take much effort to find the required material. Although many of the problems related to access have been solved in electronically available indexes and abstracts, there are still some problems related to vocabulary control, standardization of the user interface features, and so on. Evaluation of indexes and abstracts should be made in the light of the APPARATUS scheme (discussed earlier in this chapter on page 42). Evaluation of electronic indexes and abstracts involves a number of considerations, such as the indexing, the user interface, the search and retrieval features, help facilities, and so on. CD-ROM and online products vary significantly on all these issues. Some examples illustrating these points appear in Chapters 6 to 14.

Examples

CD-ROM

Anbar management intelligence (Anbar Electronic Intelligence) provides abstracts on management from more than 400 English-language journals dating back to January 1989.

BHI plus (Bowker) indexes articles from over 320 key humanities journals and newspapers, from 1985 onwards.

Dissertation abstracts (SilverPlatter Information Ltd, UK) contains bibliographic citations and abstracts on all subject areas for doctoral dissertations and master's theses completed at over 1000 accredited colleges and universities.

EconLit (SilverPlatter Information Ltd) is a comprehensive indexed bibliography with abstracts of the world's economic literature.

FT prices on CD-ROM (Financial Times Information) provides access to up to 13 years of price information, starting in 1983, from the 'back pages' of the *Financial Times*, including information on UK and European equities, commodities, currencies, indices, interest rates and UK managed funds.

INSPEC (SilverPlatter Information Ltd, UK) provides citations to and abstracts of materials on information technology, computers and computing, physics, electrical engineering and electronics.

Institute of Management international database plus (IMID plus) (Bowker) provides abstracts of journals, books, audiovisual materials, company practices, training packages and working papers in the field of management.

LISA plus (Bowker) incorporates two databases in one – *Library and information science abstracts (LISA)*, and *Current research in library and information science (CRLIS)*. It covers an international range of publications on all aspects of information handling.

ProQuest: the accounting and tax database (UMI) features abstracts of and citations to accounting, taxation and financial management journals. It contains selected articles from business journals, daily newspapers, etc.

PsycLit (SilverPlatter Information Ltd, UK) provides abstracts of the international literature in psychology and related fields.

Science citation index (Institute of Scientific Information) provides multidisciplinary coverage of over 3000 science and technology journals by title word, cited author, cited work, cited patent, journal title, author name and address. Covers a large number of subjects including agriculture, biology, chemistry, engineering, immunology, medicine, pharmacology and psychiatry.

Social science citation index compact disc edition with abstracts (SSCI CDE, 1991-) (ISI) covers 1700 of the world's most significant social sciences journals spanning 60 disciplines, as well as selectively covering items from over 5600 science journals related to the social sciences. The disciplines covered include anthropology, history, industrial relations, information science and library science, law, linguistics, philosophy, psychology, psychiatry, political science, public health, social issues, social work, sociology, substance abuse, urban studies and women's studies. A unique feature of this citation tool is that it indexes cited references of articles covered.

Online

ABI/INFORM (Dialog file 15) includes details on virtually every aspect of business, including company histories, competitive intelligence, and new product development. It contains bibliographic citations and 25–150-word summaries of articles appearing in professional publications, academic journals and trade magazines published worldwide. The full text of articles is included for about 550 of the 1000 journals. There is no print equivalent to the database.

Accounting & tax database (Dialog file 485) provides comprehensive indexing and informative abstracts of articles in prominent accounting, taxation and financial management publications from the United States and other countries. In addition to the bibliographic citation and indexing, most records contain 25–150-word abstracts.

AGRICOLA (*AGRICultural OnLine Access*) (Dialog file 10) is an extensive bibliographic database consisting of records for literature citations of journal articles, monographs, theses, patents, translations, microforms, audiovisuals, software and technical reports. Available since 1970, *AGRICOLA* serves as a document locator and bibliographic access and control system for the US National Agricultural Library (NAL) collection, but since 1984 the database has also included some records produced by cooperating institutions for documents not held by NAL.

AGRIS international (Dialog file 203) is an international information system for agricultural sciences and technology. The database serves as a comprehensive inventory of worldwide agricultural literature, reflecting research results, food production and rural development, to help users identify problems involved in all aspects of world food supply. Emphasis in AGRIS International is non-US. This file corresponds in part to the printed publication *Agrindex*, published monthly by the Food and Agriculture Organization (FAO) of the United Nations.

APIPAT (Dialog file 353): *American Petroleum Institute patent abstracts*, provides comprehensive coverage of patents related to the petroleum, petrochemicals, natural gas and energy industries. It corresponds to the following print bulletins of *Patent abstracts*: *Petroleum processes*, *Petroleum and Specialty Products*, *Chemical Products*, *Environment, Transport and Storage*, *Petroleum Substitutes*,

Catalysts/Zeolites, Tribology, Reformulated Fuels and *Oilfield Chemicals*; coverage is worldwide.

BIOSIS previews (Dialog file 555) contains citations from *Biological Abstracts®* (*BA*), and *Biological Abstracts/Reports, Reviews, and Meetings* (*BA/RRM*) (formerly *BioResearch Index*), the major publications of BIOSIS®. Together, these publications constitute the major English-language service providing comprehensive worldwide coverage of research in the biological and biomedical sciences. *Biological Abstracts* includes approximately 350,000 accounts of original research yearly from nearly 6000 primary journal and monograph titles. *BA/RRM* includes an additional 200,000 plus citations a year from meeting abstracts, reviews, books, book chapters, notes, letters, selected institutional and government reports, and research communications. US patents are included from 1986 to 1989.

Book review index (Dialog file 137) contains references to more than 2 million reviews of approximately 1 million distinct book and periodical titles. The file dates from 1969 to the present and covers every review published in nearly 500 periodicals and newspapers. Each record includes the author and title of the work being reviewed, journal name, date of review and page number. Document type indications are also included if the work is a children's book, periodical, children's periodical, young-adult periodical, reference work or young-adult book. *Book review index* corresponds to the print publication of the same name.

Derwent world patents index (Dialog files 280, 350, 351, 352), produced by Derwent Information, provides access to information on more than 18 million patent documents, giving details of over nine million inventions. Each week, approximately 20,000 documents from 40 patent-issuing authorities are added to *DWPI*.

EconLit (Dialog file 139) provides indexing and abstracts of the worldwide literature on economics, now covering more than 600 major economics journals annually. It also indexes about 600 collective volumes (essays, proceedings, etc.), 2000 books, 900 dissertations, 2000 working papers and book reviews each year. The database is produced by the American Economic Association and encompasses the bibliographic sections of both the *Journal of Economic Literature* and the *Index of Economic Articles*, as well as the Cambridge University Press journal *Abstracts of Working Papers in Economics*. Most records for journal articles, books, and working papers include abstracts.

Ei Compendex (Dialog file 8) is the machine-readable version of the *Engineering Index* (monthly/annual), which provides abstracted information from the world's significant engineering and technological literature. The database provides worldwide coverage of approximately 4500 journals and selected government reports and books. Subjects covered include: civil, energy, environmental, geological and biological engineering; electrical, electronics and control engineering; chemical, mining, metals and fuel engineering; mechanical, automotive, nuclear and aerospace engineering; and computers, robotics and industrial robots. In addition to journal literature, over 480,000 records of significant published proceedings of engineering and technical conferences formerly indexed in *Ei Engineering Meetings®* are included.

ERIC (Dialog file 1) sponsored by the US Department of Education, is a bibliographic database that contains education-related documents and journal articles. Information in *ERIC* (Educational Resources Information Center) corresponds to two printed abstract/index journals: *Resources in education* (*RIE*) and *Current index to journals in education* (*CIJE*). *RIE* announces some 14,000 documents each year, and *CIJE* some 20,000 journal articles, extracted from more than 750 serials.

Library literature (Dialog file 438) is a bibliographic database that indexes more than 229 key library and information science periodicals published in the United States and elsewhere, along with books, chapters within books, library school theses, and pamphlets. Types of periodical materials covered are feature articles, obituaries, interviews, notices of appointments and awards, regularly appearing columns, special theme issues, editorials (of reference value), letters to the editor (of reference value) and book reviews.

Summary

In this chapter we have briefly discussed the features of some commonly used reference sources. The types and examples given here are just an illustrative sample of the electronic reference sources that exist in each category. However, reference sources are not the only sources for information that one might look at in an information search process. In fact, they form only a small part of it. In order to get comprehensive information on a given subject, a user may need to look at a variety of information sources – books, journals, conference papers, reports, patents, standards, and so on that may be available in print or electronic form. Chapters 5 to 7 of this book discuss the nature of some typical information search systems that one might need to consult, viz OPACs, CD-ROM and online databases. Chapters 8 to 14 discuss the information search process in the context of specific subjects and specific types of information sources. In those chapters some examples of reference sources corresponding to the given subject, or the type of information source, will be discussed.

Chapter 5

Searching online public access catalogues

Introduction

Online public access catalogues (OPACs) are the keys to a library's collection because they allow users to find out about what books, journals, conference proceedings, reports, and so on, are available in the collection. Though OPACs are designed for all kinds of users – ranging from novice to experts – they are not always very easy to search. In other words, one needs to acquire some skills to conduct an effective OPAC search. In this chapter we discuss the general features of OPACs, then, with a view to identifying the various search and retrieval features that exist, we look at ten OPACs chosen from different libraries around the world. We have used the tabular presentation style to describe the various features of the chosen OPACs. These tables and the associated discussions will help the readers learn the various search techniques, search operators, etc, that one needs to be familiar with in order to be able to conduct successful searches on various OPACs.

OPACs

Online public access catalogues (OPACs) are interfaces between the user and the collection(s) of a library. Typically OPACs enable users to search the library's catalogue, and may also provide other facilities, such as checking borrower records, reserving reading materials, reading library news bulletins, and so on. Although OPACs made their appearance in the mid-1970s, it was only at the beginning of the next decade that a significant number of libraries switched from card catalogues to automated catalogues (Su, 1994; Large and Behesti, 1997). However, those first catalogues were usually modules linked to the automated circulation system, and had brief catalogue records and very limited functionality (Hildreth, 1988). OPACs have improved significantly since then.

Hildreth (1988) has identified three generations of OPAC development:

1 **First generation**: OPACs at the beginning were searchable typically by author, title and control number. Each record contained short and often non-standard bibliographic records.

2 **Second generation**: search functionalities improved, enabling access by subject headings, Boolean search capabilities, and browsing facilities. At this stage the user could choose from more than one display format, and some OPACs developed different interfaces for novice and expert users.

3 **Third generation**: some of the problems and confusions of the second-generation OPACs, such as the lack of assistance, non-availability of integrated vocabulary control tools, etc, were overcome in the third generation. Hildreth (1988) envisioned third-generation OPACs as having context-sensitive help facilities, controlled and natural-language search facilities, individualized display and so on.

Rasmussen (1999) suggests that third-generation OPACs are increasingly characterized by the features and facilities of the web. More and more OPACs are being made available on the web, making it possible for everyone with Internet access to search a particular library's OPAC.

OPAC search features

An OPAC is designed to tell the users about the collections of a particular library. Nowadays, with the web and common user interfaces, an OPAC can let the user search the collections of a number of libraries simultaneously.

All OPACs allow users to search a library's collection, though their search and retrieval facilities may differ. Common information retrieval facilities include:

1 Searching by author, title, call number, ISBN, etc: these are basically string or phrase search options, and consequently the user has to provide either the exact key or the first few letters/words of the search key. The user may be unable to combine search terms using Boolean or other operators.

2 Searching by keywords: the user can enter one or more keywords, and these can be combined using Boolean and proximity operators. Other operators such as truncation or limiting search options can also be used here. The operators used for combining search terms vary between systems. Some OPACs use Boolean and proximity operators implicitly, ie multiple keywords are automatically ANDed or are considered as a phrase comprising the search terms adjacent to one another. A keyword search is not limited to a specific field.

3 Searching by subject: this is a phrase search. In other words the user has to provide either the complete subject heading or the left part of the phrase. The system will automatically truncate a search term or phrase, and will retrieve items which contain its root. The user will be expected to use the headings that are valid as per the OPAC's subject headings list, such as LCSH. More and more OPAC systems are integrating vocabulary control tools, such as LCSH, for subject searching allowing the user to browse and select appropriate subject headings online.

4 Simple and advanced searching: some OPACs have different interfaces, or different sets of search options – one for novice users, providing minimum search features, and the other for expert searchers, with full search features.

5 Search output: this is usually a list of bibliographic records with some holdings information. The output may be ranked alphabetically, by publication date, or by accession date; the user may be unable to determine the usefulness of individual items without consulting the items physically. Most OPACs first display a brief record which can be expanded to show more details, such as the MARC record, and holding and availability information.

Despite several improvements in OPAC searching over the three generations, problems remain. Large and Behesti (1997) have mentioned several reasons for this. We can summarize these difficulties as follows:

1 OPAC users are not a uniform breed. They range from expert searchers to novice users. They may or may not have sufficient knowledge about the subject domain, and they have varying degrees of expectations from an OPAC search.

2 The OPAC systems themselves vary considerably in search and interface features, response time, and database content and size.

3 A typical OPAC encompasses several subjects and disciplines as well as different types of information materials – books, journals, theses, reports, reference sources, standards, patents, and so on – both in print as well as non-print media.

4 OPAC records provide metadata (data about data) in a very encapsulated form, featuring only the external parameters of information sources, such as author, title, ISBN, etc. The internal parameters, or the contents, are represented by means of keyword-assigned subject headings, and this involves too much abstraction of the contents of the information sources.

There is no unanimity on the solution to the OPAC problems: some researchers suggest improved interfaces, better online help facilities or better user instruction, while others argue in favour of sophisticated retrieval engines; still others say that OPAC records must contain more subject information to meet the varying nature of users' queries (Large and Behesti, 1997). Borgman (1996) argues that OPACs do not incorporate knowledge about user behaviour, and place too heavy a burden on the searcher for query specification.

The following sections describe the features of some selected OPACs with a view to identifying the search and retrieval features that are now available. A variety of OPACs from different parts of the world, and from different types of institutions, have been chosen in order to give a general overview of their features. As more and more library OPACs are accessible through the web, here we will discuss only the web versions of the OPACs concerned.

Features of the selected OPACs

Altogether ten web-accessible OPACs were selected for study. Three are national library catalogues: the British Library Catalogue, the Library of Congress Catalogue, and the National Library of Singapore Catalogue. The seven others are university library catalogues: two from the US (MELVYL at the University of California and PITTCat at the University of Pittsburgh); two from the UK (Star, the University of Sheffield catalogue, and the Glasgow University Library catalogue); and one each from Canada (UTCat, the University of Toronto OPAC), Hong Kong (the City University of Hong Kong), and Singapore (NTU OPAC, the Nanyang Technological University Catalogue).

The following sections describe the various features of the chosen OPACs. Our objective is not a comparative study but rather a general overview of the general and specific features of the chosen OPACs with a view to identifying the common features and facilities. Using these discussions we shall try to identify some techniques that are required to conduct a successful OPAC search.

The search interface

The search interfaces of the chosen OPACs vary. While detailed discussion of the interface features of each OPAC is beyond the scope of this book, we shall take a look at the general search options provided. Each of Figures 5.1–5.10 provides a screenshot of an OPAC search screen. Similarities as well as differences may be observed. The following general points can be made:

1 All but the NLB (National Library Board, Singapore) OPAC (Figure 5.7) provide search options such as author search, title search, etc. The NLB OPAC provides options for 'Easy Search' and 'Advanced Search', as it contains records for all the public libraries in Singapore. The other national libraries are used for reference rather than as general public libraries. The

NLB OPAC is accessed by a variety of users having different degrees of education, computer literacy, and so on.

2 The search options, and their wordings, shown on the first screen vary. In some cases (for example, Figures 5.1, 5.3, 5.4, 5.9) the search screen provides a brief explanation for each search option.

3 Some OPACs allow users to select a collection, or a specific catalogue, to search from the first screen; See, for example, Figures 5.1, 5.5, 5.6, 5.8, 5.10).

Fig. 5.1   *MELVYL catalogue (University of California)*

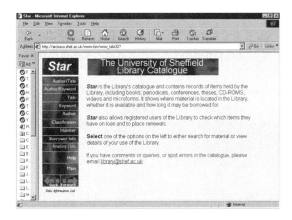

Fig. 5.2   *Star: the University of Sheffield OPAC*

Fig. 5.3   *Glasgow University Library OPAC*

Fig. 5.4   *PITTCat: the University of Pittsburgh OPAC*

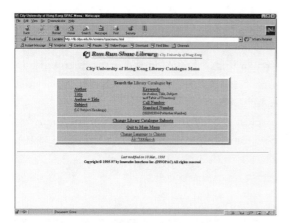

Fig. 5.5   *Library WebPAC: the City University of Hong Kong OPAC*

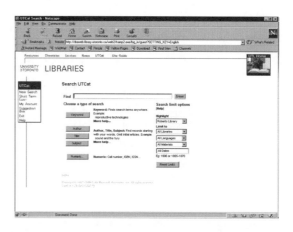

Fig. 5.6   *UTCat: the University of Toronto OPAC*

Fig. 5.7   *NLB OPAC: the National Library of Singapore OPAC*

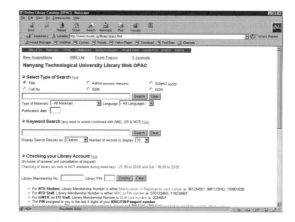

Fig. 5.8   *NTU OPAC: Nanyang Technological University OPAC*

4   All the OPACs here have 'Help' buttons, and some have links to further information about the OPAC. OPACs also provide specific help facilities for each type of search.

5   The NTU OPAC (Figure 5.8) gives all the various search options on one screen, so that the user need not move to another screen to conduct a specific type of search. It also provides context-sensitive help facilities.

6   Some OPACs, for example, the City University of Hong Kong (Figure 5.5) and the NTU OPAC, allow users to change language.

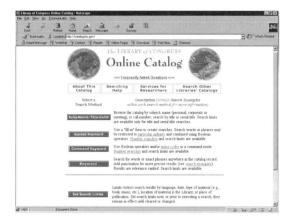

Fig. 5.9 *Library of Congress OPAC*

Fig. 5.10 *The British Library OPAC*

Selection of a specific collection to search

Some of the chosen OPACs allow users to select a specific collection to search (Table 5.1). Some allow users to select a specific type of materials, for example books, theses, reports, journals, etc. Some, for example, the NLB OPAC and MELVYL, act as a union catalogue that allows users to select a specific library to search: the British Library OPAC (Figure 5.10) allows users to select either the reference collections in London or the document supply collections in Boston Spa, for example. Allowing users to select a specific collection or a specific type of materials to search has both advantages and disadvantages. (Advanced users may prefer to focus on a specific collection or type of material, but this assumes some basic knowledge about the collection as the user is expected to select an appropriate collection, or type of material, to search. However, as this is a limiting search option, it need not be used if the user is unsure which collection or type of material to select.

Search fields

Each OPAC allows users to search on a number of specific fields (see Table 5.2). Usually OPACs allow users to conduct a known item search by certain keys, such as author, title, ISBN, etc, whereas an unknown item search is conducted by keywords and subject headings.

Table 5.1 *Choice for selection of a specific collection or type of materials*

OPAC	Search collections
British Library	User can select any of several BL collections
Glasgow University Library	There is no specific option to select a collection to search
Library of Congress	User can choose the 'Search Set Limit' button to select a specific type of material
Library WebPAC	User can select the button 'Change Library Catalogue Subsets' to select a specific collection to search
MELVYL	User can select any of the libraries of the nine University of California campuses, the California State Library, the California Academy of Sciences, the California Historical Society, the Center for Research Libraries, and the Graduate Theological Union in Berkeley
NLB	User can select a particular public library or the National Reference Library to search
NTU	User can select the 'Type of materials' option and the 'Language' option to select a specific type of material or a language to search on
PittCat	There is no specific option to select a collection to search
Star	There is no specific option to select a collection to search
UTCat	There is no specific option to select a collection to search

Table 5.2 *Choice of search fields*

OPAC	Search fields
British Library	Author's last name, author's first name or initials, organization name, title phrase/keywords, subject phrase/keywords, publisher, ISBN/ISSN, year of publication
Glasgow University Library	Author, title, author+title, keyword, subject, class number
Library of Congress	Subject, keyword, name (author), title, serial title, call number
Library WebPAC	Author, title, author+title, subject, keywords
MELVYL	Author, title, subject, and power search (allows you to search in more than 20 indexes including series, publisher, ISBN, etc, and you can limit to more than one location, format or language)
NLB	Easy search: keyword; advanced search: author, title, keyword, subject, call no., ISBN/ISSN, series
NTU	Author, title, keyword, subject, call number, ISBN, ISSN
PittCat	Author, title, keyword, subject
Star	Author+title, author+keyword, title, keyword, author, classification, number (ISBN or library allocated number)
UTCat	Author, title, keyword, subject, numeric (Call number, ISBN, ISSN)

Keyword and phrase search

Users can conduct a search on a single term/keyword or on a phrase. Searches on author, title, subject etc, can be a keyword or a phrase search. OPACs vary in terms of how the user enters keywords and phrases. For example, for a title search a user may have to enter the first few words of the title, though in some cases (for example in MELVYL), the user can search for any word in the title. Some OPACs (for example, the Library of Congress OPAC and the University of Pittsburgh OPAC), may require the user to enter a phrase in quotes. In the British Library OPAC a sequence of words entered for a search is considered as a phrase; if the words are separated by commas, a search is conducted on each word. It should be remembered that in any OPACs, when conducting a keyword search, a user is expected to enter only one keyword or a number of words interposed with appropriate Boolean or proximity operators. Otherwise, if a phrase is entered in the keyword search, the system will usually take only the first word as the search term. However, this is not the case with a subject search, where the user can enter a single word or a phrase comprising multiple keywords. All the OPACs here allow users to conduct a subject search through the Library of Congress Subject Headings List.

Search operators

The operators for Boolean, truncation and proximity searching vary. Table 5.3 shows the various search operators available in the chosen OPACs. Right truncation and wild-card or middle truncation are provided in many OPACs. However, in many cases searches are automatically carried out on certain fields such as title, author, etc. In some OPACs there is no specific operator or provision for truncation, and nor are proximity operators always provided. In some cases (for example, in the NTU and BL OPACs), proximity is assumed when more than one keyword is entered in the search box, while in others (for example, in the LC OPAC), proximity searching is performed when the option 'as a phrase' is used.

Lessons for conducting an OPAC search

As in any information search process, the first step for an OPAC search involves an analysis and understanding of the query. Once the user has a specific query, and decides to search an OPAC with a view to learning what a particular library has on a given topic, by a given author, and so on, the next step is to decide the search key(s) to be used. As we have already seen, OPACs allow a known item search by several keys such as, author, title, ISBN, etc. Searching by these keys is not difficult. For the author search, usually users enter the surname followed by the forename(s). Even if the user knows the names of more than one author

Table 5.3 *Search operators*

OPAC	Search operators			Limiting
	Boolean	Proximity	Truncation	
British Library	terms separated by commas are ANDed	none; words typed in a sequence are considered adjacent to each other in the same order as they appear	colon for a number of letters or words; hash (#) to stand for one letter	date of publication
Glasgow University Library	and, or	no specific operator	* for any number of characters	an option from: year, material, language or location may be chosen
Library of Congress	AND, OR, NOT (in capital letters); + before a term indicates that the term must appear, and ! before a term indicates that the term must not appear in the result; the option 'any of these' works as Boolean OR, and 'all of these' as the AND operator	no specific operator; the option 'as a phrase' conducts a phrase search	? for any number of characters	a field in the option: 'search in:' label may be chosen
Library WebPAC	AND, OR, NOT	no specific option	* for any number of characters	no specific option
MELVYL	AND, OR, NOT	none	* or #	an option from: location, language, date, form, date added to database

(continued)

Table 5.3 (continued)

	Boolean operators	Proximity	Truncation/wildcards	Other
NLB	AND, OR, BUT NOT	not available	* for any number of characters	>, <, or = with date for limiting a search; or English, Chinese, Malay or Tamil language may be chosen
NTU	and, or, not	no operator; in keyword search words in a string are considered as adjacent	? to search for all words with the same root and # for a character in the middle of a word	in a keyword search, search terms may be qualified with 'au' for author, 'ti' for title, and 'su' for subject; a search may be limited by date, language and material type
PittCat	AND, OR, NOT (all in upper case)	no specific operator	* for any number of characters	an option from: year, language, type, medium, location, publication status, place of publication may be chosen
Star	words in a sequence are automatically ANDed; use Boolean OR	no specific option	no specific option	an option from: date, language, format, Opus number may be chosen
UTCat	and, or, not	no specific operator	? for any number of characters	'near' specifies how many words may intervene between search terms (ignoring the word order); 'within' specifies that one term will follow another within a given number of words (word order is important while using this operator)

often it is possible to enter only one author name, because these fields do not usually allow Boolean AND searching. Usually OPACs automatically right-truncate the search keys entered for the author and title search, and this saves the user typing the full author name or full title of an item.

For an unknown item search the user can approach the OPAC through the keyword or subject search option. All the OPACs here allow users to enter a subject heading – a word or a phrase – representing a specific subject/topic. However, the user may have to enter the subject headings exactly the same way they were entered by the cataloguer at the data entry stage. All the chosen OPACs use LCSH for assigning subject headings, so the user must also use these subject headings. If the user is not quite sure of the spelling or the word order in a multi-word subject heading, it is advisable that he or she types the first word as the subject search key. The OPAC then leads the user to a portion of the dictionary beginning with that word, and against each entry the number of available items in the library will be shown. Thus the user can browse this list to pick up the most appropriate subject heading to conduct a subject search.

For conducting a keyword search, the user has to keep in mind the options for combining search terms and the corresponding operators. It should be remembered that when a keyword search option is chosen, the user is expected to enter only one word, or multiple words interposed with Boolean or proximity operators. In some OPACs, a sequence of words typed in a keyword search box are automatically considered as a phrase, ie an adjacency operator is used automatically, meaning that only those records where the keywords appear next to each other are retrieved. In some cases the user can take advantage of truncation facilities. Most OPACs allow users to combine search terms with Boolean operators, but users should check how the operators should be used. For example, some OPACs expect the user to enter Boolean operators in upper case (see Table 5.3).

The output of OPAC searches is usually not ranked, and hence the user may have to go through the entire list of retrieved items to select appropriate items. This selection is often complicated by the fact that the output records often do not include an abstract, and the user must base his or her decision on an item's usefulness by considering the title, keywords or subject heading(s).

Summary

In this chapter we have discussed OPACs and the search and retrieval features of ten systems selected from different types of libraries from various countries. The search interfaces, as illustrated by screen shots for each OPAC, vary significantly, and the user needs to learn some basic techniques in order to be able to conduct a successful search. Several researchers have discussed the changing nature of OPACs in the web environment (see, for example, Borgman, 1996; Large and Behesti, 1997; Carter and Bordeianu, 1999; Cousins, 1999; Dunsire, 1999; Holm, 1999), and some have discussed the issues to be considered for OPAC evaluation (see, for example, Anderson, S, 1998; Ashton, 1998; Kopak and Cherry, 1998).

Chapter 6

Searching CD-ROM databases

Introduction

Information sources available on CD-ROM range from common reference sources like dictionaries, encyclopedias, etc, to subject-specific sources containing bibliographic, full-text, and multimedia information. Over ten thousand information sources are currently available on CD-ROM (Chowdhury, 1999b). The usefulness of these sources depends both on their content and on the retrieval systems that come with them. In order to make effective use of information sources on CD-ROM, users need to learn about the search and retrieval techniques of each source. Some CD-ROM products can be searched using a common interface designed for all the products of the one company. For example, WINSPIRS is the search interface for all the *SilverPlatter* products (Windows version). However, the search fields, etc, depend on the content of the product and therefore vary from one CD-ROM to another.

In this chapter we shall discuss some general issues related to the searching and retrieval of information from CD-ROM products. Examples of these, ranging from common reference sources like *Books in print* to subject databases, such as *LISA plus, Ei Compendex*, and *METADEX*, and to multimedia resources, such as *Britannica CD* and the *Encarta* encyclopedia, are given to highlight the features of the various information sources available, as well as their differences. Finally, we have identified some common points that the user must consider in order to make effective use of information on CD-ROM.

CD-ROM: common search features

Basic information on CD-ROM is available in a number of published documents (see, for example, Saffady, 1992; Hanson and Day, 1994; Chowdhury, 1999b; Rowley, 1999). The following search features are commonly available, though, as we shall see later, the search syntax, operators, etc, may vary from one

CD-ROM to another (examples illustrating these search features are given later in the chapter).

1 **Keyword search**: this enables the user to conduct searches with one or more keywords, and is the most common search feature of CD-ROM databases.

2 **Phrase search**: this allows the user to conduct searches for phrases. Sometimes this is done through subject search facilities or by using proximity operators.

3 **Boolean search**: Boolean AND, OR, and NOT searches are available, though the operators used for these searches may vary from one CD-ROM to another.

4 **Truncation**: of the three kinds of truncation (left, right and middle truncation), left truncation is not commonly available in CD-ROM databases. The symbols for truncation and their syntax and effect vary, and the user has to learn these to conduct an effective search.

5 **Index and/or thesaurus support**: indexes allow users to select the search term(s)/phrase(s) from the term index, and a thesaurus allows users to consult a map of available terms to widen or narrow down a given search, as required. CD-ROM retrieval software provides index search facilities, ie users can select an index to browse and select terms from the index for searching. There may be one index file or a separate index file for each searchable field so that the user can choose a field and then browse the corresponding index file. Index search facilities are more commonly available than thesaurus facilities.

6 **Proximity search**: this allows the user to tell the search system how far apart the chosen search terms should be in the retrieved records. In some cases this is given in terms of the number of intervening words, while in others it may be possible to specify whether the search terms should appear in the same sentence, same field, same paragraph, and so on.

7 **Field-specific search**: most CD-ROM search software allows the user to specify one or more fields to search. The user may be able to select a particular field to search, and then select the search term from the index file for that field.

8 **Free-text search**: this enables the user to specify one or more search terms or phrases that are not limited to any particular field. There may also be an index for free-text search terms.

9 **Combining search sets and search refinement**: this facility enables the user to refine a given search by adding or dropping search terms or conditions. This may be done by completely rekeying an entire search expression, or by calling up a previous search set and making modifications to that. In many

cases users can save a search statement to be used as necessary.

10 **Limiting or range search**: some search software allows the user to limit a given search by adding criteria such as language, year of publication, price, and so on. In some cases, the criteria may fall within a range of values, such as items published within a certain range of years, and so on.

11 **Searching through the retrieved records**: the user may be able to select search terms from a record that has been retrieved through a previous search.

Output features

The nature of the output depends on a number of factors, such as the nature of the database, its content, organization, policies of the publisher, and so on. Some CD-ROM retrieval software automatically displays the output in a different window: in other cases the user may have to choose the view/display option to look at the records. In other cases still, the system may first display the output in brief, and the user has then to select one or more records to view the detailed display. It may be possible to choose from more than one display and print format; the output itself is usually not ranked. In some CD-ROM databases the search terms are highlighted in the output.

Sample reference and bibliographic databases on CD-ROM

Eight CD-ROM databases have been selected for a discussion on the various search and retrieval features available. Three of these, viz *Books in print*, *Ulrich's on disc* and *Multimedia and CD-ROM directory*, represent the category of general or ready reference sources; four others, viz *LISA plus, Ei Compendex, Econ-Lit* and *METADEX*, are bibliographic databases containing details of documents including abstracts; and one, *Emerald*, is a full-text database of journal articles. Brief information on these databases is given below.

Books in print, produced by the R R Bowker Company, is a comprehensive source of information on books containing bibliographic records from over 44,000 publishers. As well as books currently in print and titles to be published in up to the next six months, information is included on titles declared out of print or indefinitely out of stock since 1979. There are three search screens: Browse Index, Form Search and Search. In the first (Figure 6.1), the user can select a field from a list of nine, viz author name, ISBN, keyword, publisher name, subject, children's subject, title, title code, and series title. Once a field is chosen the user can enter a search term. The system will then show the relevant part of the index and the number of hits. You can highlight a record from the browse index and click on 'Brief display' to see basic details (title, author, price and ISBN) of the record. You can then have the full

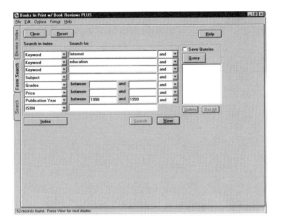

Fig. 6.1   *'Books in print' Browse Index screen*

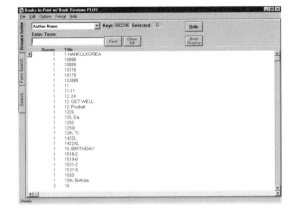

Fig. 6.2   *'Books in print' Form Search screen*

record displayed. In the Form Search mode, you can search on selected fields that appear in the boxes (Figure 6.2). You can click on the arrow in each box to see other fields. You can select a field and then enter the search term in the corresponding box, or you can click on the Index button to display the index related to that particular field. For numeric fields, such as price, year and grades, you can select a range. You can combine the search fields or terms from the same field with AND, OR, and ANDNOT operators. Brief and full records – as shown in the Browse Index example – can then be displayed. In the Search mode, you can select any search category or a combination of categories to conduct a search (see Figure 6.3). You can key in the category followed by '=' and then the search term(s), or can choose the category and click on Index to display the index. You can then key in the search term and select Find to display the index. By double-clicking on the selected term the system will automatically assign the term to the chosen category in the 'Enter search query' box.

The *METADEX* CD-ROM database from Dialog Corporation provides comprehensive coverage of international metals literature. It is part of the Dialog online database, File number 32, covering bibliographic information with abstracts on Metals, Polymers and Ceramics. Different options are available to search this database. Figure 6.4 shows the keyword search option and Figure 6.5 shows the free-text search option. In addition to keywords and phrases, users can also search by author, title words, subject headings, publisher, journal name, and so on. A search can be limited by language – there are English and non-English language records. After a search term has been selected from the list of terms (see Figure 6.4) or it has been keyed in (as in

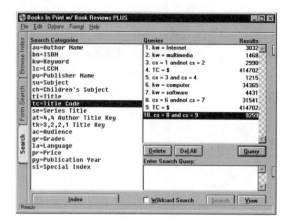

Fig. 6.3　*'Books in print' Search screen*

Fig. 6.4　*Search screen for 'METADEX' on Dialog OnDisc*

Figure 6.5), and the OK button is pressed, the system conducts a search and the first record from the output set is displayed. After a search has been conducted, users can modify the search. The Modify Search menu appears when users already have a set of records from a previous search. If users want to conduct a new search, then they have to click the New Search option which will clear the records from the last search you performed and start a new search.

Ulrich's on disc, from the R R Bowker Company, is a unique current, comprehensive and continuously updated source of information on over 200,000 periodicals and serials from 80,000 publishers in 200 countries. Annuals, continuations, and conference proceedings are included, as well as academic/scholarly publications, trade publications, consumer magazines, newsletters and bulletins, and titles that have ceased publication since 1974. The search screen and the search options are the same as those of *Books in print,* only the search fields are different (see Figures 6.6 and 6.7).

The multimedia and CD-ROM directory, from System Simulation Ltd, provides comprehensive details on over 16,000 companies, 30,000 commercially available CD-ROM and multimedia titles, their publishers and distributors worldwide. It also extensively covers multimedia software and hardware producers, production services, and other service providers, and contains information on conferences, books and journals aimed at multimedia professionals, and a glossary. Here you can search by company name or by product title. You can also find books, journals, etc, on CD-ROM and multimedia. However, title and company search form the major features of this database. In each case you will see a screen containing various search fields

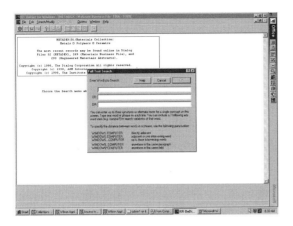

Fig. 6.5   *Search screen for 'METADEX' on Dialog OnDisc (full text search options)*

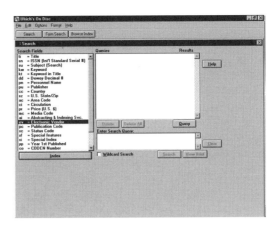

Fig. 6.6   *'Ulrich's on disc' Search screen*

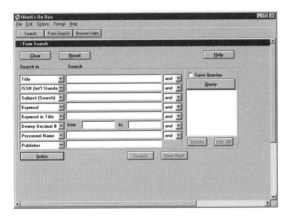

Fig. 6.7   *'Ulrich's on disc' Form Search screen*

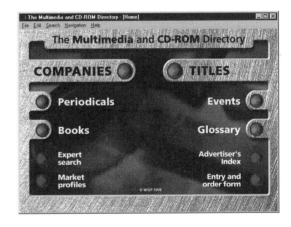

Fig. 6.8   *'Multimedia and CD-ROM directory' Search screen*

which you can select to search. You can combine the search terms by AND, OR and ANDNOT. You can click on any field and go to that index. Note that the search screen and options in each case are the same, only the fields change (see Figures 6.8–6.10).

LISA plus, produced by Bowker-Saur, comprises two different databases: *Library and information science abstracts* (LISA) and *Current research in library and information science* (CRLIS). There are three search interfaces: Browse, Easy Search and Expert Search (see Figures 6.11–6.13). In the Easy Search interface the user can enter search term(s) or phrase(s) in the appropriate

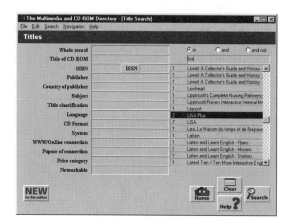

Fig. 6.9 *'Multimedia and CD-ROM directory' Title search screen*

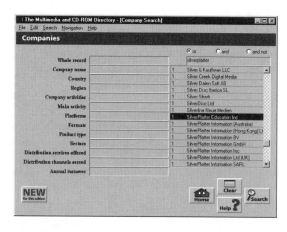

Fig. 6.10 *'Multimedia and CD-ROM directory' Companies search screen*

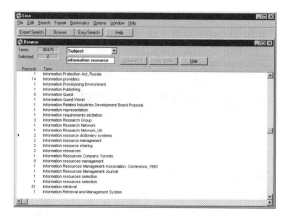

Fig. 6.11 *Browse screen of 'LISA plus'*

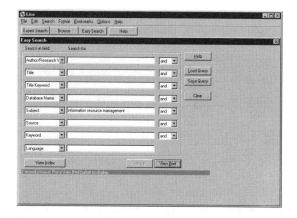

Fig. 6.12 *Easy Search screen of 'LISA plus'*

box(es) to conduct a search on the chosen field(s). A number of fields can be chosen for one search. The Expert Search interface allows the user to choose one or more fields which can combined by using appropriate search operators. Abbreviations of the fields are used before each search term, eg au = lancaster, kw = internet, and so on. In each mode of search the user can display an index file corresponding to the chosen field, browse through the index and select the search term/phrase from the index.

Ei Compendex, from KR-Ondisc, provides comprehensive coverage of the world's significant engineering and technical journal and conference literature. There are a number of search options: word/phrase search through index, author search, title word search, journal title, etc (see Figure 6.14). A search can be limited by a number of parameters, such as language, year of publication, etc.

EconLit, produced by the American Economic Association, is a comprehensive indexed bibliography with selected abstracts of the world's economic literature. Records contain basic bibliographic data plus subject and geographic descriptors. The CD-ROM runs on *SilverPlatter* retrieval software called *WINSPIRS*. There are basically two ways to search: Search and Index Search (see Figure 6.15). The search facility lets you enter one or more search terms,

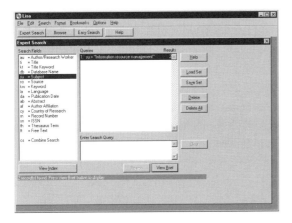

Fig. 6.13 *Expert Search screen of 'LISA plus'*

Fig. 6.14 *'Ei Compendex' Search (results) screen*

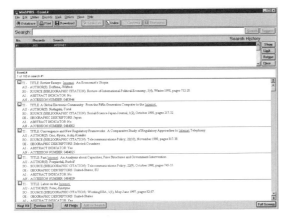

Fig. 6.15 *'EconLit' Search interface (WINSPIRS version 2.0)*

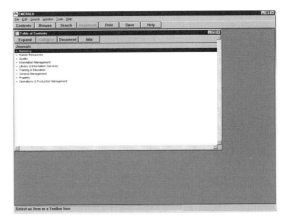

Fig. 6.16 *First screen of 'Emerald' (full-text database)*

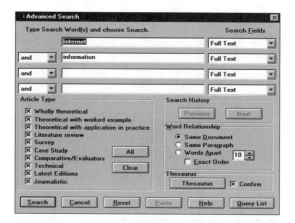

Fig. 6.17 *Advanced Search options of 'Emerald'*

and you then click on the Search button. In the index mode you can browse a portion of the index, and select a search term from there to conduct a search. The free-text index, which is a combination of a number of index files in this case, is the default one; however, you can choose other indexes too.

Emerald, a full-text database from MCB, covers more than 100 top journals across ten broad subject areas. It provides access to the full text of articles in PDF and HTML format published from 1994 to date. Abstracts of articles published between 1989 and 1993 are available. The subjects covered include marketing, information management, library and information science, human resources, general management, etc. Users can choose any subject and get a list of all the journals covered in that subject. There are different ways of searching this database (see Figures 6.16 and 6.17). You can browse through the index of a number of fields, select search terms from the index and search, or you can simply enter search terms or phrases in the search box to search. An Advanced Search option lets you formulate complex search statements. You can also choose a subject category and a specific journal from that category, and can then browse the various issues of the journal to select an article, or a part of it, and view the entire article or a specific part thereof.

Search interfaces of the selected CD-ROM databases

The user interface is probably the most important design attribute of any software program, especially in the case of CD-ROM databases. Without the retrieval engine and specifically designed user interface, the electronic databases are nothing more than efficient storage and distribution media (Chowdhury, 1999b). The user interface is the gateway through which the end-users communicate with any database. Rowley (1997) has reviewed the literature on the evaluation of CD-ROM interfaces.

Here, without focusing on the interfaces as such, we shall look into the various search and retrieval features of the CD-ROM databases under consideration. This will help clarify how the interfaces and various search and retrieval features of CD-ROM databases differ from one another; this in turn will justify the need for learning appropriate techniques for effective CD-ROM searching. Figures 6.1 to 6.17 show the search interfaces of the chosen CD-ROM products: from this small set of samples we can derive the following points.

1   Some CD-ROM products have more than one search interface, for example, *Books In Print* (Figures 6.1–6.3), *METADEX* (Figures 6.4 and 6.5), *Ulrich's on disc* (Figures 6.6 and 6.7), *LISA plus* (Figures 6.12 and 6.13), while others have one search interface giving options for both simple/novice and advanced/expert search.

2   Some search interfaces provide simple forms for the user to fill in with the appropriate search terms/phrases, and the system will then prepare the actual search expression behind the scene.

3   The search fields, ie the fields on which searches can be conducted, vary from one product to another, and they depend on the content of the database concerned.

4   If the user is unsure about a search term/phrase, it may be possible to search the index for the corresponding field and check whether the term/phrase occurs in the dictionary or not.

5   Some search interfaces have more icons than others. These are graphical user interfaces used as shortcuts for particular actions that a user is likely to perform on the interface.

6   Two types of indexing practice are followed: word index and phrase index. In the word index, each individual word in a field is indexed, while in the phrase index, a given phrase that may comprise several keyword, is indexed. The user may need to check whether a field is word- or phrase-indexed, by browsing through the index for the particular field, before entering a search term/phrase.

7   In some cases the user can see the various search sets as the search progresses. This helps the user keep track of the search process, and means the user can modify searches very easily by using a previous search set.

8   Some retrieval systems, such as *Ei Compendex* or *EconLit*, show the results instantly, while in others the user has to choose the view/display option, as in *LISA plus*.

9   The features of the search interfaces may vary significantly, and users who

are expert in searching one CD-ROM may not be able to search others with equal efficiency without some training and/or practice.

10 CD-ROM databases do not usually provide facilities for ranking the search results according to relevance.

How to conduct searches on CD-ROMs

Conducting effective searches requires knowledge of a number of techniques. Users should not only have an understanding of the nature, content and structure of the database, but also be familiar with the various options available in the search screen, the tools and techniques for searching, and the techniques and formats for display of the search output. In this section we shall see how the various search options mentioned earlier in this chapter (pp. 103–4) can be used to conduct searches in the chosen CD-ROM databases. We shall take each search option and give sample search expressions that can be used to conduct searches, which will help readers understand the various techniques that are to be learnt in order to conduct successful CD-ROM searches. Our main objective is not to compare and contrast but to give an idea of the various types of search and retrieval facilities available in CD-ROM databases.

Searching in a specific field

Searching for information in a CD-ROM database usually takes one of the two forms: field-specific or free-text search. A user may know which field to search, or might like to restrict a given search to one or more fields. This is a field-specific search. If the users are not sure of the field(s) to be searched, they can conduct a free-text search, which means that the search is not restricted to any particular field. While the free-text search is not universally available, field-specific search is the simplest form of search, and CD-ROM databases offer various options to conduct searches on one or more specific fields. The simplest option is the form search, where the user can select a specific box for a particular field (see, for example, Figures 6.1, 6.7, 6.9, 6.10 and 6.12) and can key in the search term/phrase. Which search fields can be searched in a CD-ROM database depends on the content and structure of the database concerned, and therefore they differ from one database to another. Table 6.1 shows the various search fields in the eight chosen CD-ROM databases. This indicates that to conduct a search one needs to know the various search fields that are available in a given database, and they vary even in similar databases. For example, the search fields for *Books in print* and *Cumulative book index* are not the same, although the nature and content of the two databases are similar.

Table 6.1 *Search fields of selected CD-ROM databases*

Database	Search field	Number of searchable fields
Books in print	Author, ISBN, keyword, LC control number, publisher name, subject, children's subject, title, title code, series title, 4-4* author–title key, 3-2-2-1 title key, audience, grades, language, price, publication year, special index	18
METADEX	Alloy class name, author affiliation, author name, conference location, conference title, conference year, document type, journal name, accession number, patent application date, patent number, publisher, report number, section heading code (broad subject category), subject heading, title words, and year of publication	17
Ulrich's on disc	Title, ISSN, subject, keyword, keyword in title, Dewey number, personnel name, publisher, country, US state/zip, area code, circulation, price, media code, abstracting and indexing service, electronic vendor, publication code, status code, special features, special index, year first published, CODEN number	22
Multimedia and CD-ROM directory	For titles: whole record, title of CD-ROM, ISBN, publisher, country of publisher, subject, title classification, language, CD format, system, web/online connection, purpose of connection, price category, networkable CD-ROMs	14
	For companies: whole record, company name, country, region, company activities, main activity, platforms, formats, product type, sectors, distribution services offered, distribution channels served, annual turnover	13
LISA plus	Author, title, title keyword, database name, subject, source, keyword, language, publication date, abstract, author affiliation, country of research, record number, CODEN, CATNI name, ISSN, thesaurus term	17
Ei Compendex	Word/phrase, Ei subject headings, author name, author affiliation, title words, journal name, conference title, conference location, conference sponsor, conference year, year of publication, treatment codes, language, major subject headings, EI classification codes	15
EconLit	Citation, title, author, author affiliation, source, document type, reviewed book, publication year, Festschrift honoree, descriptors, geographic descriptors, named person, abstract, abstract indicator, book review collection, references, update code, ISBN, ISSN, accession number	20
Emerald	Full text, author, article title, keyword, publication year, journal title, quality indicator, article type	8

*4-4 and 3-2-2-1 denote the number of characters that can be used to represent an element of a query; eg '4-4 author title' means that the first four characters of the query will denote the four characters of the author's name, and the next four characters, the first four characters of the title.

Keyword search, author search, subject search, etc

These are common search features. Depending on the field, the user may be able to search on words or phrases. Search terms or phrases for the same or different fields can be combined using the Boolean operators. Usually the subject field is phrase indexed, which allows the user to search single-word subjects, like 'education' or 'internet', or multi-word subjects, using phrases like 'information storage and retrieval' or 'world wide web'. However, before using a multi-word search term, it is useful to check whether the search term/phrase occurs in the index or not. Similarly, when conducting a search on the keyword field, the user should not use multiple words if the keyword field is word indexed, which assumes that the user will use single words to search. Nevertheless, it is always better to check whether a given search term occurs in the index file or not before using that as a search term. Phrases can be searched for by combining keywords to retrieve records where they appear next to each other, though the constituent terms might have been word indexed. This is possible through the use of proximity operators (discussed below). Table 6.2 shows how searches on specific fields containing keywords and phrases can be conducted in the selected CD-ROM databases. This is usually a straightforward operation: the user can simply select the chosen field and enter the search term directly or through the index. In some cases special options, for example forms (see Figures 6.1, 6.7 and 6.12) are available to conduct searches with keywords or phrases from more than one field.

Table 6.2 *Options available in selected CD-ROM databases for searches on keywords or phrases*

CD-ROM	Options for conducting search on word/phrases	Method
Books in print	Browse Index	Select a field, enter the search term in the appropriate box, and
Ulrich's on disc	Browse Index	search. In *Books in print* and *Ulrich*, you need to click on FIND
LISA plus	Browse	after entering the term, whereas in LISA plus, after entering and
		selecting the chosen term, you need to click on View Titles to
		see the results
Books in print	Form Search	1. Select the particular field, enter the search term and search.
Ulrich's on disc	Form Search	You can combine search terms, from the same or different
		fields, by Boolean operators
LISA plus	Easy Search	2. Select any particular field and choose to view the index.
		Select a term from the index and search
Books in print	Search	1. Enter the search term preceded by a field code
Ulrich's on disc	Search	(chosen from a list shown in the 'Search fields' box)
LISA plus	Expert Search	and an equals sign, and then search
		2. Select any particular field code and then choose to view
		the index. Select the term from the index to search

(continued)

Table 6.2 (*continued*)

CD-ROM	Options for conducting search on word/phrases	Method
METADEX	Browse	Keywords can be chosen from a list, or can be keyed in. If the 'Select word(s) from a list' option is chosen, a screen with a small box will appear where users have to enter a keyword, and an alphabetical list showing the keyword with the number of hits will appear. If the 'Enter word(s) to search' option is chosen, another window (see Figure 6.5) pops us where users can enter up to three keywords or phrases.
Cumulative book index	Index Search	Click on Index, and you'll see the free-text index where you can enter the search term; you will see the corresponding portion of the index in a small window. You can browse through the index window. When you select a search term from there you will see the output in the output window. Using the Search+ option, you can combine keywords and other search options by Boolean operators to formulate your search
Ei Compendex	Search/Modify	Click on 'Search/Modify' and then click on 'Word/Phrase' index. Enter the term in the small box after 'Enter' and you will see the corresponding portion of the index. Select one or more terms and click OK. You will then see a search set with the given terms in the 'Search History' window, and the output (the complete record) in the output window
Multimedia and CD-ROM directory	Title Search/ Company Search	Select a field and enter a search term or phrase. You can also display and browse the index of the corresponding field. Once you select a term/phrase from the index, it will be automatically posted on the search box for the chosen field
EconLit	Search	Enter the search term(s) in the 'Search' box and click on search; a search set will be created and shown in the search history window and out put records will be displayed in the output window. Click on Index, and you'll see the free-text index where you can enter the search term; you will see the corresponding portion of the index in a small window. You can browse through the index window. When you select a search term from there you will see the output in the output window
Emerald	Basic Search	Enter the keyword in the box for search term(s) and click on Search; the system will then conduct the search and show the no. of hits and brief information about each record (document no., title, author, document type, and quality indicator) will appear; double click on any record to see the full text. Multiple keywords can be joined by Boolean operators. Click on Browse and click on any field (author, keyword, etc) and the

(continued)

Table 6.2 (continued)

CD-ROM	Options for conducting search on word/phrases	Method
		corresponding index will be displayed; browse through the index, and double click on any term to select and search. Note that here keywords can be single words or phrases
Emerald	Advanced Search	Select a field (eg full text, author, keyword), enter search terms and select Search. You can combine search terms with any other term(s) from the same or different field combined with Boolean operators (and, or, not)

Combining search terms and fields (Boolean searching)

Boolean searching is possible in all the CD-ROM databases, though how it is carried out varies (see Table 6.3). Boolean searches cannot be conducted in the 'Browse index' mode of a CD-ROM database, for the obvious reason that only one term/phrase can be keyed in to display the corresponding portion of the index.

Table 6.3 Boolean search operators

CD-ROM	Operators	Options
Books in print	AND, OR, NOT	In the Easy Search mode you can combine terms/phrases with Boolean operators in a chosen field box, or can type one term/phrase in each box and click on a Boolean operator in the box next to the term on the right.
		In the Expert Search mode you have to type the Boolean operator to combine terms/phrases from the same or different fields.
METADEX	AND, OR, NOT	In the 'Enter Word(s) to Search' option, search terms can be combined with OR. All the three Boolean operators – AND, OR, NOT – can be used in the 'Modify Search' option
Ulrich's on disc	AND, OR, NOT/ANDNOT	In the Form Search mode you can combine terms/phrases with Boolean operators in a chosen field box, or can type one term/phrase in each box and click on a Boolean operator in the box next to the term on the right
		In the Search mode you have to type the Boolean operator to combine terms/phrases from the same or different fields
CD-ROM and multimedia directory	AND, OR, AND NOT	You can use these operators by clicking on the buttons appearing on top of the search screen. These operators can be used to combine search terms in the same field, or terms from different fields.

(continued)

Table 6.3 (continued)

CD-ROM	Operators	Options
LISA plus	AND, OR, ANDNOT (NOT can also be used in free-text search mode)	In the Easy Search mode, you can combine terms/phrases with Boolean operators in a chosen field box, or can type one term/phrase in each box and click on a Boolean operator in the box next to the term on the right.
		In the Expert Search mode, you have to type the Boolean operator to combine terms/phrases from the same or different fields. No nesting is possible*
Ei Compendex	AND, OR, NOT	Use these operators to combine search terms in the 'Modify Search Options'
EconLit	AND, OR, NOT	Use these operators to combine search terms in the 'Search' box
Emerald	AND, OR, NOT	Enter these operators in the search as well as Advanced Search mode

*Nesting means enclosing the search terms, along with the necessary Boolean and other operators, in order to set the priorities for execution of the Boolean operators.

Truncation

As noted above, truncation can be of three types, right, left and middle (or internal), though none of the sample databases provides left-truncation facilities. The symbols for truncation vary from one database to another (see Table 6.4).

Table 6.4 *Truncation search operators*

CD-ROM	Operators	Options
Books in print	* can be used for any number of characters	Truncated search can be performed in Form Search as well as in Search mode
METADEX	? – one or more can be used, with or without intervening spaces	One ? after a search term retrieves words of any length that begin with the root. To search on words that start with a word stem and that have no more than one character after the stem, one has to enter ? ? (question mark, space, question mark). To search on words that start with a word stem and that have no more than two characters after the stem, one needs to enter ?? (two questions marks, without any spaces in between)
Ulrich's on disc	* or $ substitutes for any number of characters ? substitutes for one character	* and $ can be used for right truncation only ? can be used anywhere in a word; you can use multiple ? symbols

(continued)

Table 6.4 *(continued)*

CD-ROM	Operators	Options
Multimedia and CD-ROM directory	* for at least one character ? for one character [ ] for alternative characters	Use * to search for words with the same root with any number of characters after the root. Use ? to stand for one character; you can use multiple ?. Use [ ] to retrieve records with alternative characters; for example, intern[ea]t* will retrieve both internet and international
LISA plus	$ for any no. of characters ? for one character	Right and middle or internal truncation is allowed. Both the symbols can be used for right as well as middle truncation. You can enter the symbol as appropriate in the Easy Search as well as the Expert Search mode. Multiple ? can be used
Ei Compendex	? for any no. of characters A combination of ? and space can be used to conduct different types of truncation	To search on words that start with a word stem and that have no more than one character after the stem, enter ? ? (question mark, space, question mark). For example, ROBOT? ? retrieves robot and robots. To search on words that start with a word stem and that have no more than two characters after the stem, enter ?? (two question marks). For example, ROBOT?? retrieves: robot, robots, robotic
EconLit	* for any number of characters ? for a single character	Right truncation and middle truncation are allowed. The truncation symbols can be used anywhere in the search term except as the first character; multiple ? can be used
Emerald	? for any number of characters	Use ? for right as well as middle truncation

Index and/or thesaurus support

CD-ROM databases allow users to select and browse index files corresponding to the chosen fields. This facilitates searching in many ways. For example, the user can decide which search term/phrase to use for a given field, and may even conduct the search without having to key in the search term. Some databases also have an integrated thesaurus that can be used while searching. This does not only facilitate the choice of the most appropriate search term/phrase, it also helps the user reformulate the query by choosing narrower, broader or related terms. Table 6.5 shows the index and thesaurus facilities available in the chosen CD-ROM databases.

Proximity search

CD-ROM databases allow users to conduct proximity searches in order to specify how closely the terms prescribed in a search expression should appear, in which order they should appear and so on. The operators for proximity searches vary among the CD-ROM databases (see Table 6.6).

Table 6.5 *Options for conducting an index search*

CD-ROM	Options for index and/or thesaurus support
Books in print	The index is available through Browse Index mode. The user can select a field from a list of nine (author name, ISBN, keyword, publisher name, subject, children's subject, title, title code, and series title). The user can then enter a search term and click on the FIND button. The system will show the part of the index and the number of hits
METADEX	In the 'Word Search Option' users can choose the option 'Select word(s) from a list'
Ulrich's on disc	You can choose a field from either the Search or the Form Search mode. In each case you can display and browse the corresponding index and select a term/phrase from the index
Multimedia and CD-ROM directory	For each field you can display the index, browse through it and select a term/phrase for searching
LISA plus	The thesaurus may be accessed via the Browse window by clicking on the Index drop-down list and selecting Thesaurus Term; highlight the required term and click View Titles. In the Expert Search mode, enter the thesaurus term in the Search Query box, click on OK or press Enter. Press the 'View Brief' button to display the results of the search ie the thesaurus block. A thesaurus term can be selected to conduct a search in the database.
Ei Compendex	In order to conduct a search, you need to choose an index: author, subject heading, keywords, etc, and then the corresponding index will be open for you to browse and to select the search term
EconLit	You can toggle between the search and index button. By choosing the index button, you can display and browse the index file (the default is free text) of several fields
Emerald	In the Advanced Search mode, you can choose one or more fields to search, and once you have entered a search term corresponding to a field, you can click on the 'Thesaurus' button to get other words corresponding to the search term

Table 6.6 *Proximity search operators*

CD-ROM	Operators	Options
Books in print	NEAR	Although it is mentioned in the help file, this option does not seem to work
METADEX	Write two or more words consecutively to search as a phrase. Use period(s) (.) for one or more intervening words. Use underscore (_) for words in the same paragraph. Use asterisk (*) for words in the same field	A search expression 'artificial intelligence' will be searched as a phrase. A search on 'artificial . intelligence' will retrieve artificial intelligence, as well as phrases such as artificial machine intelligence. A search on 'information_management' will retrieve records where both the terms occur in the same paragraph, while a search on 'information*management' will retrieve records where both the terms occur in the same field

(continued)

Table 6.6 (continued)

CD-ROM	Operators	Options
Ulrich's on disc	none	–
Multimedia and CD-ROM directory	# adjacent in the same order #n within n words in the same order ## adjacent in any order ##n within n words in any order	eg personal # computer eg information #2 retrieval eg information ## systems eg information ##2 management
LISA plus	ANDx or NEARx: Locates both words, in any order within x words in the same field. NOTx: locates the first word, but not the second within x words in the same field. WITH: locates both words in adjacency, forward order only, in the same field. WITHx: locates both words, forward order only, within x words in the same field.	Proximity search is only allowed for the Free Text search. It can be used in both the Easy Search and Expert Search modes
Ei Compendex	Write two or more words consecutively to search as a phrase. Use period(s) (.) for one or more intervening words	A search expression 'artificial intelligence' will be searched as a phrase, ie the words next to each other in the same order. You can specify the maximum no. of intervening words by one or more periods, eg information . management will retrieve both information management and information resource management
EconLit	NEAR indicates adjacent in any order in the same sentence; NEAR n specifies the maximum number of words	Use the NEAR operator to specify that the search terms should appear in the same sentence in any order. Use NEAR n to specify the maximum number of words that may occur between two search terms that appear in the same sentence
Emerald	same document, same paragraph, words apart, exact order	In the Advanced Search mode, you can choose any of the four options to conduct a proximity search

Free-text search

Instead of searching in a specific field, in some cases the user might like to conduct a search in all or many different fields. This is possible through what is known as the free-text search facility. In some cases, the default setting is the free-text search, ie whenever a user enters a search term it is searched in all or a number of selected fields. The facilities available for free-text searching in the selected CD-ROM databases are shown in Table 6.7.

Table 6.7 *Free-text search options*

CD-ROM	Options for free-text searching
Books in print	Not available
METADEX	Can be conducted through the 'Word Search' option
Ulrich's on disc	None
Multimedia and CD-ROM directory	You can choose the 'whole record' option and enter a word or phrase to search for it anywhere in the record
LISA plus	Here a free-text term is any single word taken from any field in the record, with the exception of Stopwords*. Free text differs from keyword searching in that a space between two terms is treated as meaning true proximity in relative position and order. For example: ft=catalog$ will retrieve all references that have 'catalog' as the first seven characters of the term; ft=line, will retrieve all references that contain the term 'line', including 'line management', author/research worker 'Line, Maurice B.'; ft = public libraries will retrieve all references where the term 'public libraries' occurs, but it will not retrieve records with the combinations, 'libraries public' or with the phrase 'public and academic libraries'. If a term is entered in the Search Mode without an operator a free text (ft) will be automatically carried out
Ei Compendex	No free-text search is possible: you have to choose an index (ie a field) to conduct a search
EconLit	The search term may appear any field
Emerald	In the Search option, or using the 'Full text' option in the Advanced Search mode, you can conduct a full-text search, ie a search on any part of the document

*Stopwords are the common words that may occur in any text, such as 'a', 'an', 'of', 'the', etc. A file of these common words is created which is used to prevent them from being indexed by the database. This is called a stopword file.

Search refinement

A given search can be refined by adding or dropping one or more search terms or criteria, such as limiting the output to a given language, year of publication, price range, and so on; see Table 6.8 for some of the options available.

Table 6.8 *Options for search refinement*

CD-ROM	Options for search refinement
Books in print	One or more search terms from the same or different fields may be added in the Form Search and Search mode. A range search can be conducted using any of three fields, viz publication year, price and grades.

(continued)

Table 6.8 (continued)

CD-ROM	Options for search refinement
	If any of these fields is chosen in the Form Search the user is asked to enter values within two boxes prefixed 'between' and 'and'. In the Search mode several symbols, such as $=$, $<$, $>$, $<=$, $>=$, and $^\wedge$, can be used to indicate range for numeric searches
METADEX	There are three Modify Search Options that can be used to modify the current set of records retrieved: 'Limit by including additional criteria (AND)', 'Limit by excluding additional criteria (NOT)', and 'Expand by including alternate criteria (OR)'. The 'Limit to Same' option allows users to search for terms/phrases in the same document, field or subfield
Ulrich's on disc	You can toggle between the search and the output window. In the Form Search mode you can add terms to the same or different fields to modify a previous search. In the Search mode you can use the 'cs' (combine set) option to combine two sets; you can add one or more search terms to an existing set
Multimedia and CD-ROM directory	You can toggle between the search and the display window. If you have already searched for a term in a particular field, you can display the result and from there can return to the search screen and add another search term/phrase in the same or different search fields to modify the query
LISA plus	One or more search terms or phrases from the same or different fields can be used to refine a search. Language and publication date can be used to limit a search. In the Expert Search mode, the combine search (cs) command is used to combine the results of two or more previous searches or to see records of a single previous search (For example, cs=1 AND 2; cs=10 NOT 3); or use the # operator to label each set to be combined; for example, #1 AND #2; #10 NOT #3, which will produce the same results. A number of symbols, such as $=$, $>$, $<$, $,=$, $>=$, and $^\wedge$ (to indicate range) are used for numerical searches, for example with publication year
Ei Compendex	The Limit to Same option allows you to further specify records. The document option restricts your search to terms in the same document type as found in the previous search; field restricts your search to terms in the same field as found in the previous search; subfield restricts additional terms found in the same subfield as found in the previous search
EconLit	As the searches build up, the sets are shown in a separate window. You can call up any set and modify it. You can also choose the 'Limit' option to limit your search by the type of material, publication year, and so on
Emerald	A number of options for search refinement are available in the Advanced Search mode

Features of multimedia information sources on CD-ROM

So far we have seen the search and retrieval features of CD-ROM databases containing textual information, both bibliographic and full text. Here we shall briefly discuss the features of two popular multimedia information sources, the *Encarta reference suite* and *Britannica* CD.

Encarta reference suite 99

This is a popular multimedia reference source from the Microsoft Corporation. It comprises five CDs with *Microsoft encarta encyclopedia deluxe* 1999, *Microsoft encarta virtual globe* 99 and *Microsoft bookshelf* 99, and provides:

- more than 5000 new or updated articles, some with links to web resources
- media including images, sounds, videos and interactive charts
- geographic information, including a virtual tour facility with panoramic views of exciting places to explore
- a research organizer that helps the user collect and organize information for reports and other research projects.

The search interface of *Encarta reference suite* 99 is quite simple to use. Figure 6.18 shows the first screen: the user can click on any option to begin a search. The search is conducted through a tool called the *pinpointer* (Figure 6.19). When a search term is keyed in, the corresponding portion of the index is displayed. The user can click on any word/phrase listed and the output will be shown as in Figure 6.20. The user can also change the search category from the *pinpointer* (Figure 6.19).

Fig. 6.18 *Encarta encyclopedia*

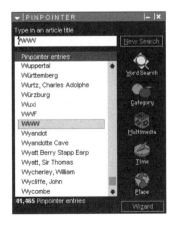

Fig. 6.19 *The 'Encarta' pinpointer*

If users change to the Multimedia search category, they will see the screen shown in Figure 6.21, which gives various multimedia search options. By clicking on Virtual Tours (Figure 6.22), the user will be prompted to insert the *Virtual globe* CD, and then the search screen shown in Figure 6.23 will appear. The user will then have the chance to locate a place, get geographical and other information about a place, take a virtual flight across a region, or to take up learning options through games, and so on (see Figure 6.24).

Fig. 6.20 The 'Encarta' output screen

Fig. 6.21 'Encarta' multimedia search

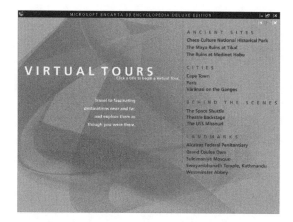

Fig. 6.22 'Encarta' virtual tours

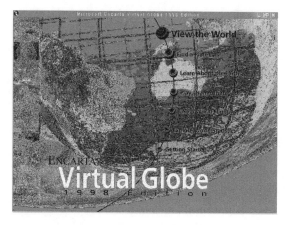

Fig. 6.23 'Encarta' virtual globe

Microsoft bookshelf enables the user to search for a quotation, find the meaning of words, synonyms, etc, learn about various styles, and so on (see Figure 6.25). To search for a definition, for example, you first enter a word or phrase in the Find box (Figure 6.25). If you want to find a quotation on a subject, for example on marriage, first select Quotations from the right part of the screen and then enter marriage in the Find box and click Enter. You'll then be taken to the output screen as shown in Figure 6.26.

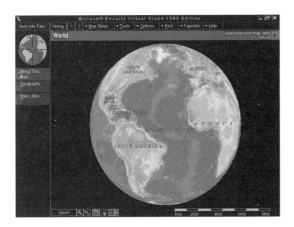

Fig. 6.24 *'Encarta' virtual globe search features*

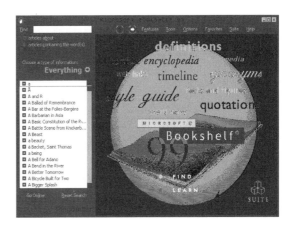

Fig. 6.25 *Microsoft bookshelf*

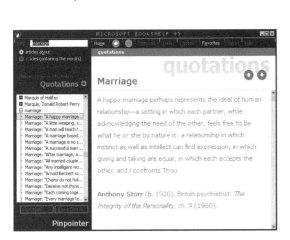

Fig. 6.26 *Output screen for a quotation on marriage from a 'Bookshelf' search*

Fig. 6.27 *'Britannica CD' opening screen*

Britannica CD

The *Encyclopedia Britannica* on CD is a popular reference source used all over the world. The user can conduct a full-text search by entering a natural language query in the search box, or just by entering a word or phrase. The first screen of *Britannica CD* is shown in Figure 6.27. There are two basic search options: full-text search and browse titles. The search screen for the full-text search option is shown in Figure 6.28.

In order to conduct a search the user simply enters a word, phrase or sentence in the search box (Figure 6.28). For example, a user looking for information on the web may key in 'WWW' in the search box (Figure 6.28). The corresponding

Fig. 6.28 *'Britannica' full-text search screen*

Fig. 6.29 *'Britannica' full-text search on 'WWW'*

Fig. 6.30 *Result of search shown in Fig. 6.29*

Fig. 6.31 *'Britannica' browse title screen*

portion of the terms dictionary will be displayed (Figure 6.29). The user then clicks on World Wide Web and sees the output screen as shown in Figure 6.30.

If the user chooses to browse titles the screen shown in Figure 6.31 appears; the user can then browse an alphabetical list of titles. As the figure shows, there are a number of search controls.

Summary

In this chapter we have discussed features of CD-ROM databases and have considered a number of appropriate examples. The databases come with proprietary interfaces, and the user needs to know the various search options, features of the search interface(s) and, moreover, the various search and retrieval facilities. The search output is not ranked; hence the user may need to spend more time establishing which records are of most use.

The same CD-ROM database may be available from a number of publishers, eg *Ei Compendex*, *ERIC*, and so on. Hence, one has to be careful in selecting the right CD-ROM database from the right publisher. Several authors have suggested criteria for the evaluation of CD-ROM databases (see, for example, Rowley, 1997; Mambretti, 1998; Chowdhury, 1999b). We can summarize these points as follows:

1   reputation of the publisher
2   database content and coverage
3   amount of data
4   currency of data and frequency of updates
5   technical quality, including the manuals and user support
6   type and appropriateness of data
7   richness and/or specialty of content
8   degree of interactivity
9   convenience and speed of access to the data
10   useful life of the product.
11   user interface
12   post-processing (presenting in a form accessible to the user)
13   standardization
14   cost
15   system requirements.

Many CD-ROM producers offer web access to their products. For example, the CD-ROM databases produced by *SilverPlatter* can be accessed through its web interface, *WebSPIRS* (**http://www.silverplatter.com/erl/webspirs4.htm**), and the *Encyclopedia Britannica* is available online. The future of the CD-ROM industry in the context of the Internet and the web has been discussed by several authors (see, for example, Tedd, 1995; Rowley, 1997, 1999; Mambretti, 1998; Chowdhury, 1999a, b).

Chapter 7
Searching online databases

Introduction

Online information retrieval involves searching remotely located databases through interactive communication using computers and communication channels (Chowdhury, 1999b). The phrase online searching was originally used to describe the process of directly interrogating computer systems to resolve particular requests for information. Now the phrase is used to denote searches that are conducted by means of a local computer that communicates with a remote computer system containing databases. Users can access the database(s) via an online search service provider (also called vendor). The search process is interactive and the user can conduct the search iteratively (repeatedly) until a satisfactory result is obtained.

With the advent of the Internet and world wide web online searches can be conducted on information sources that are distributed all over the world. To search these information sources, we can go straight to the web page where the information is located, provided we know the URL (uniform resource locator; the address of the web page, simply speaking). Alternatively, we can try to locate the information source(s) by using web search engines (retrieval programs used to search the web), such as *AltaVista* or *InfoSeek*, or through subject directories or gateways (directories that can be navigated to reach a particular information source or a group of similar sources), such as *Yahoo*, *SOSIG* or *Biz/ed*.

In this chapter we shall restrict our discussions to the former type of online service, i.e. the traditional online service characterized by a remote online database search service offered commercially by a search service provider or vendor. A major advantage of this kind of online searching is that it is designed to be pay-as-you-go, and therefore each search session can be costed. Another advantage is its speed and currency of data. Originally online search services were very expensive and rather complex, and therefore would require an intermediary to help end-users conduct an effective and efficient online search. However, over the years online search services have become less expensive and more user-friendly. As a result, they can now be used directly by end-users themselves without the need for an intermediary.

Development of online searching

According to Walker and Janes (1993) the first major online dial-up service was *MEDLINE*, the online version of MEDLARS (Medical Literature Analysis and Retrieval System), which was followed in 1972 by the offer of commercial online services from Dialog (Lockheed) and ORBIT (SDC). Since then many organizations have offered online databases and search services. By 1975 there were as many as 300 public access databases from a range of different vendors (ibid). Initially the majority of online databases were used to provide bibliographic references as the output of search session(s), and thus were called bibliographic or reference databases. More recently an increasing number of databases are becoming available that retrieve actual information rather than mere bibliographic references. These databases are either full text, where the complete texts of documents (including graphics and pictures) are available, or data banks that contain machine-readable numerical (often combined with textual and graphical) data.

Rowley (1999) identifies three generations of online searching:

1 The first generation, up to 1981, was characterized by dumb terminals, slow transmission speeds and mostly bibliographic databases.
2 The second generation, which continued through the 1980s, was characterized by PCs as workstations, medium transmission speeds, bibliographic as well as full-text databases and interfaces directed to end-users.
3 The third generation, which started at the beginning of the 1990s, has been characterized by multimedia PCs, higher transmission speeds, bibliographic as well as full-text databases, and improved user interfaces, help and tutorial facilities.

To this we can add a fourth generation, which started at the end of the 1990s with web access to online search services. users can go directly to the web address of an online service provider to log in to the service. Web-based online search services, such as *DialogWeb*, *Ovid Online*, *OCLC FirstSearch*, etc, provide fast and easy access to online databases with a number of search and retrieval facilities. The qualities of online search services coupled with the advantages of the web have brought significant developments to online search systems and have made online searching more directed towards the end-users.

The growth in the database industry can be interpreted in terms of the number of vendors or service providers, database producers, databases, database records, and online searches. There are a number of publications which regularly record the growth of online information retrieval; the most prominent publication in this field now is the *Gale directory* (Kumar, 1999), and the most prominent author is Martha Williams who writes up detailed statistics in each of the biannual issues of the *Gale directory*, and regularly reviews new databases in each of the six issues of the journal *Online Information Review* (previously *Online and CD-ROM Review*). The following two paragraphs provide a glimpse of the online information market (Marcaccio, 1989; Williams, 1998; Chowdhury, 1999b).

From 1975 to 1988 database records have increased by a factor of 39.71; the number of records increased from 52 million to 2.25 billion. The number of database producers has expanded, leading to a growth factor of 11.54. The average database contained 173,000 records in 1975 and 558,000 in 1985. In the sixties and seventies most databases were produced by government organizations such as NASA (National Aeronautics and Space Administration), AEC (Atomic Energy Commission), etc. In the eighties, the commercial databases grew rapidly from 22% in 1977 to 57% in 1985 and 65% in 1988. From 1985 to 1988 the number of bibliographic databases increased from 1094 to 1162. Similar growth over this period in other kinds of databases are: full text 535 to 1285, directory 287 to 613, dictionary 10 to 32. The total number of databases in 1985 was 3010, which rose to 4042 in 1988. In 1988 the number of databases in major subjects stood at business, 1815; consumer interests, 186; general, 301; health and life sciences, 433; humanities, 84; law, 441; academic, 29; news, 428; social sciences, 460; and science, technology and engineering, 1184.

From 1975 to 1997 the number of databases grew from 301 to 10,338 (ie by a factor of 34), and the number of records grew from 52 million to 11.27 billion (ie by a factor of 217), and, excluding the very large databases (11.26%) and their records (at least 1 million each), the average database contains 121,000 records. About 70% of these databases are word-oriented (textual): among these over the last 20 years the number of bibliographic databases have decreased, while full text databases have increased from 28 to 51%. North America is in the forefront, having produced 64% of all databases, followed by Western Europe (28%), with the rest of the world producing 8%. The number of databases in 1997 were: 3039 in business; 1889 in science, technology and engineering; 1680 in consumer interests; 1154 in health and life sciences; 626 in humanities; 1208 in law; and so on.

Each issue of *Online & CD-ROM Review* reports and reviews the new CD-ROM and online databases that have appeared during the past six months.

These new additions indicate the growth in the database industry: in the March 1999 issue of the *Gale directory of databases* (Kumar, 1999) there were the following new additions compared with its previous (September 1998) edition:

- 222 new science, technology and medicine databases, of which 82% were totally new, while 18% were old databases either published by a different vendor or appearing in a new medium (Williams and Smith, 1999)
- 143 new social science and humanities databases, of which 70% were totally new (Williams and Burgard, 1999), and
- 118 new business and law databases, of which 57% were totally new (Williams and Gaylord, 1999).

Online search services

There are various components of an online search service:

1 information providers or database producers, which provide the resources to be accessed online;
2 search service providers or vendors, which provide access to the databases and software for conducting searches
3 communication links, such as the Internet, which connect the user with the search service provider and the database(s), and
4 a local workstation through which the user is linked to the service.

Online search services vendors provide value-added processing to the databases and offer search services (Wynar, 1998). There are different types of online search services (Rowley, 1999), such as:

1 the traditional online search services that offer a range of databases, eg Dialog and Questel-Orbit
2 specialist online search services that offer access to special types of databases, eg DBE-Link, which offers access to German language and other European databases
3 search services offered by database publishers, eg EBSCO search service or UMI's ProQuest Direct
4 platform-independent search services that provide access to CD-ROM and online databases through the web, eg Ovid Technologies
5 bibliographic utilities that offer access to a select range of databases, eg OCLC FirstSearch.

Details of these online search services are available in a number of recent publications (see, for example, Forrester and Rowlands, 1999; Large et al, 1999; Rowley, 1999), as well as from the websites of the search services concerned.

Basic steps for an online search

The steps involved in an online search vary from system to system, because each system has its own custom-built interface that allows specific types of search and specific operators for specific search commands. Nevertheless, graphical user interfaces have made the task of searching quite easy, especially with the introduction of web-based interfaces. The following are the basic steps necessary to conduct an online search:

1 Study the search topic and develop a clear understanding of the information requirement. This is a critical step and depends on a number of factors, such as the nature and requirements of the user, how well the user can express his or her information needs, how much the user already knows, how the user is going to use the information, and so on. This happens before the actual search process begins and is often conducted through a series of dialogues between a searcher and an information intermediary. In the absence of an intermediary, users themselves have to clearly delineate their information requirements.

2 Have access to an online search service arranged. This can be done through subscription or licensing agreement. The access right has to be obtained before the search begins.

3 Log on to the service provider. This is usually done through the web interfaces of the online search service providers. At this stage the user needs to know the relevant URL as well as the user ID and password.

4 Select the appropriate database(s) to search. This is a critical and often a difficult task. The success of a search largely depends on the choice of database. Users can select one or more databases to search using the same interface, and most search services allow users to browse through the database categories to select the appropriate databases(s). Dialog has a unique facility called DIALINDEX search (see p. 141) which enables the user to see how many times a given search term occurs in a set of chosen databases. This information can guide the user in selecting the appropriate database to conduct the actual search.

5 Formulate search expressions. This vital step may involve a number of activities, some of which may be carried out before going online. The first is the selection of appropriate terms and/or phrases, which may require the user to consult dictionaries, thesauri, etc. Once the appropriate search terms and/or

phrases are chosen, the search expression can be formulated. At this stage the user should have an understanding of the nature, content and structure of the chosen database(s). The user also needs to know which fields are indexed and therefore can be searched, and so on, and what search facilities are available, such as Boolean searching, truncation, field-specific searching, proximity searching and what the appropriate operators are. The search operators and syntax for formulating search expressions vary from one search service to the other, and often there are different interfaces for novice and expert users. Users wishing to use an expert search interface, which may be command-driven, must have a knowledge of the various search commands, their order of execution, and so on.

6   Select the appropriate format, from a number of predefined options, to display the retrieved records. There may be charges for the records displayed: for example, when searching Dialog, charges incurred include output and search-time costs, as well as telecommunications charges; prices also vary by database. Therefore care should be taken in deciding which record(s) to have displayed and in which format. If the option to display the full record(s) is chosen, the process may be time-consuming, depending on the network traffic. It may be more efficient to choose the brief display option, and then select records from this list for full display.

7   Reformulate your query, if necessary. This may mean going back to step 4 or step 5: online searches are usually iterative processes, meaning that the user conducts several searches, compares the results, and modifies search statements or conducts a new search in order to get the best results.

8   Select the mode of delivery. You may download all the chosen records online to your local computer or send an offline request.

Features of selected online search services

In the following sections we shall discuss the features of five of the most popular online search services to give a general idea of the various search and retrieval options available. We will look at the web versions of these services as users are most likely to access online searching through their web interfaces. The five online search services under consideration are: DialogWeb, OCLC FirstSearch, STN Easy, Ovid Online and LEXIS-NEXIS. Some screenshots to illustrate the search process are included, and the search operators and search commands for each service are presented in tabular form. Full details of these search services are available at the relevant websites: DialogWeb (**http://www.dialogweb.com**); OCLC FirstSearch (**http://www.oclc.org/oclc/menu/fs.htm**); Ovid Online (**http://www.ovid.com/**); STN Easy (**http://stneasy.cas.org/html/english/login1.html**) and LEXIS-NEXIS (**http://www.lexis-nexis.com/lncc/**).

DialogWeb

DialogWeb is the web interface of Dialog, the oldest and largest of the five online search service providers considered here. It offers the largest variety of search operators and search commands, and provides easy access to over 600 databases with:

- company information – both directory listings and financial information
- industry information – trends, overviews, market research, and specialized industry newsletters and reports; US and international news – an extensive collection of newspapers and newswires from North America and Asia; US government news – including public affairs, law, and regulatory information
- patents and trademarks information – a worldwide collection for research and competitive intelligence tracking
- chemistry, environment, science and technology information – technical literature and reference material to support research needs
- social science and humanities information – including education, information science, psychology, sociology and science, from public opinion, news and leading scholarly and popular publications.
- general reference information – people, books, consumer news, and travel.

Users can search and retrieve information from all these sources using

- guided search mode, which does not require knowledge of the dialog command language
- command search mode, which allows experienced users to use the dialog command language
- database selection tools, which help users pinpoint the right database for a search
- integrated database descriptions, pricing information, and other search assistance
- easy to use forms to create and modify Alerts (current awareness updates).

Dialog search results are available in HTML or text formats. Users can choose to have records displayed or to have search results sent via e-mail, fax or postal delivery.

Steps for a DialogWeb search

The first step of a Dialog search involves logging on to the system. You need to have a Dialog account in order to obtain the necessary user ID and password.

For information on how to obtain these, consult Dialog's website (**http://prod-ucts.dialog.com/products/dialog/price_list/back0100.html**). The log-in screen (Figure 7.1) where these are entered is reached by going to the DialogWeb homepage (**http://www.dialogweb.com**). The log-in screen also provides information about DialogWeb and a preview and search tips.

After logging on, you will automatically be taken to the Guided Search page (Figure 7.2).

Guided Search

Guided Search is designed for novice to intermediate searchers. You can use the Guided Search when you

- do not know the Dialog commands and/or databases
- are trying out a new subject area and are not familiar with the databases or search terminology
- need an answer to a frequently asked question.

To undertake a Guided Search for information on, say, digital libraries, the procedure is as follows.

Step 1: Choosing databases
To begin our Guided Search, we click the New Search button and choose from the list of eight main subject categories (Figure 7.2). Each category is further divided into focused search topics. For our search on digital libraries, we can select the appropriate category as follows:

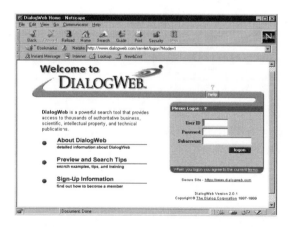

Fig. 7.1   *DialogWeb homepage*

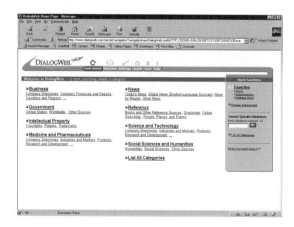

Fig. 7.2   *Dialog database categories in Guided Search mode*

Social Sciences and Humanities > Social Sciences > Library and Information Science

We now see a list of databases that cover library and information science (Figure 7.3).

Step 2: Choose your search option
In Guided Search there are two search options:

1 **Targeted Search**: this is available in some, but not all, subject categories. It is a ready-made search form with databases pre-assigned to the form.
2 **Dynamic Search**: this is available in all subject categories. The Dynamic Search form varies according to the category or database that is selected. A Dynamic Search can access many more databases compared with the Targeted Search, and is more flexible.

Targeted Search

This is the easier type of search to perform. You can enter the search word/phrase as 'Words in Title' or as the 'Main Subject' (see Figure 7.4). If we enter 'digital libraries' in the Main Subject box, we then see the output screen as shown in Figure 7.5.

Dynamic Search

This is available at various points in the search category selection process, or when we use the Quick Functions option in New Search and enter a specific

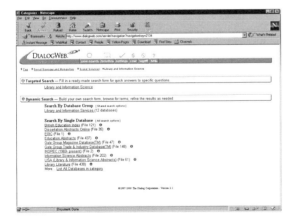

Fig. 7.3 *Dialog databases on library and information science*

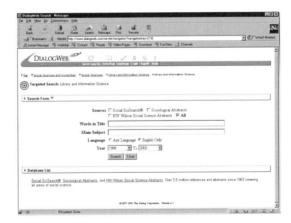

Fig. 7. 4 *Dialog Targeted Search*

database number for our search. The Dynamic Search capability is available no matter what category or database we have picked. In a category with many databases assigned to it, we can search:

- all of the databases together
- a group of similarly designed databases together, or
- one of the assigned databases individually.

If we choose the 'Dynamic Search' option and decide to conduct a search on all 12 databases under the 'Library and Information Science' category, we shall then see the Dynamic Search screen as shown in Figure 7.6.

The Dynamic Search forms also offer the following options:

- Navigation: the search category selections are displayed at the top of the form. To return to a category or option, we can click the search category or option name.
- Run Saved Strategy: if we have already saved a search strategy, we can run it against the selected databases by clicking on this option.

A list of the databases used in the search is displayed at the bottom of the form. We can click the information icon (i) to find out more about the database content and pricing.

At the Dynamic Search screen you can enter a search term or phrase and conduct your search on subject, author, descriptor or title field. You can also

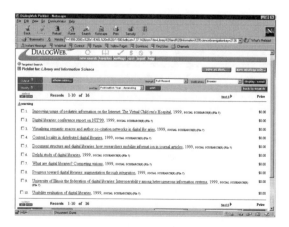

Fig. 7.5 *Dialog Targeted Search results on 'digital libraries'*

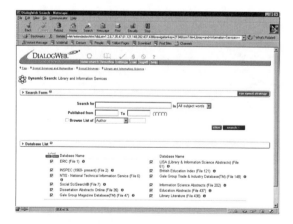

Fig. 7.6 *Dialog Dynamic Search screen*

restrict your search by year of publication, or can browse the list of items by author or year of publication.

Picklist

The search results from a Targeted Search or a Dynamic Search will appear on a Picklist page (Figure 7.5), which provides a quick view of the resulting records. From here the user can choose to:

- display specific records in more detailed formats or have records sent via e-mail, fax or postal delivery
- rearrange the order in which the records are displayed
- refine the search strategy
- remove duplicate records
- view the prices for all format options
- save the strategy for future use
- create an Alert for automatic updates on the search topic.

We can now choose to view results by checking one or more boxes and then selecting the display button, or we can display any one record just by clicking on the hyperlinked title. In any case, we can choose the format for display from the Format box. We can choose to sort the records according to criteria chosen from the 'Sort by' box. We can refine the search expression by clicking the Back to Search button, and then can edit, add, or delete information from the search form. Suppose, we click on item 7 from the Picklist (Figure 7.5), we shall then get the output (the full record) as shown in Figure 7.7.

Print and/or save records

Once we display the records, we can choose to print or save them at no extra cost. After selecting the desired records, we can select Browser for Print/Save from the destination drop-down list, at which point only the text of the records displays: no checkboxes or buttons appear, making it easy to download or print records. Post-processing the record is easy too: to save records, we can use Save As with a .txt (text) or .html extension (eg dlib.txt or dlib.html).

Command Search

This is designed for intermediate to experienced Dialog searchers. It provides complete command-based access to Dialog's extensive collection of databases, and assumes the user is familiar with the various Dialog commands. Additional features include: built-in tools such as Bluesheets (database descriptions) and pricing information, database selection assistance to help pinpoint the right databases for a search, and easy-to-use forms to create and modify Alerts (current awareness updates). The Command Search main page (Figure 7.8) allows users to begin inputting Dialog commands right away. A Command Search contains

- a textbox for entering Dialog search commands
- a Submit button that sends the command, and
- a Previous button that displays your most recent command entries.

The Command Search main page, reached from the search screen (Figure 7.2) by clicking on 'Command Search', has links to the Databases feature, product support information, and Guided Search. You can move between Guided Search and Command Search, but the sets you create in one search mode can't be transferred to the other. Steps for conducting a command search can be summarized as follows.

Step 1: Choose database(s)
The first step in conducting a command search is to select the appropriate databases. DialogWeb simplifies the selection of databases by arranging them by subject in the Databases feature. The 'All Categories' page appears when we click the Databases button on the navigation bar or click on Databases on the DialogWeb main page. Dialog offers two multiple-file search options:

1   The first search option, OneSearch, allows you to conduct a full search of a collection of related databases (up to 60), browse the indexes, or display

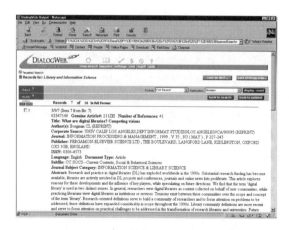

Fig. 7.7   *Dialog display of a full record*

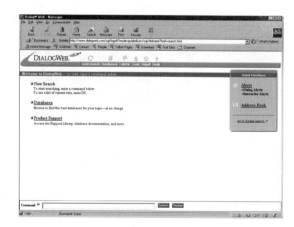

Fig. 7.8   *Dialog Command Search screen*

records. You can search using OneSearch categories or mix OneSearch categories and file numbers (eg B medicine, 11, will open all the databases in the Onesearch category 'medicine' as well as file number 11, ie the PsycInfo database).

2 The second option, DIALINDEX, is particularly useful when you do not know which databases to search or when you want to do a comprehensive search and cover everything on a topic. DIALINDEX is a master index to most of the Dialog databases, and it allows you to compare the number of records retrieved from a group of databases.

For our search on digital libraries, we will choose the Databases option, and then DIALINDEX. The Databases option lets us choose the best databases for our search by allowing us to preview search results across a group of databases. We can follow the database category listing to choose the appropriate databases. For our search on digital libraries, we can select the category as follows:

Social Sciences and Humanities > Social Sciences > Library and Information Science

A list of databases (Figure 7.9) is now displayed. We can key in the search phrase ('digital libraries') in the box preceded by the Dialog search command S (or 'select'). We are then shown the occurrence of the search phrase in the chosen databases (Figure 7.10). This will help us choose the appropriate database(s) for our search.

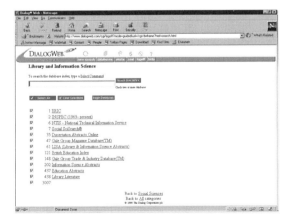

Fig. 7.9 *Dialog list of databases on library and information science*

Fig. 7.10 *DIALINDEX results*

Choose a database

If the search has revealed databases of interest, we must search these to view the records. We can click 'Begin Databases' to enter the files that we have checked and run the same strategy, or we can choose the database(s) to search by entering the file numbers and even change our search strategy in the command line.

Step 2: Dialog Command Search

Once the databases are chosen, we see the Dialog Command Search page. It can also appear:

- after we log in — if it is set as the default
- when we click the Command Search link from the main Guided Search page, or
- when we click the Begin Databases button from the list of databases as selected.

The appropriate Begin command (B) is inserted in the command line automatically when a search has been done in Databases and one or more databases have been selected. We can add the Current command to our Begin statement by typing in the word 'current' following the command. This allows us to search only the current year plus one back year, and narrows the search results at the beginning. We can click the Submit button or press Enter on the keyboard to start our search.

To begin searching, we enter any Dialog command followed by the search term(s) in the search box. For our present example we can enter: S digital (W) libraries.

Step 3: Add to search

We can refine our search and include 'electronic libraries' through the expression:

```
S (digital OR electronic) (W) libraries
```

This search statement will retrieve records on electronic as well as digital libraries by selecting those records where 'digital' and 'libraries' or 'electronic' and 'libraries' occur next to each other in the same sequence. We can retrieve more records by truncating the search term libraries as follows:

```
S (digital OR electronic) (W) librar?
```

Various other modifications may be made by using appropriate search commands; for example, we can limit the search to one or more fields, or limit the results to a language, year of publication, and so on.

Step 4: Displaying records

A search history of all the sets appears, and we can now view some of the records from our search. It is a good idea to display a few records in Free format before displaying the records in the Long or Full format. The type of format, which determines the amount of information to be displayed for each record, is chosen from the Format list box: Free, Short, Medium, Long, Full and KWIC (keyword in context). We can also indicate the number of records to display – the default is 10, and a maximum of 99 records can be specified. We also have the option of using a Type command to display records. We can also enter the From Each command along with the Type command when we search more than one database at a time. This enables us to see a sampling of records from each database in our search.

Dialog search operators

Dialog offers a number of search features, such as Boolean searching, proximity searching, truncation, field-specific searching, limited searches, and so on. These features and the corresponding operators are shown in Table 7.1.

Table 7.1 *Dialog search operators*

Search operator	Example	Description
Proximity operator: (W)	S information (W) system S information (2W) system	Requests adjacent terms in the order given. You can specify the maximum no. of intervening words. In the second example, there may be at the most two words in between 'information' and 'system'
Proximity operator: (N)	S information (N) system S information (2N) system	Requests adjacent terms in any order. You can specify the maximum no. of intervening terms. In the second example, there may be at the most two words in between 'information' and 'system'
Proximity operator: (S)	S solar (S) energy	Requests that terms should be in the same subfield
Proximity operator: (L)	S solar (L) cell	Requests that terms should be in the same descriptor field
Proximity operator: (F)	S information (F) system	Requests that terms should be in the same field
Open truncation ?	S computer?	Open truncation: any no. of characters can appear after the root

(continued)

Table 7.1 *(continued)*

Search operator	Example	Description
Truncation operator: ? ?	S cat? ?	Maximum of one character can appear after the root
Truncation operator: ??...	S comput??	As many characters as question marks can appear after the root
Internal truncation: ?	wom?n	Replaces the '?' with one character
Field-specific search		
Suffix code	S Internet/ti,de	Suffix codes restrict retrieval to Basic Index fields.
Prefix code	S au=Chowdhury,G.	Prefix codes are used to search the Additional Indexes; from one to seven prefix codes can be used
Limit suffixes	S Internet/1999	Used with the Select command to restrict the search by any of several criteria
Range searching	S internet/1998:1999	Useful for limiting the search results. A colon (:) is used to indicate a range of sequential entries to be retrieved in a logical OR relationship.
Numeric searching	S EM=100 S EM>1k	The relational operators >, <, >= , <=, = can be used. In the first example, the system will retrieve records with employees of 100, and in the second those with employees of more than 1000
Boolean AND	information AND Internet	Retrieves records with both the terms
Boolean OR	information OR Internet	Retrieves records with at least one term
Boolean NOT	Internet NOT WWW	Excludes those that contain the search term following the NOT operator

Essential Dialog commands

There are a number of Dialog commands that can be used in the Command Search mode. These are for expert users and must be keyed in according to the prescribed syntax. Some commands, for example, Display, Field, Format, Type, Print, Rates, etc, are now available as buttons in the DialogWeb interface, and a simple click performs the corresponding operation. However, some commands still require to be keyed in to perform an operation; some of these are shown in Table 7.2.

Table 7.2 *Some essential Dialog commands*

Command	Example	Description
Begin, or B	B 61 B 1, 61	Opens one or more databases for searching
Current	S 61 current 2	Used to narrow the search to records from the most recent year(s) within a file. In the example, the file number is 61 and the year is restricted to the two most recent
Find, or F	F internet F world wide web	Can be used in place of the Select or S command to conduct a search. The difference with Select is that it does not need a proximity operator to search for a phrase
Help, or ?	Help field 1	Produces help. For example, the command shown here will show the list of fields for Dialog file 1
Save	Save <name>	Saves the entire search strategy since the last Begin command in a file with the given filename
Select, or S	S digital (W) libraries	The most essential Dialog command: it is necessary to conduct any search unless F is used
Select Steps, or SS	SS internet AND information	Creates a set for each search term/phrase and one for the entire search. This is useful when a multi-word search term is given; later on, you can just call up the set with any constituent term to conduct another search
Sort	Sort s1/all/au,ti	Sorts the results of a search set (set1 for the given example) by one or more sort keys (here author and title). Each database has a list of sort keys that can be used. You can click on the 'Sort' button to get a list of sort keys for a given database
Rank	Rank de,id	Conducts a statistical analysis on the existing search set. Dialog extracts the specified fields from the record and lists them in a ranked order.

OCLC FirstSearch

This service gives library users access to 85 online databases and more than 5 million full-text articles (**http://www.oclc.org/oclc/menu/fs.htm**). It includes the following OCLC databases:

- *OCLC WorldCat* (the OCLC Online Union Catalog): contains more than 41 million books, videos, sound recordings, maps, scores, manuscripts, archives and more, representing over 370 languages
- *OCLC ArticleFirst*: journal article citations from some 13,000 serials and 18 million articles
- *OCLC ContentsFirst*: complete contents pages from 13,000 journals

- *OCLC FastDoc*: the full text of over 1.5 million articles from approximately 1000 journals available for fast online full-text delivery
- *OCLC NetFirst*: finds URL addresses of Internet-accessible information resources, including web pages, electronic discussion groups, video catalogues, FTP sites, listservs, newsletters, electronic journals and gophers; the user can go immediately to hot-linked records
- *OCLC Union Lists of Periodicals*: includes more than 7 million local data records (LDRs) that are linked to over 750,000 bibliographic records in *WorldCat*.

Steps for an OCLC FirstSearch

User authorization and a password are needed to access the OCLC FirstSearch service. OCLC provides access to it only through libraries on a subscription or per-search basis.

After we log in we see a screen (shown in Figure 7.11) that briefly describes the OCLC FirstSearch Service and also provides various options. On the left side of the screen we can see a list of database categories: selecting one of these leads us to a number of databases that we can choose to search.

Thus, the second step is the selection of the appropriate database(s) to search. For our search topic digital libraries we choose the database category 'Social sciences', which takes us to the social sciences databases (see Figure 7.12). From here we choose 'Library Literature' and are then shown the basic search screen in Figure 7.13, which provides brief information about the chosen database. We can enter a word or a phrase to search, and the search can be restricted to a particular field (chosen from a drop-down box). The search fields are: article con-

Fig. 7.11 *Opening screen of OCLC FirstSearch*

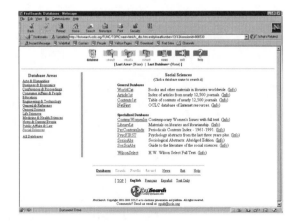

Fig. 7.12 *Databases covering social sciences in OCLC FirstSearch*

tent, author, place of publication, publisher, sources, standard number, subject, subject heading and title. There is also a button to select the Advanced Search option (see below). The various search options provided by OCLC FirstSearch are shown in Table 7.3.

Table 7.3 *OCLC FirstSearch operators*

Search operator	Example	Description
Truncation: +	cancer patient+	Finds records containing 'cancer' and 'patient' or 'patients'
Boolean AND	nursing AND education	Finds records containing 'nursing' and 'education'
Boolean OR	education OR research	Finds records containing either 'education' or 'research'
Boolean NOT	nursing AND education NOT research	Finds records containing 'nursing' and 'education' but not 'research'
Parentheses: ( )	nursing AND (education OR research)	Finds records containing either 'education' and 'nursing' or 'research' and 'nursing'
Proximity: W	information W retrieval	Finds records containing both terms in the same order with no other term between them
Proximity: W and a number (1–25)	information W3 retrieval	Finds records containing both terms in the same order with at most 3 intervening terms
Proximity: N	information N management	Finds records containing both terms adjacent to each other but in any order
Proximity: N and a number (1–25)	information N2 management	Find records containing both terms in any order with at most 2 intervening terms

Basic search

Figure 7.13 shows the screen for a basic search. By clicking on the arrow beside the box we can select one of the indexes listed, such as subject, author and title index. The default is the subject index. If we want to use more than one index in a search, we need to use the Advanced Search option. The index we choose tells *FirstSearch* which parts, or fields, of each record to scan for the search term. If we type 'digital libraries' in the 'Word, Phrase' box and choose the Subject index, *FirstSearch* searches for the words in fields containing subject information. For most databases these fields include titles, abstracts, subject headings, and descriptors. We can also click on the 'Advanced Search' option.

Advanced search

Figure 7.14 shows the Advanced Search screen of *OCLC FirstSearch*. Again the Index box is used to choose an index. The box lists the keyword and exact-

Fig. 7.13 *The OCLC FirstSearch screen after the 'Library Literature' database has been chosen*

Fig. 7.14 *OCLC FirstSearch Advanced Search*

phrase indexes available for the chosen database. We can use a separate 'Word, Phrase' box and Index box for each index that is to be included in the search. Selecting the default index at the bottom of the list is the same as selecting the Subject (keyword) index.

We can limit the records by year, document type and language. The categories available vary by database. With either a Basic Search or an Advanced Search we can limit the records on the Search Results screen after *FirstSearch* has processed the search. With the Advanced Search we can also limit records on the search screen before *FirstSearch* processes the search.

Sample search (advanced)

Having entered a search expression: *digital W libraries*, and limited the search to subject (keyword), years 1997–1999, and English language only, we obtained the result screen shown in Figure 7.15. Here we can display records by clicking on the hyperlinked title, thus obtaining the full record, as shown in Figure 7.16.

STN Easy

This provides access to STN International, a service operated jointly by the Chemical Abstracts Service (CAS) in North America, the Japan Science and Technology Corporation (JST) in Asia, and FIZ-Karlsruhe in Germany for users in Europe. To conduct a search, users need to go to the STN Easy Website (**http://STNEasy.cas.org**), and log-in (Figure 7.17). The STN Easy search system has been improved recently, and the log-in screen provides links to detailed descriptions of the new features of the system. STN Easy now offers three types of searches, viz Easy Search, Advanced Search and CAS Number Search.

Easy Search

Easy Search is designed for infrequent searchers who want general science and technology information about a subject. Users enter search terms in the search box and press the 'Search' button (see Figure 7.18). More than one search term can be combined with the Boolean AND, OR, NOT, and NEAR operators. The search is carried out in the basic indexes of five general science databases, viz CAplus, JICST-EPLUS, SCISEARCH, CONF, and NTIS. Users can refine a search too. The search output page shows the total number of answers from the five databases.

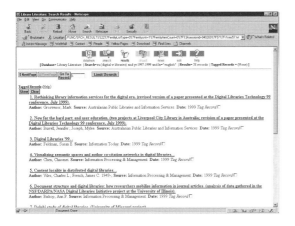

Fig. 7.15 *Search results from OCLC First-Search*

Fig. 7.16 *Full record in OCLC FirstSearch*

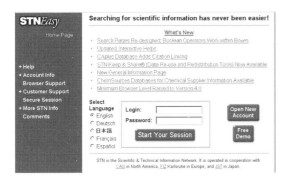

Fig. 7.17 *The 'STN Easy' Log-in Screen*

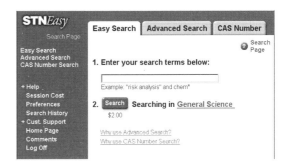

Fig. 7.18 *The Easy Search interface of 'STN Easy'*

Advanced Search

The Advanced Search is designed for those who want to search for data in a specific science and technology discipline or those who need more power and precision for a search. Here users first must select a search category which tells STN Easy which databases to search. Figure 7.19 shows the Advanced Search screen of STN Easy. Advanced Search provides tremendous search power: a wide variety of fields, browse index, and more than 30 sci/tech categories. Users first click on the 'Select your category' button (Figure 7.19) whereby a list of all the database categories will pop up. Beside each database category there is a folder icon which can be clicked to get a list of databases covered by that category. Users can deselect databases to be searched simply by unchecking them from this list.

Once a database category has been selected, users choose Boolean operators and search fields, and then enter search terms into the boxes. A number of search operators are available in STN Easy (see Table 7.4). All the most commonly used fields are available for searching. They are listed in alphabetical order in the drop-down box where the search field is selected. Up to ten rows of search boxes can be added. Users may now select more than one language and document type by holding the control key and clicking on the language or the document type sought. Browse Index can be scrolled for up to 70 terms.

After pressing the search button, the answer page appears. Answers to the search are listed consecutively by database. To view the section of answers for a specific database, users simply need to click on the database name at the top of the screen. They can refine a search and can choose the option to show the duplicates. On top of the search output screen there is an option 'Find documents citing this reference.' This link finds citations (the titles of articles that cited the given retrieved article) in both the CAplus and SCISEARCH databases. According to the STN source (**http://stneasy.cas.org** *What's new for July, 2000*) 'as of late May (2000), approximately 22 million citations have been

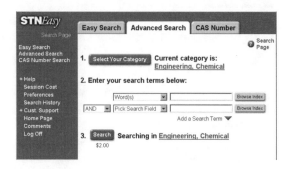

Fig. 7.19 *The Advanced Search screen of 'STN Easy'*

Table 7.4 'STN Easy' search operators

Search operator	Example	Description
Right truncation: ?	chromatogra?	Finds records on 'chromatogram' and 'chroma-tography'
Boolean AND (or the 'all word' option)	protein AND carbohydrate	Retrieves records containing both search terms
Boolean OR (or the 'any word' option)	protein OR carbohydrate	Retrieves records containing either of the search terms or both
Boolean NOT	alcohol NOT methanol	Retrieves records containing 'alcohol' but not 'methanol'
Parentheses: ( )	AIDS AND (children OR women)	Retrieves records containing 'AIDS' and 'children', as well as 'AIDS' and 'women'
Quotes	'methylated spirit'	Retrieves records containing the phrase
Proximity: NEAR	Mars NEAR life	Retrieves records containing all the search terms appearing in the same sentence

included for complete coverage of nearly 1300 of the core journals; partial coverage of 5300 other journals and miscellaneous publications; and basic patents (examiner citations) from the U.S., Germany, EPO, and WIPO.'

In addition to the easy and advanced searches, STN Easy allows users to conduct the CAS Number Search that allows users to get a CAS Registry Number for a chemical name, or get the name of a chemical whose CAS Registry Number is known to the user. The interface for this search is very simple. The user simply enters the CAS Registry Number or the chemical name in the search box and clicks on the 'Search' button. The STN Easy search system automatically determines which categories contain additional information about the chemical name or CAS Registry Number that a user searched and lists those categories at the end of the display as links.

Ovid Online

Ovid Technologies has been in the information retrieval industry since 1988, providing access to a number of academic, corporate and medical databases. *Ovid Online* is its online access tool, which makes available over 90 commercial bibliographic databases and hundreds of full-text journals. The databases include definitive bibliographic resources in many research areas. For medicine and allied health, Ovid offers MEDLINE and EMBASE; for nursing, CINAHL; for bioscience, the BIOSIS databases; for general reference, *Current contents*, *Newspaper abstracts* and *Wilson readers' guide abstracts*; and so on. *Ovid Online* covers a wide range of subjects such as business, humanities, engineering, agriculture, science and technology, and social sciences.

Steps for an Ovid search

Ovid Online offers two pricing options: Fixed Fee annual subscription access that includes database fees and in some cases telecommunications costs; and Pay-as-You-Go, assessed on time in database and number of records viewed, printed or saved. The first step in searching Ovid is to log in, and then choose a database to search. The user can then choose between the Basic Search (Figure 7.20) and the Advanced Search (Figure 7.21). The Basic Search allows the user to search by keyword(s) and/or author. The search can be restricted to a particular type of material or by year of publication (see Figure 7.20). The search term can be truncated by appending a $ sign. The various search operators used in Ovid Online are shown in Table 7.5.

Table 7.5 *Ovid search operators*

Search operator	Example	Description
Unlimited truncation: $ or :	disease$	Retrieves all possible suffix variations of a root
Limited truncation: Sn	cat$1	Specifies the maximum number of characters that may follow the root
Mandated wild card: #	wom#n	Can be used within or at the end of a word to substitute for one character
Optional wild card: ?	Colo?r	Substitutes for one or no character
Boolean AND	computer AND communications	Find records containing both the search terms
Boolean NOT	search engines NOT directories	Excludes records containing the term that follows NOT
Boolean OR	search engines OR robot programmes	Retrieves records with either of the search terms
Proximity: ADJn	information ADJ2 management	Specifies the maximum number of words that may appear between two search terms (an adjacency operator is automatically inserted when multiple search terms are entered consecutively)
Frequency of occurrence of words: FREQ	Internet.tx./freq=10	Specifies a threshold of occurrence of a term. The sample search expression will retrieve only those records in which the term Internet appears at least ten times. This is very useful for full-text searches

The Advanced Search screen provides a number of search options, including Boolean search, field-specific and limiting search, truncation, and so on. The user can click on any of the search options, and then the corresponding screen for author search, title search, keyword search, etc. will appear. The Advanced

Fig. 7.20 *Ovid Basic Search screen*

Fig. 7.21 *Ovid Advanced Search screen*

Search screen shows the search sets and the corresponding results as the search progresses (Figure 7.21). Against each search set there is a Display button, which can be used to display the corresponding search results. Figure 7.22 shows a sample search output screen. Ovid enables expert users to use the command line syntax to conduct complex searches, bypassing the button bar to save time. Some important commands are shown in Table 7.6.

Table 7.6 *Important Ovid search commands*

Search command	Syntax	Description
Change database	..c/x	Changes to database x
Command line limit	Limit n to x	Limits set n by command line limit x (consult the database field guides for the list of command line limits)
Display search sets	..ps	Displays the complete search strategy during the current session
End search	..o	Ends a search session and returns to the log-in page
Execute search strategy	..e/x	Executes search strategy x
Field search	x.yy.	Searches for the word/phrase x in the field yy
Index display	..root x.yy	Displays alphabetic position x in index field yy
Limiting search	..L/n yr=x	Limits search set n to publication year x, where x is a 2-digit year or hyphenated 2-digit year range (eg '98-99')
Save search (temporary)	..sv x	Saves search strategy temporarily (for 24 hours) with name x
Save search (permanent)	..sv ps(x)	Saves search strategy permanently with name x
Search more than one field	x.yy,zz	Searches for the word/phrase x in the fields yy and zz

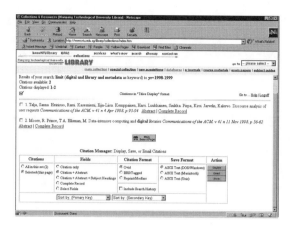

Fig. 7.22 *Ovid search output screen*

LEXIS-NEXIS

The LEXIS-NEXIS Group makes its information products available via the web, online dial-up, CD-ROM and books. With the web version of LEXIS-NEXIS (http://www.lexis-nexis.com/lncc/), users can access information from authoritative sources, with valuable enhancements such as indexing, linkages and segmentation from 10,200 databases. The user can search

- 24,871 sources, 18,871 on news and business and 6000 on legal information
- 26.5 million images/attachments.

The LEXIS service, the first commercial, full-text legal information service, began in 1973 to help legal practitioners research the law more efficiently. The companion NEXIS news and business information service was launched in 1979 to provide recent and archival news and financial information. Since then, NEXIS has become the largest news and business online information service, comprehensively coveirng company, country, financial, demographic, market research and industry reports. Its access to thousands of worldwide newspapers, magazines, trade journals, industry newsletters, tax and accounting information, financial data, public records, legislative records and data on companies and their executives – makes LEXIS-NEXIS one of the most popular online search services.

LEXIS-NEXIS commands

LEXIS-NEXIS has a long list of search commands which are used to conduct a command search. Table 7.7 provides search command equivalents for function keys used with some LEXIS-NEXIS products.

Table 7.7 *LEXIS-NEXIS Search operators or connectors*

Search operator	Example	Description
OR	doctor OR physician	Links synonyms, alternative forms of expression, acronyms, and so on: the example finds either 'doctor' or 'physician'
W/n	doctor W/5 malpractice	Links search words and phrases to create concepts: the example finds 'doctor' within five or fewer words of 'malpractice', regardless of which word appears first; the *n* stands for a number from 1 to 255; word order is not specified
W/p	doctor W/p malpractice	Looks for documents with search words in the same paragraph: the example finds 'doctor' in the same paragraph as 'malpractice'
W/s	doctor W/s malpractice	Looks for documents with search words in the same sentence: the example finds 'doctor' in the same sentence as 'malpractice'
AND	doctor AND malpractice	Links words or phrases that must both appear anywhere in the same document, no matter how close or far apart: the example finds both 'doctor' and 'malpractice' anywhere in the same document.
PRE/n	southwest PRE/1 air OR airline	Requires both words to appear in the document; the first word must precede the second word by n words. Use this connector when a different word order would change the meaning. The example finds 'Southwest Air' or 'Southwest Airlines'
AND NOT	doctor AND NOT malpractice	Excludes documents that contain the word or phrase following NOT
Truncation: ! or *	employ! or employ*	Retrieves all items with 'employ' as the root
Variant forms of words: **	fly**	Looks for all forms of a word by using a double asterisk (**): the example finds fly, flew, flown and flying

Searching LEXIS-NEXIS

LEXIS-NEXIS has four different pricing plans for searching services:

- a flat rate on a monthly basis
- an hourly charge based on database time
- a transactional rate based on search charges and volume discounts
- special rates for government offices and agencies.

Users must choose either the Boolean search method or the 'Freestyle' method. The former uses words and connectors to create phrases and concepts based on specific rules of search logic. For example, to find documents on employee drug tests, you might use this search request:

drug W/5 test OR screen! W/10 employ!

(See Table 7.7 for LEXIS-NEXIS)

The Freestyle feature allows the user to formulate queries using plain English, and can be used in virtually all LEXIS-NEXIS services, including news, business and financial sources as well as case law, statutes, administrative material and more. For example, you may enter the following as a search using the Freestyle feature:

Under what circumstances can biological parents regain custody of their adopted children after an adoption?

Once the search expression has been entered, the user can follow the prompts that appear on the screen to:

- edit the search description
- enter/edit mandatory terms
- enter/edit restrictions (eg date)
- enter synonyms and related concepts, or
- change the maximum number of documents (the default setting is 50).

Once documents have been retrieved, the user can:

- browse documents in the SuperKWIC format used in LEXIS-NEXIS
- view the location of the search terms in the documents
- view number of documents containing the search terms, or
- change the document order.

Figures 7.23 and 7.24 show the LEXIS-NEXIS search and output screens.

Special features of the five chosen search services

Each online search service has some unique features, some of which are highlighted in Table 7.8.

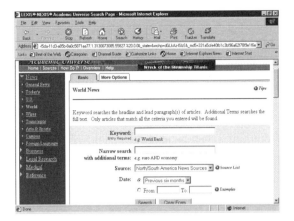

Fig. 7.23 *LEXIS-NEXIS search screen*

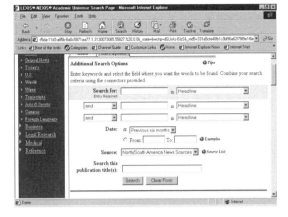

Fig. 7.24 *Additional search options of LEXIS-NEXIS*

Table 7.8 *Special features of five search services*

Search service	Special features
DialogWeb	• Targeted Search for novice users and Dynamic Search for expert users • The Database Directory allows users to browse Dialog databases by subject • Integrated *Bluesheets* provide information on the database content, capabilities, fields, pricing, etc. • A new web interface to Alerts makes it easier to set up current awareness profiles • DIALINDEX tells the user which database(s) contain information on the search problem • The user can sort the search results
OCLC FirstSearch	• Basic and advanced search features cater for novice and expert users • Each search screen shows brief details of the chosen database
STN Easy	• The Analyze command extracts how many times a term occurred in a field in an answer set for statistical analysis • The Transfer command is used to extract terms from an answer set in one or more files and automatically search them in other files. One may search the extracted terms in the same or a different field. • The STN index quickly determines the files that contain information on the user's search problem. It enters the files that contain hits, conducts the search and displays the search results
Ovid Online	• Automatically maps the search term to the controlled indexing language of the database for precise retrieval • The FREQ operator specifies the mininum occurrence of a term, and the system will retrieve only those records in which the term appears at least as many times as the threshold value, a very useful feature for full-text searching
LEXIS-NEXIS	• The Freestyle feature uses a new and evolving technology, associative retrieval, which lets users enter a search description in plain English • Variant forms of a word can be searched by using double asterisks (**) after a search term • Numerous search commands are available for expert searchers

Summary

In this chapter we have discussed the basic steps for conducting an online search, and have looked at the features of five online search services. All of these have web interfaces and offer a number of search and retrieval features, though they differ in terms of their database coverage, search interface and output features. Issues to be considered when evaluating and selecting online search services have been proposed in the literature (see, for example, Rowley, 1999 and Forrester and Rowlands, 1999). They include the following:

1 databases offered
2 search and retrieval facilities
3 search interfaces: simple and advanced user interfaces
4 database structure and record formats
5 cost
6 time required for searching
7 cross-database searching facility
8 communication facility
9 support services, and
10 additional facilities, such as current awareness and selective dissemination of information services (like the Dialog Alert service).

With the development of their web interfaces, online search services have become quite easy to use, but the user still needs some training and practice to become an expert and efficient online searcher. Users need to be familiar with the search interface and also need to know the various search options. Formulating the most appropriate search expression is not always easy, and one may have to make several attempts, by formulating new search sets and/or modifying search sets, to get optimum results. However, trial and error can be expensive, as the longer the user is connected to the system and the more records are displayed, the greater will be the cost (see Figure 7.25).

Initially online search services were very expensive, but over the years more flexible pricing systems have come about (Webber, 1995, 1998). However, price is still a factor and a major concern for the users as well as the service providers. Webber (1998) comments that while there are some general trends in online pricing, there seems to be no general solution to the pricing conundrum of online search services. She further argues that the complicated multipart pricing system continues, and that vendors' increasing sophistication in using price as part of the marketing mix may lead to a wide range of pricing strategies aimed at different market segments, and this will eventually make prices of online services more difficult to evaluate and compare.

Fig. 7.25 *Cost of a Dialog search session*

Many important databases that have been (and are currently) available through online search services like Dialog are now available free, as a result of the changes in the business strategies of the information industry that have taken place with the advent and proliferation of the web (see Chapter 15). These changes, coupled with the entry of more players onto the online market, will force online service providers to become more innovative and competitive.

Chapter 8

Science and technology information sources

Introduction

A large number of subjects come under the general heading of science and technology. Volume 1 of *Walford's guide to reference materials* (Mullay and Schlicke, 1999) lists 22 subheadings: agriculture and livestock; anthropology; astronomy and surveying; biology; botany; building industry; chemical industry; chemistry; communication; earth sciences; engineering; household management; industries, trades and crafts; mathematics; manufacture; medicine; natural history; palaeontology; patents and inventions; physics; transport vehicles; and zoology. A much greater number of subjects is to be found in Dewey Decimal Classification classes 500 and 600, which cover science and technology respectively.

Several thousand CD-ROM and online information sources covering different areas of science and technology are now available. In fact, this is the fastest growing area of the database industry. Information sources in science and technology come in a wide range of formats, including books; monographs; journal, conference and workshop papers; theses and dissertations; technical reports; company and product literature; laboratory manuals and handbooks; standards and patents; engineering drawings and specifications, and so on. Common reference sources, such as dictionaries and encyclopedias, bibliographies, indexes and abstracts, biographies, handbooks and manuals, yearbooks, maps and atlases, etc, also form a significant part of scientific and technological information sources.

Long lists of CD-ROM and online information sources on science and technology are available in a number of publications (see, for example, Bopp and Smith, 1995; Balay, 1996; Lea and Day, 1996; Katz, 1997; *Multimedia and CD-ROM directory*, 1998; Wyner, 1998; Kumar, 1999; Mullay and Schlicke, 1999). A select list of CD-ROM and online database on different areas of science and technology is given in Appendix 1. News and reviews of the new science and technology databases appear regularly in *Online & CD-ROM Review*.

This chapter discusses some basic issues related to the searching of electronic information sources on science and technology, and then describes the features of some selected sources to give an overview of the search and retrieval features available. We will thus consider both the specific nature of this category of information sources and the basic techniques necessary for successful searching.

Searching CD-ROM and online information sources in science and technology

Appendix 1 lists over 70 information sources covering different areas of science and technology. Some of these sources are unique and are available only in one format (only on CD-ROM, say) and/or from only one producer or vendor, while others are available in different formats and from different vendors. In other words, in some cases, the same information source may be available on CD-ROM, through online search services, or through the web; the same database may also be available from a number of CD-ROM vendors or online search service providers. However, the search interface as well as the search and retrieval features vary from one version to another. Hence, even if the database is the same, the user needs to be familiar with different sets of skills depending on the format or vendor.

If a database is available on CD-ROM then the search and retrieval techniques discussed in Chapter 6 are applicable. However, these techniques are also affected by the nature and content of the database. For example, CD-ROM databases on different subjects may have different searchable fields, may or may not have an associated thesaurus file, may allow a specific type of searching, and so on. Likewise, if the database is available online then the search and retrieval features discussed in Chapter 7 are applicable, but the search and limiting fields may differ depending on the nature and content of the database. In general users may be able search on any field (free-text search) or on one or more specific fields, may key in search terms/phrases or select them from the corresponding index file, and may combine search terms using the various search operators. It is helpful for the user to have an understanding of the nature of the database concerned (its content, various search fields, indexing techniques ie whether word- or phrase-indexed, limiting fields, cost per search where applicable, and so on) as well as of the search system itself (search interface, search modes, search techniques and operators, and techniques for formulation and modification of queries and for the display and/or printing of the search output using the appropriate format).

In the following sections we shall briefly discuss the features of some information sources covering different areas of science and technology. The databases in question are available in different formats: on CD-ROM, through online search services and through the web. Our basic objective is not to give a comparison of the information sources as such, but to highlight the various search and retrieval features of the chosen sources. It is hoped this will help readers appreciate the need to be familiar with various search and retrieval techniques in order to conduct successful searches of scientific and technological information sources.

Three versions of Ei Compendex

Discussed below are the features and search interface of the CD-ROM, web and online versions of this database.

Ei Compendex on CD-ROM

Features of the CD-ROM version of *Ei Compendex* have been discussed in Chapter 6; Figure 6.14 shows the search output screen. The user can search by word/phrase, Ei subject headings, author name, author affiliation, title words, journal name, conference title, conference location, conference sponsor, conference year, year of publication, treatment codes, language, major subject headings, and Ei classification codes. The user clicks on 'Search/Modify' and then on 'Word/Phrase' index. Enter a term in the small box after 'Enter' and you will see the corresponding portion of the index. Select one or more terms and click OK. You will then see a search set with the given terms in the 'Search History' window, and the output (the complete record) in the output window.

Unlike an online search service provider such as Ovid (see p. 151), which gives a common search interface that can be used to search a number of databases, *Ei CompendexWeb* is a database available directly on the web, and has its own search interface.

Ei CompendexWeb

Ei CompendexWeb is a bibliographic database of engineering research literature, containing over five million records from over 5000 engineering journals and conferences covering the period 1970–2000. *Ei CompendexWeb* from Elsevier Engineering Information Inc, is now available on the web through the search interface called *Engineering Village 2*. There are two basic modes of searching: quick search and expert search.

Quick Search

The quick search mode (Figure 8.1) allows users to select a database from a range of databases that are available through Engineering Village 2. Users can enter a search term/phrase or can select the term/phrase by clicking on the

'Index of Terms' option. Users can also specify a field to search. After entering a search term/phrase in the box (see Figure 8.2), users can click on the 'add fields' button that will show a list of available fields to search. Users can also specify the search period by entering the required years in the 'Search From' option. The Simplified Form does not support manual construction of queries using operators within the search window. For more complex searches using various search operators or nesting, the expert search interface can be used. Users may have the option of sorting the results by Relevance or Ei Publication Date. With Relevance selected, the records are retrieved by an exact match, and then ranked by the proximity and frequency of the search terms. With Ei Publication Date selected, the records are also retrieved by an exact match, and then sorted with the most recent publications at the top of the list.

If users choose the 'All fields' option and enter a term/phrase, the system will search for the term/phrase in all the indexed fields. However, one can limit a search to a specific field. For example, 'Author Search' allows users to search for articles by a specific author, and 'Author Affiliation Search' allows users to search by the affiliation of the first author of each article. Users can also use the index to perform an author affiliation search. Ei Subject Terms are subject headings assigned by indexers from the Ei Thesaurus. The asterisk (*) is used as the wild card to search on variations of a root word.

Once a search is conducted, the system comes up with the retrieved records containing bibliographic details and abstract. The output screen also shows the total number of records retrieved.

Fig. 8.1 *'Engineering Village 2' Quick Search screen for searching 'Ei Compendex Web'*

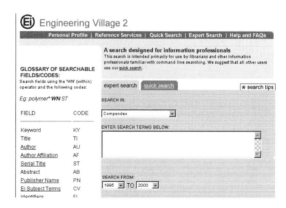

Fig. 8.2 *'Engineering Village 2' Expert Search screen for searching 'Ei Compendex Web'*

Expert Search

The expert search screen (Figure 8.2) allows users to construct complex queries, using Boolean, proximity, and stemming operators. One can also control multiple steps of a search by nesting, and can search either a single field chosen via the drop-down menu, or a combination of fields. If no operator is used between two or more terms, the system will consider as a phrase and will search accordingly. However, in order to denote the proximity of two search terms, the 'near' operator can be used between terms, for example:

```
alkali near metals
gallium near arsenide near materials
```

The asterisk (*) is used as a wildcard, to specify any characters that might appear after the search term. The dollar sign ($) is used to search for words that have the same linguistic root as the search term. For example, $manager retrieves 'managers', 'managerial' and 'management'. Note that although the $ sign is used at the beginning of a search term, it does not work as a left truncation symbol; the truncation, as illustrated by the above example, is still the right truncation.

A search can be limited to a specific field, and users can choose the field code as listed on the left side of the expert search screen (Figure 8.2). Users can also limit their search within a range of years by entering the appropriate years in the boxes below the 'Search From' option (see Figure 8.2)

Ei Compendex on Ovid

The search interfaces for *Ei Compendex* on Ovid Online are shown in Chapter 7 (Figures 7.20–7.22). In the Basic Search mode you can enter a word or phrase for keywords or author, and can limit your search results by year, latest update, English language, journal articles or conference papers. In the Advanced Search mode you can enter a keyword or a phrase, or you can enter a keyword/phrase and map that onto the subject heading. This is a unique feature, whereby you will see a list of words/phrases that map onto the subject heading corresponding to the term/phrase entered, and you can choose any term from the list. You can limit your search results by year, latest update, English language, journal articles or conference papers.

Discussion of Ei Compendex

As we have seen, the search interfaces as well as the search features vary between the CD-ROM, Ovid Online and web versions of the database. This shows that users need to learn the features of a particular version of a database in order to be able to conduct successful searches.

The options available for searching a database depend on the database concerned, and therefore even if we use the same online search service, the search and retrieval features may vary. For example, for the *NTIS* database, the basic and advanced search features of Ovid are not as many as are available for searching *Ei Compendex* (Figures 8.1 and 8.2). Figure 8.3 shows that in the Ovid Basic Search mode, you can enter keywords or author or both to search. In the Advanced Search mode (Figure 8.4) you can search *NTIS* by entering a word or phrase for author, keyword, title, etc. You can also combine search sets. Unlike the search facilities for *Ei Compendex* (Figure 8.2), there is no option for limiting the search.

Applied Science and Technology Index on OCLC FirstSearch

Applied Science and Technology Index, produced by H W Wilson, is accessible through OCLC FirstSearch. This database covers over 350 periodicals on subjects such as chemistry, computer technology, data processing, energy-related disciplines, engineering, mathematics and physics. There are two search interfaces: basic and advanced. In the former (Figure 8.5) users can enter a search term or phrase and can choose a field on which to conduct the search. If users are not sure about the search term/phrase, they can choose from the list of fields and then browse the index for the field chosen. In both interfaces, a brief description of the chosen database appears.

In the advanced search mode (Figure 8.6) users can combine searches on various fields using Boolean operators. The advanced search interface also allows users to browse the index of a chosen field. In addition it allows users to limit a search by year and document type. Other features of OCLC FirstSearch, for example the Boolean and proximity operators, truncation, etc (see Table 7.3,

Fig. 8.3 NTIS *on Ovid (Basic Search mode)*

Fig. 8.4 NTIS *on Ovid (Advanced Search mode)*

Fig. 8.5   'Applied science and technology index' on OCLC FirstSearch (Basic Search screen)

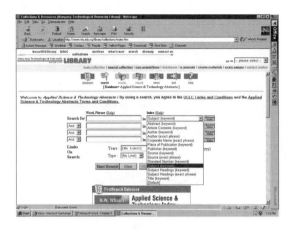

Fig. 8.6   'Applied science and technology index' on OCLC FirstSearch (Advanced Search screen)

p. 147) can be used to search the *Applied science and technology* database through the Advanced Search screen of OCLC FirstSearch.

Wilson applied science and technology abstracts on Dialog

Dialog file 99 contains the *Wilson applied science and technology abstracts* database, which provides abstracting and indexing of more than 400 English-language scientific and technical publications. Non-English-language periodicals are indexed if English abstracts are provided. Periodical coverage includes trade and industrial publications, journals issued by professional and technical societies, and specialized subject periodicals, as well as special issues such as buyers' guides, directories and conference proceedings. The various information retrieval features of Dialog, discussed in Chapter 7, can be used to search this database. The Rank feature of Dialog can be used to prepare, say, a list of required reading, eg

```
SELECT WASTE(W)(MANAGEMENT OR DISPOSAL OR RECYCLING)
RANK JN
```

This will retrieve records on waste management, waste disposal and waste recycling. The output records will be sorted and listed by journal name.

Figures 8.7 and 8.8 show the brief output of a Dialog search and a sample record of *Applied science and technology abstracts*.

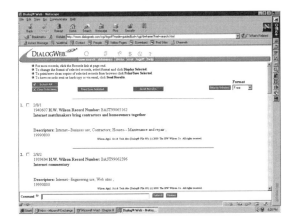

Fig. 8.7 *Picklist screen for a simple Dialog-Web search on 'Wilson applied science and technology abstracts database'*

Fig. 8.8 *Full record of a DialogWeb search on 'Wilson applied science and technology abstracts'*

Grolier multimedia encyclopedia

So far we have considered bibliographic or reference information. In this section we shall see how to search a full-text database containing multimedia information. Our chosen example is the *Grolier multimedia encyclopedia*, available online at **http://gme.grolier.com/**. This online multimedia encyclopedia contains:

• text: 37,000 articles
• multimedia information: features an atlas, pictures, sounds, flags and time-lines
• *Brain Jam*, a monthly electronic magazine; and
• Grolier Internet Index, an easy-to-access authoritative collection of web links.

In the search screen of *Grolier multimedia encyclopedia*, users can search on the titles or full text of articles simply by entering one or more search terms or phrases in the search boxes. Users can choose to search for the terms/phrases in the 'Article Text' or 'Article Title' boxes. Search terms can be combined by using the Boolean operators (AND, OR, or NOT). Users can choose to search on a particular category of information, such as life sciences, physical sciences, technology, etc. They can also search for specific types of information such as maps, pictures, facts, and so on.

The advanced search options allow users to further refine a search and choose a subject category. By default searches are conducted on the article titles in the encyclopedia. By selecting one or more of the optional data types users can modify and limit a search to pictures, maps and fact boxes. The encyclopedia by default also searches all subject categories, but users can limit this by selecting a specific category or categories.

The Advanced Search options allow you to further refine your search both by Search Choices (data type) and by subject category. By default searches are conducted on the article titles in the encyclopedia; you can modify one or more of the optional data types (pictures, maps and fact boxes). The encyclopedia by default also searches all subject categories, but you can limit this by selecting the category or categories that you wish to search. Click the Reset button to quickly return to the default settings.

There are three different types of truncation facilities:

- ? (single character): for example, *Anders?n* would yield results containing *Andersen* or *Anderson*.
- $ (one character or none): for example, the expression *Col$r* will produce results containing *Color* as well as *Colour*.
- * (any number of characters or none; ie wild card): for example searching for *manage** will produce results containing *manage, manager, managers, management*, etc.

There are also different types of proximity search facilities (see Table 8.1).

Table 8.1 *'Grolier multimedia encyclopedia' search operators*

Operator	Action
word W/n word	Searches for word pairs in which the second term occurs within a specified number of words after the first. For example, *information w/2 management* will retrieve *information resource management*
word ADJ word	Searches for adjacent words: equivalent to the W/n operator with a defined range of one word. For example, *information ADJ retrieval* will retrieve *information retrieval*
word SAME/n word	Searches for word pairs that occur – in any order – in the same paragraph or in a specified range of paragraphs
word NOTSAME word	Returns articles in which, in any one paragraph, the first search term occurs but not the second
~	The fuzzy search operator retrieves articles that contain words with spelling similar to that of the query term. For example, *mathematic* will retrieve no articles, but *math~matic* will return 691 articles containing terms such as mathematics
exact phrase operator	retrieves articles that contain exact matches of the query terms, ie this is an option which will conduct a search for a phrase.

Once a search is complete, the number of articles found and a listing of relevant documents are displayed on the Search Results screen. These are ranked according to relevance. The document title is displayed as a hypertext link to the article, picture, map, etc. A representative sample of the document's content is often provided to help users determine whether that document is of interest. This text is selected from information in the document by the search software, using search algorithms, and as a result the information may appear in incomplete sentences.

If there is any image associated with the text, it can be retrieved by clicking on the picture button shown on top of the output screen. Users can go to the related articles by clicking on the 'Link' button that appears on top of the output screen containing the full text. Users can also retrieve images by conducting a search with an appropriate keyword/phrase, and then checking the 'Picture' box on the search screen.

Summary

In this chapter we have talked about CD-ROM and online information sources on science and technology. We have noted that the same database may be available on CD-ROM as well as through online search services. Again, the same database may be available through a number of vendors – CD-ROM as well as online. We have also seen that the same database searched on different media may produce different results with the same search expression (see, for example, p. 164, *Ei Compendex*, etc). We have observed that users need to know various search and retrieval features to be able to move from one platform to another, for example, from the CD-ROM to the online version of the same database. Users need to be familiar with the various fields that can be searched and the various search facilities – for example, Boolean searching, proximity searching, truncation, limiting searches, and the corresponding search operators. Similarly, they should also be aware that the techniques for modifying a query, and as we have seen in this chapter, differ from one system to another. The same is true for the output features, viz viewing, sorting, ranking, saving, printing, etc, of the output records. Searching a full-text database may require the searcher to select additional search options/buttons. For example, in the case of the *Grolier multimedia encyclopedia*, we saw that users can choose between searching on the title field only and conducting a full-text search.

Other features that are characteristic of scientific and technological information sources may be useful keys for searching, such as chemical names and structure for chemical databases, scientific and popular names of objects in botanical, zoological, biological, medical and biomedical databases, and so on. Patents and standards information is another category of sources heavily used in science and technology information systems: these are discussed in Chapter 13.

Chapter 9
Social sciences and humanities information sources

Introduction

Volumes 2 and 3 of *Walford's guide to reference material* (Day and Walsh, 2000, and Chalcraft et al, 1998) list a total of 43 major divisions for describing information sources on social sciences and humanities. Though some of these divisions refer to the form of materials rather than subjects, such as biography, bibliography, organizations and associations, the number of subjects is still quite high. Consequently, there are a large number of CD-ROM and online databases on social and humanities subjects. There are a number of publications that list and review various information sources on social sciences and humanities (see for example, Bopp and Smith, 1995; Balay, 1996; Lea and Day, 1996; Katz, 1997; Chalcraft et al, 1998; Wynar, 1998; Day and Walsh, 2000). A select list of relevant sources available on CD-ROM and/or as online databases appears in Appendix 2. This list is not exhaustive, but illustrative of the various types of information sources that cover this area of study. In this chapter we discuss the features of some selected CD-ROM and online databases in order to give an idea of the various types of information sources, their search and retrieval features and so on. We have chosen some sources that are available on various platforms (search service providers, for example) with a view to showing how versions of the same database differ in terms of their search interfaces as well as the search and retrieval facilities. We have done so in order to highlight the various points that a user might need to consider to conduct searches on social sciences and humanities sources.

How to search information sources on social sciences and humanities

Searching CD-ROM and online information sources in this field, as with any other subject, needs an understanding of the features of the chosen database, the search interfaces, search and retrieval facilities, and so on. Users need to have an understanding of the structure of the chosen database, in terms of the search fields, indexing techniques, such as word and phrase indexes, the various search and limiting fields, etc. Some CD-ROM and online (web) resources have specially designed user interfaces, while in others the common interface of the search service provider, like Dialog, Ovid, etc, or the CD-ROM vendor, for example SilverPlatter, has to be used. In either case it is helpful for the user to be familiar with the search interface features. As shown in the following sections, different information sources have various features, and users need to learn those in order to be able to conduct successful searches.

Features of selected CD-ROM sources on social sciences and humanities

In the following sections we shall look at the features of some selected information sources in order to get an idea of the nature of the databases in this subject category as well as their search and retrieval features. While some of these sources are unique and are available only from one producer or vendor, others are available in different formats. We shall consider the features of some databases that are available on CD-ROM, through online search services and on the web.

'PsycLIT' on CD-ROM

This version of *PsycLIT*, available from SilverPlatter, runs on *WinSPIRS* software (the Windows version of SilverPlatter information retrieval software). The search screen is the same for all the SilverPlatter databases. However, compared with others (for example, *EconLit*, discussed below), this database has certain specialities. It has an associated thesaurus that can be used for formulating search expressions. In order to use this thesaurus the user keys in a word or phrase in the search box and then clicks on the Suggest button, whereby a list of related terms will appear. For example, if we enter the search phrase 'child abuse' and then click on the Suggest button, we would get a list of suggested terms/phrases as shown in Figure 9.1. Search results can be limited by a number of parameters, such as media type, document type, author, publisher. Users can also select search terms or phrases through the various indexes: these include free text (the default index), media type, document type, author, author affiliation, publisher, publication year, etc. Users can get a full record (as shown in Figure 9.2) by selecting a record from the search output window and then clicking on the 'All Fields' button.

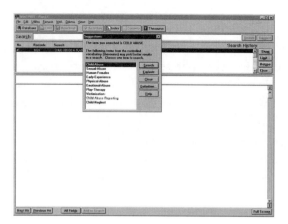

Fig. 9.1   *Use of the thesaurus for searching 'PsycLIT' on 'WinSPIRS'*

Fig. 9.2   *A Full record from 'PsycLIT' on 'WinSPIRS'*

'EconLit' on CD-ROM

This version of *EconLit*, available from SilverPlatter, also runs on *WinSPIRS* software. Figure 9.3 shows a sample search screen. The top part of the search screen contains the search box, the search buttons and the search history box showing the various search sets and the corresponding hits. The bottom part of the screen shows the search results. The user can scroll through this screen to see all the search results, each of which contains brief information on the record; the user can select one or more records and can click on the 'All Fields' button to see more details. By clicking on the 'Limit' button and choosing the appropriate option the search results can be limited by document type, publication year and abstract indicator. By clicking on the 'Index' button the user can browse and select terms from the index file. The default index file is called the 'Free Text Index', which contains index terms from various fields. However, users can click on the 'Change' button to choose from a list of the available indexes: free text, document type, publication year, abstract indicator and update code.

'EconLit' through Ovid Online

Users can search *EconLit* using either the basic or the advanced search screen of Ovid Online. With the basic search screen, users can enter keywords in the keywords search box, and/or can enter author names in the author search box. The advanced search screen allows users to enter a search term or phrase to conduct a search. A search can be limited to the latest updates, journal articles or abstracts, or can be limited by year. A search can be conducted on all fields, or the user can choose from a total of 28 fields. After a search is conducted the user is shown the search results, but in the advanced search option the user can see the search history as well (Figure 9.4) . This helps users modify the query, if necessary, more easily. The output screen gives brief information on the records, and users can click on the 'Abstract' or the 'Complete reference' option to get further details. Users can also choose more than one record and an appropriate format for display of records from the output screen.

'EconLit' through DialogWeb

EconLIT, Dialog file 139, provides abstracts of the worldwide literature on economics, now covering more than 600 major economics journals annually. In addition, the database indexes about 600 collective volumes (essays, proceedings, etc), 2000 books, 900 dissertations, 2000 working papers, and book reviews each year. The database is produced by the American Economic Association and encompasses the bibliographic sections of both the *Journal of Economic Literature* and the *Index of Economic Articles*, as well as the *Cambridge University Press Journal*. Most records for journal articles, books and working papers include abstracts. The *EconLit* database on Dialog can be searched by entering the database number with the command 'B' or 'Begin'. Alternatively, users can choose this database through the database category or thorough the DIALINDEX search (see p. 141). The various search and retrieval features of Dialog discussed in Chapter 7 can be used to search this database. A simple search 'S electronic and commerce' on this database, produced the output shown in Figures 9.5 and 9.6.

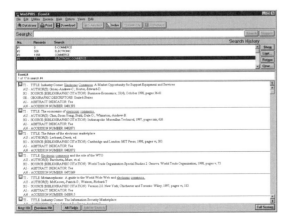

Fig. 9.3 *Sample search screen of 'EconLit' on 'WinSPIRS'*

Fig. 9.4 *Result of a search on 'EconLit' through Ovid Online*

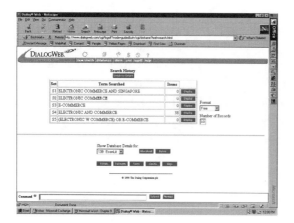

Fig. 9.5   *Dialog search hits on 'EconLIT'*

Fig. 9.6   *Output of a Dialog search on 'Econ-LIT'*

Discussion

The above examples show some of the differences in the search interfaces and features provided by the three different systems for the same database. It is interesting to note from Figure 9.5 that Dialog searches did not find any hit for the search expressions 'electronic commerce and Singapore', or 'electronic commerce', or 'e-commerce', nor even when the proximity operator was used between the two search terms 'electronic' and 'commerce'. However, a search on 'Electronic commerce' retrieved some records from the same database on CD-ROM and Ovid Online. It is also interesting to note that though the search expressions differed, the first record retrieved by both Ovid and Dialog is the same (see Figures 9.4 and 9.6).

ERIC (Educational Resources Information Center) database
'ERIC' on the web

ERIC is now available on the web (**http://ericae.net/aesearch.htm**) with a simple search interface (see Figure 9.7). Users can enter one or more words or phrases in the 'Enter terms' box. They can choose to search for the exact match of the search term(s)/phrase, or can choose to match some or most terms. A search can be limited by fields (author, title words, and descriptors and identifiers), by type of material (book, dissertation, conference paper, journal article, etc), or by the time period. Users can decide to display only the title, the title with short notes, or title with long notes. The search results to be displayed can be restricted to 10, 20 or 30 at a time. Figure 9.8 shows a sample search output screen. Users can select one or more records from the output screen to see the full record, as shown in Figure 9.9.

Fig. 9.7   *Search 'ERIC' on the web: the search interface*

Fig. 9.8   *'ERIC' on the web: the search output*

Fig. 9.9   *Full record from the 'ERIC' database*

Fig. 9.10   *The advanced search screen for searching 'ERIC' on Ovid Online*

'ERIC' on Ovid Online

The basic and advanced search options and the search interfaces are broadly the same as those shown earlier for other Ovid Online databases (see also Chapter 7). The advanced search interface offers an additional option, 'Map Term to Subject Heading'. As shown in Figure 9.10, users can enter a keyword or phrase and then choose this option to see the corresponding subject headings (see Figure 9.11). From the advanced search screen users can conduct a search on all the fields (the default option) or can choose from a list of 29 fields. Users can also choose a field and display the corresponding index to search.

Fig. 9.11 *Mapping keywords on subject headings in 'ERIC'*

'ERIC' on Dialog

ERIC (Dialog file 1), is a bibliographic database that contains education-related
documents and journal articles. Information in *ERIC* corresponds to two
printed abstract/index journals: *Resources in Education* (*RIE*) and *Current Index
to Journals in Education* (*CIJE*). *RIE* announces some 14,000 documents each
year, and *CIJE* announces some 20,000 journal articles, extracted from more
than 750 serials. The *RIE* subfile includes records of many different types of
documents: research/technical reports, conference papers, conference proceedings, programme descriptions, opinion papers, bibliographies, state-of-the-art
reviews, legal/legislative/regulatory materials, dissertations, classification
schemes, teaching guides, curriculum materials, lesson plans, course descriptions, pamphlets, guides, and so on.

There are 8 main search fields, viz, abstract, author, descriptor, identifier,
journal name, publication date, publication year, and title, and 18 additional
search fields, such as *ERIC* document number, ISBN, clearing-house number,
corporate sources, country of publication, etc. The various search and retrieval
features of Dialog (see pp. 135–45) can be used to search this database. Figures
9.12 and 9.13 show the screens of a sample search and its corresponding output.

Discussion

The search interfaces, and the corresponding search and retrieval features, of
the three systems for searching the *ERIC* database – *ERIC* on the web, *ERIC* on
Dialog and *ERIC* on Ovid Online – are quite different. Thus the user may need
to use different techniques, depending on the search system, to access the same
database. For example, a search on 'internet education' on the *ERIC* database

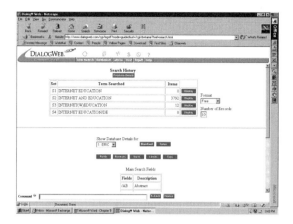
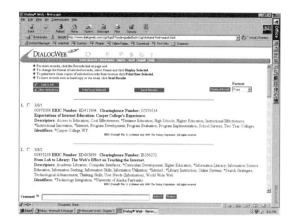

Fig. 9.12 *Search on 'Internet education' on 'ERIC' through DialogWeb*

Fig. 9.13 *Output of a search on 'ERIC' through DialogWeb*

on Dialog produced no results, which means that the phrase 'internet education' was not indexed. We then conducted a Boolean AND search that retrieved 3792 hits, and then a proximity search that retrieved 12 records (see Figure 9.12). When the same database was searched using Ovid Online 34 records were retrieved (Figure 9.10), and using the web interface 2458 hits were produced from 1990 onwards. So the same search phrase may not be appropriate for different search systems, and the user may need to reformulate the search expression.

Summary

Databases differ from one another in terms of their nature, content, interface as well as their search and retrieval features. Users need to be aware of the basic techniques appropriate for searching CD-ROM and online databases (as discussed in Chapters 6 and 7) in order to conduct successful searches. The following general points may be useful for anyone searching a social science and humanities database.

- Usually the search system comes with two search interfaces, one for novice users and the other for experts. The simple search interface may be easier to use, but may not be suitable for formulating complex search queries and thus to pinpoint a search.
- Each database has a number of fields that can be searched, and there are some fields that can be used as limiting fields.
- It may be useful to know the indexing policy, ie whether the various fields have been word indexed or phrase indexed, or both.

- Users need to know how to display the index of a given field in order to select appropriate search terms.
- Users may need to modify queries, and therefore may need to know how to display a previous search set and/or how to combine two or more search sets.
- Users need to know how to select an appropriate format for displaying the search results. It may be possible to set the number of search results to be displayed, and the format in which they appear. Such options may be available on the search screen itself, though in some cases users may need to click on other buttons to activate these options.
- It may be useful to check whether the search system allows the user to save a query for future use.

Chapter 10
Business information sources

Introduction

Business information includes marketing, accounting, product information, finance and investment, corporate information, company profile, and so on. The growth of business information collections in all sectors during the past few years has mainly been due to business end-users' becoming increasingly aware of the importance of information as a tool for competitiveness in the marketplace (Scott and Wootliff, 1992). Information sources that are relevant to the business community are published by a number of organizations, including government bodies, national and international organizations, statutory boards, companies, commercial publishers, and so on. Lists of a number of CD-ROM and online information sources are available in different publications: see, for example, Daniells, 1993; Diaz, 1997; Shelfer, 1997; Burke and Hall, 1998; Burtler, 1999; Kumar, 1999; *Multimedia and CD-ROM directory*, 1998; Day and Walsh, 2000. A list of selected CD-ROM and online business information sources appears in Appendix 3.

Identifying the right business information source is often a demanding task, as is searching the chosen source and retrieving the right information. This chapter describes the features of some useful business information sources and illustrates the different search and retrieval features available in electronic business information sources. The examples given are illustrative rather than comparative or exhaustive, and they are intended to give a general idea of what search and retrieval features are available.

How to search information sources on business

It is important that users are aware of the differences between information sources, in terms of database content, search interface, search and retrieval facilities, and source format (CD-ROM, web, or online search services). Features of five business information sources are discussed in the following sections.

ABI/INFORM

This is one of the most popular business information sources. It is available in a number of different formats and from different vendors, such as UMI, Silver-Platter and Dialog. The version we will discuss here is the *ProQuest ABI/INFORM global* database from UMI (available on the web at **http://www.bellhowell.infolearning.com/proquest/**. Through this database one can search 1000 premier worldwide business periodicals for information on advertising, marketing, economics, human resources, finance, taxation, computers and more. The database also contains information on more than 60,000 companies.

There are two search interfaces, viz basic and advanced (see Figures 10.2–10.3), both of which allow simple or complex searches to be constructed. In the basic search interface, users can limit the date, eg to the backfile (1986–97) or current file (1998–present), and can specify the publication type (such as periodicals, newspapers, reference books, or all) and whether to search in the citations and abstracts or the full text of the article). Boolean and proximity search facilities are available, and users can truncate the word or phrase or can use wildcard characters. Two types of field-specific search are available: the *primary field* search – eg *ABS (information management)* will retrieve the term 'information management' in the abstract field – and the *special field* search – eg *DTYPE(review)* will retrieve only a review type article. A search can also be limited to specific dates of publication (eg past 7 days, past 30 days, past year, and so on. For example, a search expression *PDN(>02/26/2000 AND <03/03/2000)* will look for articles published within seven days, ie from 26 February 2000 to 3 March 2000. In this interface phrases of more than two words should be enclosed in quotation marks. Searching is not case-sensitive. Once users have finished searching they can display the results or view the marked articles by using any of the options provided at the foot of the screen (Figure 10.4).

In the advanced search interface users can also select the backfile or current file, and can limit the search to a specific month of a year or a range, and can specify the publication type as before and the type of article (such as product review, commentary, editorial, interview, statistics, all article types). Users can again choose to search in the citations and abstracts or the full text of the articles, but they can also specify which fields to search (eg publication title, image caption, geographical name, product name, etc); by default the system will search all the nine basic fields, viz, author, abstract, article title, company name, etc. A simple search for 'information resource management' in the publication title field and 'knowledge management' in the article title field, with the search restricted to 'all types of article' in the 'periodicals' publication type, published

Fig. 10.1 *Sample screen of 'ABI/INFORM Global'*

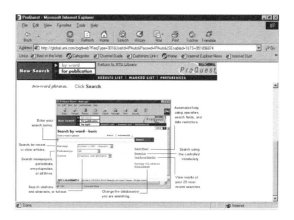

Fig. 10.2 *Basic search interface of 'ABI/INFORM Global'*

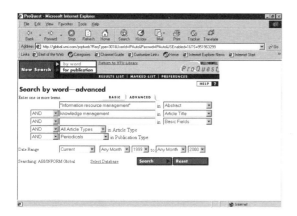

Fig. 10.3 *Advanced search interface of 'ABI/INFORM Global'*

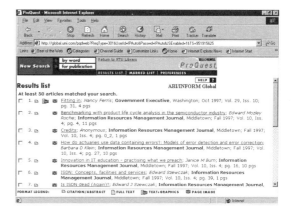

Fig. 10.4 *Sample results from the basic interface of 'ABI/INFORM Global'*

between June 1999 and February 2000, retrieved two articles (see Figure 10.5 and 10.6). Other search options, like spelling variants (eg labour or labor) and related terminology (eg employment, job, work), are also available. Users can select search options, set e-mail format, set or change image quality, change password, configure their browser, and so on, by using the 'Preferences' option.

Dow Jones Interactive

The *Dow Jones Interactive publications library* includes more than 2200 trade and business publications from around the globe. These include the *Wall Street Journal*, the *Far Eastern Economic Review* and *Barron's*; articles are available in

Fig. 10.5 *Sample results from the advanced interface of 'ABI/INFORM Global'*

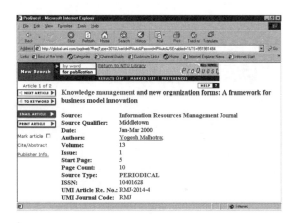

Fig. 10.6 *Sample full record of 'ABI/INFORM Global'*

full text. *Dow Jones Interactive* is a customizable, enterprise-wide business news and research solution. It integrates the content of top national newspapers, Dow Jones and Reuters newswires, business journals, market research reports, analyst reports and websites. Access to third-party databases, such as *Dun and Bradstreet corporate profiles* for US companies, *Dun's market identifiers* (sales report, employees report, etc), *Investext* research reports on companies and industries worldwide, or *Tradeline-trading* histories for equities and derivatives worldwide, is chargeable; the cost of such access varies. Components include: business newsstand, publications library, web centre, custom clips, company and industry centre, historical market data centre, company/industry quick search and the *Wall Street Journal* interactive edition. The database can be searched by word, company, industry and person. Sample search screens of *Dow Jones Interactive* are shown in Figures 10.7 to 10.9.

Users can search for words or phrases from either all or a selected list of publications. Using the 'Look for words in the . . .' menu, the full article, headline only, lead paragraph only, or headline and lead paragraph can be searched, and the date (such as current year, current and previous year, all dates) or date range can be specified. Headlines can be sorted by relevance, by current date, or by oldest date. While searching *by company* you can enter either the company name or the company symbol (the latter can be looked up if necessary). Searching by person will look for articles by a person or about a person. Date and publication type can be specified, if necessary, in all cases.

An advanced search facility is also available in the publications library, which is useful for more experienced searchers. To make search statements (for word or phrase searcher only) more precise Boolean AND, OR and NOT operators can be used. Proximity and truncation search facilities are also available.

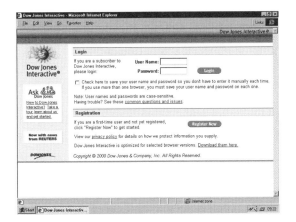

Fig. 10.7 *Log-in Screen of Dow Jones Interactive*

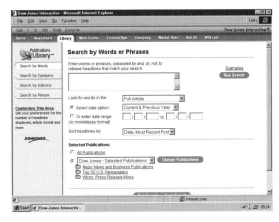

Fig. 10.8 *Sample Screen of Search by Words (Dow Jones Interactive)*

The 'Web Center' of *Dow Jones Interactive* is a service that helps users gather relevant business information published on the web. More than 2000 business websites are reviewed (Figure 10.9). It is possible to search all these websites, or, by entering words or phrases with appropriate logical operators, to restrict the search to particular categories, such as top news sites, non-English language sites, regional sites, reference and news sites, and industry-specific sites. A search can be conducted in all languages or in a specific language, such as, English, Dutch, Spanish and so on. The results can be sorted by relevance or by date. Users can also use the directory where thousands of sites selected by Dow Jones editors are listed alphabetically.

The 'Company & Industry Center' enables users to conduct in-depth

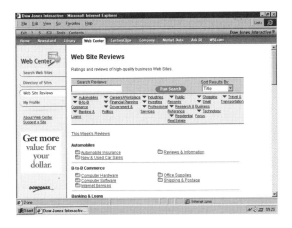

Fig. 10.9 *Sample screen of Web Site Reviews (Dow Jones Interactive)*

research on a company, industry, country or market by making data available from leading research and financial information providers. Information can be obtained by quick or advanced searching. In quick searching, simply type the company name or symbol to obtain company information, business description, corporate performance, stock performance, and so on.

The 'Historical Market Data Center' provides quick access to detailed pricing and dividend histories for worldwide securities, including more than 330,000 active and inactive stocks, mutual funds, corporate bonds, government securities, market indices and options. Users can also get historical exchange rate reports comparing the rate of one currency with another or others. There are two separate component areas, or channels: historical pricing and exchange rates.

LEXIS-NEXIS

NEXIS is one of the world's largest online libraries of international news and information. It has a collection of full-text databases offering a comprehensive source of electronic information for business, financial, news and market information research. At present there are more than 170 libraries with more than 5600 databases available in NEXIS. LEXIS is one of the world's leading online legal research services. It provides access to a comprehensive collection of full-text primary legal source materials. LEXIS users have access to millions of pages of law reports, unreported cases and statutory texts (see Chapter 11 for details), which are organized in different libraries according to jurisdiction.

The LEXIS-NEXIS Group makes its premium branded information products available via the web, dial-up online, CD-ROM and books (**http://www.lexis-nexis.com/lncc/**). *LEXIS-NEXIS* users can access information from authoritative sources enriched with valuable enhancements such as indexing, linkages and segmentation. The information is contained in

- 2.5 billion searchable documents
- 26.5 million images/attachments
- 10,200 databases
- 24,871 sources, 18,871 of which are news and business and 6000 legal.

The NEXIS news and business information service was launched in 1979 to provide recent and archival news and financial information. Since then it has grown to become the largest news and business online information service, including comprehensive company, country, financial, demographic, market research and industry reports. Providing access to thousands of worldwide newspapers, magazines, trade journals, industry newsletters, tax and accounting information, financial data, public records, legislative records, data on companies and their executives makes the *LEXIS-NEXIS* service (Figure 10.10) an indispensable tool for gathering information and providing accurate answers.

In basic searching (see Figure 10.11), the headline and lead paragraph(s) of articles are searched by keyword. A search can be narrowed down with the use of additional terms; this option searches the full text. There is a list of sources to choose from, such as North/South America News Sources or Asia/Pacific News Sources; the date can also be specified. In the Additional Search Options screen (Figure 10.12) specific fields can be searched, such as headlines, caption, or author. Search terms can be combined by using logical and proximity operators. A search can be limited to documents from a specific publication: users can choose the Source List link to see the sources available for this search.

Global Market Information Database (GMID)

GMID, from Euromonitor International, provides data on countries and markets – offering historical statistics and forecasts, information sources, brand and company information, plus full-text market analysis. It provides access to the following seven unique information resources:

- **Detailed Market Size Data**: this module provides size data for 330 consumer products across 49 countries in the world. In order to facilitate analysis and usage, data are presented in comparative tables and there are a range of built-in functions that allow users to manipulate data.
- **Country Marketing Parameters:** this is a compilation of demographic, economic and background marketing statistics for 209 countries in the world.

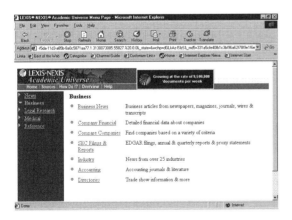

Fig. 10.10 *Sample screen of LEXIS-NEXIS*

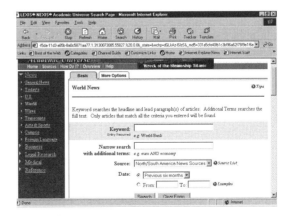

Fig. 10.11 *Basic search screen of LEXIS-NEXIS*

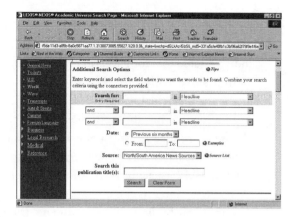

Fig. 10.12 *Additional search options of LEXIS-NEXIS*

The content varies widely, from the length of the average working week, to the number of hospital beds, or the size of the population aged over 65 years. The data are presented in comparative tables and there are a range of built-in functions that allow users to manipulate and analyse the results.

- **Marketing Forecast Data**: this database contains market forecasts for 330 consumer products with demographic breakdowns and economic forecasts up to the year 2010.

- **Brand and Company Information**: this database gives access to 100,000 consumer brands and the 12,000 companies that own them. This database allows the user to find out (1) the major companies in a country or sector, (2) the top brands in a country or sector, (3) Who owns a particular brand in a specific country, and (4) The brands owned by a particular company.

- **Business Information Sources**: this database contains over 29,000 sources of business information. The information sources range from trade associations and industry journals to business libraries, national statistical offices and private research publishers. The categories of information sources include: business directories, chambers of commerce, databases, electronic publications, government departments, industry and trade journals, market research agencies, online hosts, private research publishers, syndicated surveys, trade associations, and trade development organizations.

- **Marketing Profiles**: this database contains 6000 market profiles, and provides instant overviews of the major market factors in the world's leading industrialized countries, such as UK, USA, France, Germany, etc. The statistical, text and graphical data are presented in a format suitable for an instant understanding of the key market parameters.

- **Full Text Market Analysis**: this module provides access to research reports providing in-depth analysis of global consumer markets. As an optional addition to the Global Market Information System there are different types of reports to address different information needs, from country by country studies to global strategic analysis.

Figure 10.13 shows the welcome or first screen of GMID. In order to search any particular service, users need to click on the icon for the service appearing on top of the welcome screen. When we click on the first icon, ie, to search for marketing parameters, we find the corresponding search screen displayed in Figure 10.14. On this search screen, the authors conducted a search for 'population and India' and obtained 36 records, as shown in Figure 10.15. If we click on the 'Continue' button shown in Figure 10.15, we find another tabular output screen, part of which is shown in Figure 10.16. Here, users can display the data differently by selecting a particular year. Users can also choose to display the data on a 'per capita' basis.

Search options vary slightly depending upon the item being searched. The following search options are available:

- For searching for country data (Marketing Parameters Option in Figure 10.13) there are subject search, country search and combined search options.
- For searching for consumer market sizes, there are product search, country search and combined search options.
- For searching for forecast data, there are product search, country search and combined search options.

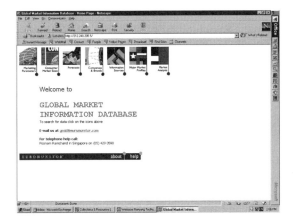

Fig. 10.13 *Global Market Information Database: Welcome screen*

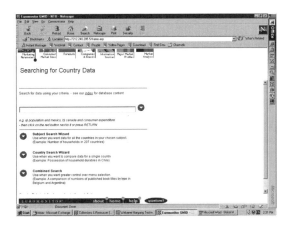

Fig. 10.14 *GMID search screen – searching for country data*

Fig. 10.15 *Results of a search conducted on the search screen of GMID shown in Fig. 10.14*

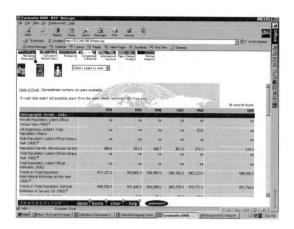

Fig. 10.16 *Tabular representation of data from GMID*

- For searching for companies and brands there are two options: company profile search and brand search.
- For searching for business information sources, there are index (country and topic index) and menu searches (where users can select more than one item from each list and from as many of the lists as wanted) options.
- For searching for market profiles and market analysis reports, users can search for the text of reports/analyses, titles of reports/analyses or can browse reports/analyses by categories.

Users can enter a search term or phrase in the search box that appears on the search screen (see Figure 10.14). Search terms can be combined using the Boolean 'and', 'or', 'and not' operators. Search terms can also be nested (bracketed) for formulating complex Boolean searches. For truncation '*' can be used as a wildcard. The operator 'near' (which in this case will retrieve records containing both the terms occurring within eleven words of each other) can be used for conducting a proximity search.

Moody's Global Company Data

This is an extremely useful database on CD-ROM providing information on over 16,000 companies throughout the world. It is a full-text database containing textual and numerical information on each company. Each record contains information on a company's history, business, properties, subsidiaries and officers, as well as relevant financial information. The user can search and display the textual information on any of the fields or can display the entire record. The user can choose the currency in which the financial information is expressed, and the data can be displayed in tabular as well as graphic formats. The first screen is called the 'Information Desk'. The database can be searched by entering a company name in the search box. As a company name is entered in the box, the corresponding alphabetical portion of the index file showing company names appears in the box below, in the 'folders' area. Once a company name is selected the full text of the record appears at the bottom of the search window, the 'list' area. Users can scroll through the full records or can select other options such as 'highlights', 'history', 'business', etc, to display the particular portion of the records. The user can move between records by clicking on the icons for the previous and next records. Once a particular company is selected the user can display some of its information using the 'graphs' button. The user can then choose between different types of information, such as the balance sheet, financial performance, net income, etc, and also the type of graph to be displayed, such as '2D Bar', '3D Bar', '2D pie', 3D Pie', etc.

The user can search all fields or select a specific field, such as 'History', 'Business' or 'Property' and the user can also select a currency. The number of companies found will be shown in the search portion of the Information Desk at the top of the screen; the list of companies found will be displayed in the List portion of the Information Desk, and the first company on the list will be shown in the folders area. By clicking the Find icon on the first search screen the user can get another small window where the company name to be searched can be entered. Here the user can choose the option 'Find company in list' or 'Find word in folder'. The 'Select Companies' button on the first search screen produces a small window displaying the list of companies in alphabetical order; the user can mark one or more companies from the entire list of 16,314 companies to conduct a particular search. The search results can be sorted by a particular field or by date, in ascending or descending order. The user can export one or more records in a pre-defined or user-defined format. The search operators such as 'Equal to', 'Does Not Equal', 'Greater Than', 'Less Than' or 'Between' can be used, and the period of the search can also be selected from 'Annual' or 'Quarterly'.

Summary

We have seen that business information sources vary in terms of their content, interface and search and retrieval facilities. Users should be aware of the differences in order to retrieve information effectively. In addition to the basic search techniques (discussed in Chapters 6 and 7), users of business information sources can take advantage of specific items of information that can be used as the search keys, such as company name, product/service name, country or branch location, etc. In some cases users may specify specific items to sear ch or view, such as news sources, balance sheet, financial performance, net income, and so on. Some business information sources, for example *Dow Jones Interactive*, provide a number of information services, each having a specific set of search options. Users need to be familiar with these in order to conduct successful searches.

Chapter 11
Legal information sources

Introduction

Legal information sources can largely be divided into two distinct categories: primary sources and secondary sources. The former are records containing the law itself, such as acts of parliament and reports of cases, while the latter include treatises, commentaries, journals and other sorts of publications that are broadly speaking about law and are not in themselves sources of legal authority (Blunt, 1980). In recent years, we have witnessed a significant growth in the number and variety of materials added to law library collections. The growth in the body of primary law has also had a significant impact on the growth and revision of both case digest and secondary sources of materials that discuss, synthesize and analyse the primary law (Svengalis, 1991).

Legal information sources are numerous. First, there is the legislation, the enactments of parliament, made either directly or through the powers delegated to such bodies as government departments, local authorities, etc. In many countries there is also a written constitution, standing above all other legislation. Then there is the judge-made law, the decisions of courts of law. Bills also form a significant part of legal information sources. The legislative process in parliament, of which the end result is an act, begins with the first reading of a bill, and thus a bill may be defined as a draft version of a proposed act (Blunt, 1980). There are also a number of government publications that are closely associated with the parliamentary legislative process, and hence these publications can also form part of legal information sources. Reports of parliamentary debates may be required by lawyers for a variety of reasons, especially for the light that they may shed upon the intentions of the parliament with regard to a particular enactment. Law and arbitration reports and gazettes, which contain published accounts of legal proceedings, account for a significant portion of legal information sources. There are also digests and indexes that are important reference tools facilitating the access to, and selection of, law reports. Standards and patents literature, as well as common reference sources, such as bibliographies, encyclopedias, etc also form part of legal information sources.

There are a number of published sources that list various legal information sources (see, for example, Day and Walsh, 2000; Balay, 1996; Lea and Day, 1996; Wynar, 1998). A select list of CD-ROM and online legal information sources appear in Appendix 4. In this chapter we shall take a look at some legal information sources with a view to understanding their basic characteristics, their search and retrieval features and so on.

Features of selected legal information sources

Techniques for searching legal information sources are somewhat different from those used in searching other sources, for example the science and technology or social science and humanities sources discussed in Chapters 8 and 9. For example, in the case of legal documents certain parameters, such as the date, the type of court, the country or state where the lawsuit took place, the source for legal reviews and commentaries, etc, are very important. Such fields are unique to the legal information sources, and not available in the case of information sources in other disciplines.

LEXIS-NEXIS academic universe

This database at (**http://web.lexis-nexis.com/universe**) provides access to a wide range of news, business, legal and reference information. It couples the convenience of the Internet with the power of *LEXIS-NEXIS* services so that users can quickly and easily retrieve documents that meet their specific research needs. Figure 11.1 shows the interface of *LEXIS-NEXIS academic universe*. It provides access to five areas:

- News, which allows users to search the full text of the day's news or search back more than 20 years
- Business, which allows users to retrieve full-text company news and financial information
- Legal research, which allows users to search full-text federal, state and international legal materials
- Medical, which allows users to search full-text and abstracted medical and health information
- Reference, which allows users to search general reference sources.

The legal information on *LEXIS-NEXIS* is categorized under several headings:

Fig. 11.1 *LEXIS-NEXIS academic universe*

- **Secondary Literature**
  - Legal News: articles from legal newspapers, magazines and newsletters
  - Law Reviews: articles from law reviews
- **Case Law**
  - Get a Case: federal and state legal cases
  - Federal Case Law: decisions from all federal court levels
  - State Case Law: state high court and appellate decisions
  - Area of Law by Topic: cases on a variety of topics
- **Codes & Regulations**
  - Federal Code: federal code, US constitution and court rules
  - Federal Regulations: federal regulations, agency opinions and US attorney-general opinions
  - State Codes: statutory laws, court rules from all states and attorneys-general opinions from all states
  - EU Law (CELEX): European Union law
  - Tax Law: The US *IRS Bulletin*, tax regulations and more
- **Patent Research**
  - Patents: all US patents from 1971 to present
  - Class: patent numbers by classification
  - Manual: manual of classification
- **Career Information**
  - Martindale-Hubbell Law Directory Listings: details on more than 900,000 lawyers and law firms around the world
  - Law School Directories: details on over 250 US schools
  - Choosing a Law School: NALP's *Degrees of difference.*

Users can click on any category to get the search screen for that category; obviously it helps to know which category is most appropriate for a given query. Figure 11.2 shows the search screen for the Legal News category.

Users can review the Finding Information section of the help pages to learn how to build a successful search. The Keyword search option is the simplest form of search: articles retrieved will contain the search terms in the headline or lead paragraph(s) of the document. The use of additional words or phrases, which will be searched for in the full text of a document, narrows a search. You can also narrow a search to documents published on a specific day or within tha specified date range. You may either select a predefined date range from the drop-down list or enter your own custom date range. A range of date formats is supported.

Search screens vary between categories. For example, the Get a Case search screen (Figure 11.3), is different from that for the Legal News category (Figure 11.2). Figure 11.4 shows the simple output of a search in the Federal Case Law category using the keywords 'computer software'. The search output contains brief information: the user can select records or clicked on the hyperlink to obtain the full text. Users can select to view the output using three other formats: expanded, KWIC and full. The results are sorted by default. User can sort the output by relevance, select one or more records to view the full text, print or save the results, or can modify the search.

'Accounting and Tax' database on DialogWeb

This database provides comprehensive indexing and informative abstracts of articles in prominent accounting, taxation and financial management publications from the United States and other countries. The subjects covered include

Fig. 11.2 *LEXIS-NEXIS academic universe Legal News search screen*

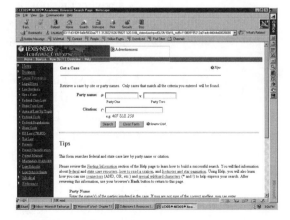

Fig. 11.3 *LEXIS-NEXIS academic universe Get a Case search screen*

accounting, bankruptcy, finance, legal changes, local taxes, federal taxes, the US tax code, international tax issues, etc, and the document types indexed include books and monographs, journal articles, theses and dissertations, newsletters and newspaper articles. Records can be searched by words in the company name, abstract, title, descriptor and geographic name. The company names, descriptors, journal names, journal codes, ISSN, etc can be searched as a phrase. Search results, the output of a simple search and the full text of a document on this database are shown in Figures 11.5, 11.6 and 11.7 respectively.

Fig. 11.4 *LEXIS-NEXIS academic universe output of Federal Case Law keyword search*

Fig. 11.5 *Dialog 'Accounting and tax' database search results*

Fig. 11.6 *Dialog 'Accounting and tax' database search output*

Fig. 11.7 *Full text of a document from the Dialog 'Accounting and tax' database*

'US Copyrights' database on DialogWeb

US Copyrights provides access to registration details for all active copyright and registrations on file at the US Copyright Office. The database has been designed primarily as a fast screening tool for checking the ownership and registration status of a particular work, and it is also useful for checking a particular individual's or entity's portfolio of registered works. There are three types of records: monograph records, serial records and legal document records. Monograph and serial records contain information on the initial registration and renewal of a work. Legal document records contain information on assignments and other information pertaining to the ownership status. Each record contains the title of the work, the owner's name, the registration number, an indication of whether the work is published or unpublished, the class and retrieval code assigned by the US Copyright Office, and other pertinent information about the work and nature of the registration. Registered works that have been renewed are also in the database, with the status designation of renewal. *US Copyrights* includes works registered under the Copyright Act of 1976 and subsequent amendments, including the Semiconductor Chip Protection Act of 1984. Records can be searched by owner or claimant, title, assignor or assignee, author, named title, title of the registered work, registration number, etc. Figures 11.8 and 11.9 show the results and output of a simple search.

Summary

Our discussions of a small sample of information sources on law and related subject reveal some important points. *LEXIS-NEXIS*, one of the most heavily used information sources, is organized by various categories. In order to search

Fig. 11.8 *Results of a search on the Dialog 'US copyrights' database*

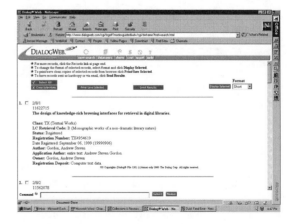

Fig. 11.9 *Output of a search on the Dialog 'US copyrights' database*

efficiently the user must make an informed choice of which category is most relevant. The search strategy employed will differ according to the category chosen: for example, for searching in the Get a Case category users need to enter a party name, whereas the Legal News category can be searched by keyword(s) and here date is very important. The two examples of legal databases available on Dialog show that a knowledge of what fields can be searched is particularly useful in the context of legal information sources. The user who is aware of these search fields and how they are indexed, and who is familiar with the chosen search system's interface, search options, search syntax, output features, and so on, is well prepared to conduct successful searches on legal information sources.

Chapter 12
Health information sources

Introduction

Medical information sources were among the first to appear in electronic form, about three decades ago, for local as well as online access through the National Library of Medicine (NLM) in the US. Many online and CD-ROM databases on health and related subjects have appeared since. Now users have a choice from a large number of sources available on CD-ROM, through online search services, and on the web. Although *MEDLINE* (MEDLARS onLINE) is the largest and the most frequently used database – available through a number of CD-ROM and online vendors as well as on the web – there are many other information sources in this area that are available in print as well as electronic form. Major electronic information sources in health and related disciplines include abstracts and full texts of medical journals and conference papers, research reports, theses and dissertations, clinical practice guidelines and regulations, radiology images, treatment options, drug and patent information, laboratory techniques and instruments, environment and safety standards, as well as ready reference sources like dictionaries, encyclopedias, directories and biographies. There are many sources that list these various kinds of health information sources: see, for example, Balay, 1996; Lea and Day, 1996; Schnell, 1997; *Multimedia and CD-ROM directory*, 1998; Mullay and Schlicke, 1999; Kumar, 1999; Booth and Walton, 2000). A select list of CD-ROM and online health information sources appears in Appendix 5.

How to search health information sources

As the list of information sources in Appendix 5 shows, a wide variety of health information sources are available. The techniques for searching these sources vary from one type to another. In order to utilize the wide array of health information sources effectively, users need to learn the appropriate techniques. Here we shall discuss *MEDLINE*, *UnCover* and some health information sources that are accessible through OCLC FirstSearch. Our discussion will not only apply to the databases in question but will also highlight some general points that users need to consider while searching other health information sources.

'MEDLINE' on the web and through Dialog

MEDLINE is one of the oldest, largest and most popular databases on medical and health sciences. It is produced by the US National Library of Medicine and is available on CD-ROM and online through a number of vendors. It has recently become available on the world wide web.

'MEDLINE' on Internet Grateful Med

PubMed is the National Library of Medicine's search service providing access to over 11 million citations in *MEDLINE, ProMEDLINE* and other related databases (**http://www.ncbi.nlm.nih.gov/PubMed/**). Internet Grateful Med (IGM) is a world wide web application that searches *MEDLINE* using the retrieval engine of NLM's PubMed system (**http://igm.nlm.nih.gov/**).

Internet Grateful Med (IGM) searches *MEDLINE* and 14 other related databases (for the list of databases see Figure 12.1). Users need to select a database from the list appearing on the left of the IGM screen (Figure 12.1) and click on it. Once a database is selected, a search screen, as shown in Figure 12.2, appears.

In the first part of the search screen (Figure 12.1) there are three text boxes where users can type in query terms. In each box, users can enter a search term or phrase and can select a field from three choices: Subject, Author Name and Title Word. Search terms in each box can be combined with those in the other by Boolean operators AND and OR. The Find MeSH/Meta Terms option at the

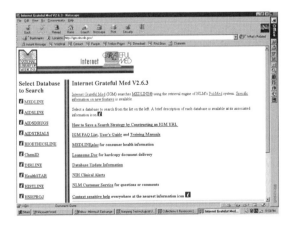

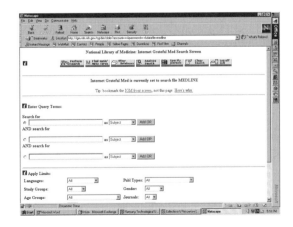

Fig. 12.1 *First screen of the 'Internet Grateful Med'*

Fig. 12.2 *IGM search screen*

top of the search screen is used to find concepts in the thesaurus. Internet Grateful Med sends every search expression to NLM's (National Library of Medicine) PubMed retrieval engine. PubMed performs a set of Automatic Term Mapping functions on the search terms it receives. The terms entered by the user are matched against a MeSH Translation table, a Journals Translation table, and a phrase list. These functions are active only for subject searches, not for author name searches or title word searches.

In the second part of the search screen (Figure 12.2), users can enter options to limit a search. The limiting options are: Languages (English, French, German, Italian, Japanese, Russian, Spanish, or All Non-English); Publication Types (Clinical Trial, Editorial, Letter, Meta-Analysis, Practice Guideline, Randomized Controlled Trial, or Review); Study Groups (Study Groups – human or animal – characterizing participants or experimental subjects described in an article); Gender (Female or Male); Age Groups (Newborn, Child, Adult, etc); Journals (users can specify a pre-defined journal list), and Year Range. After entering the search terms and the limiting options, if any, users have to click on the 'Perform Search' option appearing at the top of the search screen. Once this is done, the system will conduct a search and the results will be shown in the output screen shown in Figure 12.3.

The output screen shows the number of hits and displays 20 records at a time. Brief information on each record appears giving title, author, source, and so on. Users can click on the Full Citation or Related Articles button against each output record. They can select more than one record and can click on the Fetch for Display button appearing on top or at the bottom of the output screen. The output records can be saved by clicking on the Download to Disk option.

Fig. 12.3 *Output of a search on 'MEDLINE' in IGM*

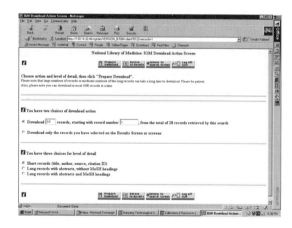

Fig. 12.4 *Download results screen of IGM*

As soon as this option is chosen, users will see the screen shown in Figure 12.4. Users can save all the records or only selected records. Regarding the format, users can choose to save short records with title, author, source, and citation ID. They may also choose long records with abstracts, with or without the MeSH headings. Once this is done, the downloading operation can be initiated by choosing the Prepare Download action.

'MEDLINE' on Dialog

MEDLINE is a major information source for biomedical literature. It corresponds to three print indexes: *Index Medicus*, *Index to Dental Literature*, and *International Nursing Index*. Additional materials not published in *Index Medicus* are included in the *MEDLINE* database in the areas of communication disorders, and population and reproductive biology. *MEDLINE* is indexed using NLM's controlled vocabulary, MeSH (medical subject headings). An online thesaurus is available to aid in locating MeSH descriptors. Abstracts, which are taken directly from the published articles, are included for over 59% of the records added from 1975. Records added before 1975 do not contain abstracts; records added from 1985 to the present have abstracts for about 69% of the records. Approximately 400,000 records are added per year, of which more than 85% are in English.

The extensive search and retrieval features of Dialog, discussed in Chapter 7, can be used to search the *MEDLINE* database. However, there are some special operators that can be used in searching this database. For example,

* the (L) operator can be used to link descriptors and subheadings:

```
S ASPIRIN(L)AE
S BLINDNESS(L)CHEMICALLY INDUCED
```

* the explode operator (!)can be used to search narrower descriptors in the MeSH vocabulary:

```
S DIABETES MELLITUS!
```

* the online thesaurus can be used to check and select MeSH thesaurus terms:

```
E (ACUPUNCTURE)
```

* the MAP can be used to take CAS registry numbers to another file:

```
MAP RN TEMP
```

A given search can be limited by a number of parameters, such as abstract/no abstract, English/non-English language materials, human subject, major descriptors and publication year. The search output can be sorted by author, corporate source, journal, publication year and title. A simple search was conducted on *MEDLINE* with the following search expression: S AIDS AND CHILDREN AND AFRICA; the output screen is shown in Figure 12.5. From here we can choose to display the results in Free format (see Figure 12.6), and then choose one record to display in Full format (see Figure 12.7).

Discussion

Comparing the steps involved in searching *MEDLINE* on Dialog with those on the PubMed website, we can see that there are some differences in the steps that are to be followed for the search and display of records. There are also some differences in terms of the search facilities and operators. Figures 12.2 and 12.6 show that the number of hits retrieved by the same search expression can differ significantly, even on the same day, between the Dialog and PubMed searches. Results can be affected by several factors, such as the up-to-dateness of the databases or the nature of the indexing. This shows that while searching a database it is extremely important to note the platform that is being used: different techniques, operators, etc may be needed when the user changes from one online search service to another or to the web version of the same database.

Searching medical information through UnCover (http://uncweb.carl.org/)

UnCover is a database of current article information taken from well over 18,000 multidisciplinary journals, and contains brief descriptive information for over 8.8 million articles that have appeared since late 1988. It is easy to use, with keyword access to article titles and summaries. *UnCover* also provides an online periodical article delivery service and a current awareness alerting service.

- *UnCover SOS* is a method of document delivery created for users who simply want to forward orders to *UnCover*. It aims to continue a tradition of responding to customer needs and provide the most innovative, automated and efficient document delivery available.
- *UnCover Reveal* is an automated current awareness service that delivers the table of contents of users' favourite periodicals directly to their e-mail address. The Reveal service also allows users to create search strategies for their favourite topics. Keyword or author searches result in a list of individ-

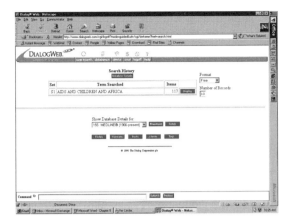

Fig.12.5 *'MEDLINE' search results on Dialog-Web*

Fig. 12.6 *Dialog Picklist showing 'MEDLINE' search results in Free format*

Fig. 12.7 *'MEDLINE' search result in Full format on Dialog*

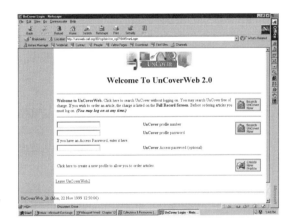

Fig. 12.8 *UnCover first screen*

ual article citations. Articles may be ordered from *UnCover* by e-mail reply or by printing the list and faxing the order.

Searching the *UnCover* database is free (see Figure 12.8): users pay only for the articles that they order. Users can search the journals by using the simple search interface shown in Figure 12.9. The results of a simple search for medical information in *UnCover* are shown in Figure 12.10; Figure 12.11 shows a full article record.

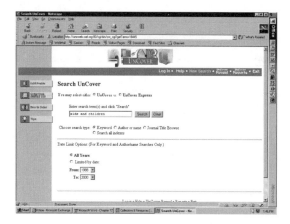

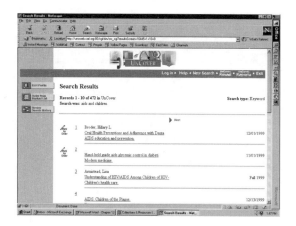

Fig. 12.9 *Searching in UnCover*   **Fig. 12.10** *Search results from UnCover*

Health information sources on OCLC FirstSearch

Some important health information sources are available via OCLC First Search. These include:

- *FactSearch* database is a guide to statistical statements on current social, economic, political, environmental and health issues, derived from newspapers, periodicals, newsletters and other documents from all over the world.

- *HealthRefCtr – Health reference center – academic* provides access to nursing and allied health journals, plus a wide variety of personal health information sources: journals, newsletters, pamphlets, reference books and more. More than 40 full-text nursing and allied health journals, as well as leading medical journals, provide the latest information specific to students' courses and careers.

- *HRCtr – Health reference center* is a multi-source database for health and wellness research. Rich with full text documents, *Health reference center* draws from medical and consumer periodicals, health newsletters, reference books, referral information, topical overviews and pamphlets. Designed especially for lay research, *Health reference center* provides information in terms that the non-medical-professional can understand.

- *MDX health digest* contains abstracts of medical and health information.

All the databases are accessible through the OCLC FirstSearch search screen (see Figures 12.12 and 12.13, showing similar search screens for the *Health reference center* and the *MDX health* databases respectively). However, the searchable fields differ from one database to the other. For example, there are 16

Fig. 12.11 *Full article record in UnCover*

Fig. 12.12 *'Health reference center' on OCLC FirstSearch*

searchable fields for the *Health reference center* (abstract, accession number, author, case name, company name, industry codes, product information, publisher, source, standard number, subject, subject heading, text, title, update date and year) but only 8 searchable fields for the *MDX health digest* (abstract, author, comment, index term, MeSH heading, source, subject and title). In both databases there is a subject field which actually refers to keywords: the subject heading field, is thus called in the *Health reference center* database, but is referred to as the MeSH heading for the *MDX health digest*. The user can click on the right-hand box to display the list of searchable fields. A search can be conducted on a chosen field, or a field index can be browsed to select the search term.

There are two search interfaces: the basic search (the default option; see Figures 12.12 and 12.13) and the advanced search (Figure 12.14). In the basic search interface, users can enter one or more keywords on a field selected from a drop-down box. Users can also browse the index of a chosen field, which shows a portion of the index with an indication of the number of records for the browsed keyword/phrase. Users have the same options in the advanced search mode, but can combine search terms from up to four fields, and can limit a search by several parameters: year, availability, format, article type and audience. Figure 12.15 shows the result of a search on the *Health reference center* database. The user can select one or more records to display the full details (see Figure 12.16).

Fig. 12.13 *'MDX health digest' on OCLC FirstSearch*

Fig. 12.14 *'Health reference center' advanced search screen on OCLC FirstSearch*

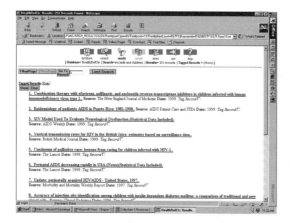

Fig. 12.15 *'Health reference center' search results*

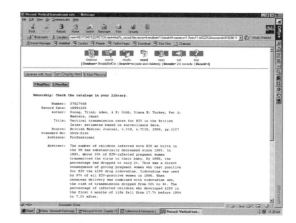

Fig. 12.16 *'Health reference center' sample full record*

Summary

In this chapter we have described the features of some very useful electronic information sources on health and related disciplines. Users may need to follow different steps to search the same database when it is available on a different medium. The search interface may remain the same for various databases when they are searched through the same vendor, but the searchable fields may differ. Fields, operators, search strategy formulation, output features and terminology all differ between the various databases and service providers. Familiarity with these differences will ensure more efficient searching.

Chapter 13
Standard and patent information sources

Introduction

Standards and patents form a significant part of the collections of scientific, technical and industrial information systems. They are also used in commercial as well as academic and research libraries. Patents and standards have some specific characteristics that make them different from traditional bibliographic and textual information sources. In this chapter we briefly discuss the features of standard and patent literature and then discuss how these sources can be searched. A select list of these sources is given in Appendix 6.

Standards

Standards and specifications consist of descriptions of technical features of products, materials, processes and services that may be useful for a purchaser; patents are the rights given to protect the intellectual property rights for an invention. The Standards Council of Canada defines a standard as 'a published document which contains requirements, procedures or definitions for a specific activity' InNOVAcorp, n.d.). A standard may discuss the safety, performance, or quality requirements; it may outline materials that should be used or tests that should be conducted; or it may define product dimensions, terms or how a service is provided (Allott, 1992). A standard usually has an identifying alphanumeric label that consists of an acronym for the organization which produced it and a number specifying the subject and publication year. For example, ISO2709:1978 denotes that the standard was number 2709 of those produced by the ISO (International Organization for Standardization) in 1978. Standards ensure that we have safe products, and that products perform as they should. There are basically five classes of standards:

- International standards are, as the name implies, established at the international level. The most recognized international standards organization is the ISO.
- Regional standards encompass broad geographical areas. Those produced by CEN, the European Committee for Standardization, are an example.
- National standards are produced by national organizations. Examples are: ANSI (American National Standards Institute), CSA (Canadian Standards Association) and BSI (British Standards Institution).
- Government standards are produced by government for government. Military specifications produced by DOD (the US Department of Defense) are an example.
- Voluntary or industry standards are generally produced by industry associations, such as ASME (American Society of Mechanical Engineers), ASTM (American Society for Testing and Materials), IEEE (Institute of Electrical and Electronics Engineers) and SAE (Society of Automotive Engineers).

Patents

Patents, registered trade marks and service marks, and registered designs are known collectively as industrial property (Sibley, 1992). These are the monopoly rights, given to a person or an organization, which can be used to protect intellectual property. The rights that come with a patent, and what is patentable, depend on the country that grants the patent. Patent rights can be sold or licensed to third parties, and these rights are applicable in one or more countries that grant them. Given the highly technical nature of intellectual property protection, the authority of patent information sources becomes a crucial area (Pillow, 1997).

Patent literature is complicated because an inventor must obtain a patent in each country where he/she intends to get protection on a given invention. Therefore, many patent publications may arise from the same invention. The documents from various countries that describe the same invention are referred to as a patent family (Pruett, 1986). Patent documents published throughout the world provide a unique source of technical information, much of which is not available from other sources. Collections of national and foreign patent documents are held in national patent offices, together with the name indexes and search tools (Sibley, 1992), but a number of patent information sources are now available on CD-ROM and online.

How to search standard and patent information sources

Standards and specifications can be formulated by companies, trade associations and professional societies, government agencies, national standards institutions, and regional and international standardizing agencies. There are three common types of questions about standards and specifications: (1) verification, eg what is ISO 2709 or BS 5723; (2) equivalence, e.g. what is the international standard that is equivalent to BS 6523; and (3) availability, eg what standards exist for the manufacture of CD-ROM discs? In addition, sometimes users need to know whether or not an existing standard has been withdrawn or superseded. Answers to these types of questions can be found by searching the standards handbook produced by the standard producing agencies, or by a search on standards databases available on CD-ROM or online. The standard number is one of the most useful search keys in addition to the subject and keywords.

Patent documents contain both bibliographic data, generally confined to the front page, and technical information, which is generally confined to the body of the specification and includes the title and abstract. There are usually two types of technical information: that relating to the invention itself, the 'invention information', and the 'additional information', which may be useful for future patentability searches (Sibley, 1992). The information on the front page of patent documents is generally presented in a form recommended by the World Intellectual Property Organization (WIPO). Patents are organized according to the International Patent Classification (IPC) system. Patents are searched to establish the state of the art or to establish the novelty of inventions. Such searches are carried out using the patent as well as the literature on the subject concerned. Another important type of search is called the infringement search, which is carried out to establish that an organization's product, process or apparatus does not infringe a valid patent. There are three basic parameters involved in a patent search: the subject area, the country and the time.

Features of selected standard and patent information sources

In the following paragraphs we shall discuss the features of some standard and patent information sources with a view to highlighting some points that a user may find helpful in order to conduct successful searches on these sources.

'The ISO catalogue' on the web

The ISO home page (**http://www.iso.ch/**) provides access to the *ISO catalogue*, as shown in Figure 13.1. The user can click on either the HTML or database of international standards, among other options. In both HTML and database versions users need to click on a chosen category of standards that leads them to the sub-categories. In the database version the categories and sub-categories chosen, ie the hierarchy, is shown on the output screen. The search screen (Figure 13.2) includes a search criteria box and a classified list of patent categories to browse. The user can click on any category to get a list of subcategories, and

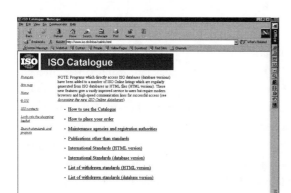

Fig. 13.1 *The 'ISO catalogue' on the web*

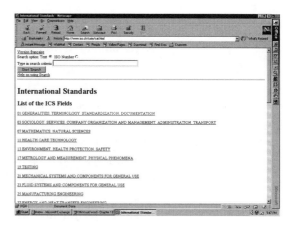

Fig. 13.2 *'ISO catalogue' search screen*

Fig. 13.3 *ISO list of information science standards*

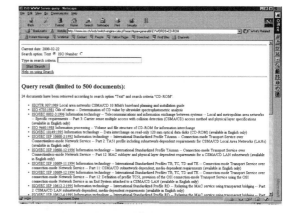

Fig. 13.4 *Results of text search on 'ISO CD-ROM' standards*

may follow this to get a list of standards in a specific (sub)category. For example, the list of information science standards shown in (Figure 13.3) was obtained by this process. Clicking on any standard number produces the relevant details. If the user already knows the specific standard number, he or she can click on ISO Number and enter it in the search criteria box (Figure 13.2), thus retrieving the specific standard without browsing. If the user wants to know what standards are available on a given subject, the text search option allows specific terms or phrases to be entered in the search box. A text search on CD-ROM standards, for example, would produce a list as shown in Figure 13.4.

British standards

Information on British standards can now be obtained from the BSI website (**http://www.bsi.org.uk**). From the BSI home page (Figure 13.5) the user clicks on the *British standards online* option, which links to the search screen (Figure 13.6). The user can enter the standard number, if known, in the search box. The results of a search for BS 5723 are shown in Figure 13.7.

British standards online provides two modes of search: simple and advanced (Figure 13.8). In the simple search mode the user can search by standard number, title or keywords, and among current, withdrawn or draft standards. A search can also be limited by year and month. In the advanced search mode, users can search by keywords in the abstract, or can look for a British standard by entering an equivalent international standard number. Other search keys include withdrawn standard number, committee reference number, and so on (see Figure 13.8). The limiting search facilities by the year and month are available in the advanced search mode too.

IBM patent search (Intellectual Property Network)

The IBM patent search site (Intellectual Property Network) (**http://www.patents.ibm.com/**) allows access to US Patent & Trademark Office patent descriptions and over 1.4 million European Patent Office and World Intellectual Property Office patents and applications, going back to 1971. The images of nearly all US patents and the images of the EPA and WIPO documents are available free. It provides simple as well as detailed search facilities for patents (Figure 13.9). Users can enter a search term/phrase or a patent number to con-

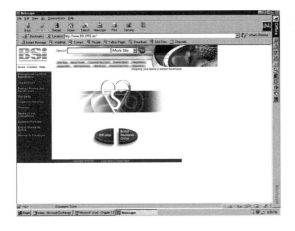

Fig. 13.5 *BSI home page*

Fig. 13.6 *'British Standards online' search screen*

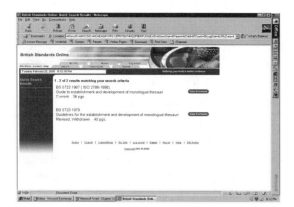

Fig. 13.7 *'British standards online' search results*

Fig. 13.8 *'British standards online' simple and advanced search screen*

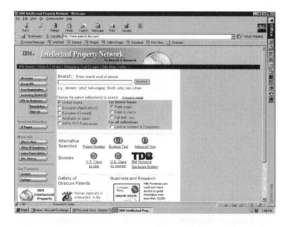

Fig. 13.9 *IBM patent database search screen*

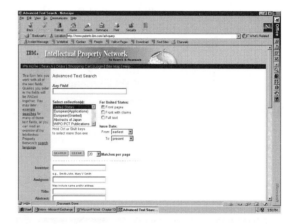

Fig. 13.10 *IBM patent Advanced Text Search screen*

duct a search. Advanced text and Boolean search options, and browsing facilities for US patents by title and class number, are also available. Searches can be limited by country, or to the front page, front page with claims or full text of the patent documents. The advanced text search screen (Figure 13.10) allows users to search on fields such as inventor, assignee, title abstract, attorney/agent/firm, related information, international classification, application date, application number, patent number, claims, examiners, US reference, other references, government information and maintenance status code. Search keys entered in more than one field are automatically ANDed. Browsing by title and class number is also possible from the advanced search screen. Users can also choose the 'Any field' option to enter their search key. An 'Any field' search on 'digital libraries' retrieved 20 US patents, as shown in Figure 13.11. Users can select one or more patents from the output screen to see the brief or full patent text and images.

esp@cenet

esp@cenet is the online patent search system (**http://ep.espacenet.com/**) of the European Patent Office. It allows users to search for (1) patents, in their original language, from the European Patent Office as well as the World Intellectual Property Organization and (2) patent applications with an English abstract and title from 30 million patent documents worldwide or from Japan. Searches can be conducted in English, German and French. Simple searches can be conducted by entering the patent number, company name or text words and phrases. Figure 13.12 shows the search interface for **esp@cenet**.

'Derwent world patent index' on Dialog

Derwent world patent index (*DWPI*) provides access to 18 million records covering patents from the following authorities: Argentina, Australia, Austria, Belgium, Brazil, Canada, China, Czechoslovakia, Czech Republic, Denmark, European Patent Office, Finland, France, Germany, Germany (East), Hungary, Ireland, Israel, Italy, Japan, Luxembourg, Mexico, Netherlands, New Zealand, Norway, Patent Cooperation Treaty, the Philippines, Portugal, Romania, the Russian Federation, Singapore, Slovakia, South Africa, South Korea, the Soviet Union, Spain, Sweden, Switzerland, Taiwan, United Kingdom and the United States of America. Each record in the database describes a single patent family

Fig. 13.11 *IBM patent search results*

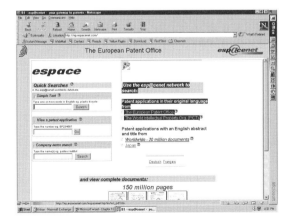

Fig. 13.12 *The 'esp@cenet' search interface*

containing data from the first publication of an invention, known as the basic patent, as well as any further published patents relating to that invention, known as equivalents. The records contain bibliographic data, Derwent-assigned titles, abstracts, general indexing and in-depth chemical and polymer indexing. Additionally, electrical and engineering drawings are present in records dating back to 1988, and chemical structure drawings are present in records dating back to 1992. Since 1999 additional abstracts and indexing features have been provided. The alerting abstract (formerly known as the basic abstract) is organized into paragraphs with informative, searchable paragraph headings. The alerting abstract also contains a 'novelty' paragraph describing the non-obvious improvements over previous technology. A 'technology focus' abstract contains separate paragraphs providing different technological viewpoints of the invention. The extension abstract, available only in file 350, provides a detailed summary of a patent, which bridges the gap between the concise abstract summary and the full-text patent document. Files 351 and 352 are identical in coverage but are split by geographical access, with the former available to users worldwide except in Japan, and the latter available to users in Japan only. File 350, *Derwent world patents index extension (DWPIX)* provides additional search capabilities for Derwent subscribers. A companion file, *Derwent patents citation index (DPCI)*, file 342, details examiner and author patent citations for patents from the 16 largest patent-issuing authorities. Users can search on the basic index fields, such as abstract, basic abstract, extension abstract, title, novelty, technology focus, etc. There are also a number of additional index fields that can be searched, such as application country, priority application country, application date, application number, author/inventor, patent assignee company, designated states and cited patents.

'European patents fulltext' on Dialog

Each record in this database consists of bibliographic, administrative and legal-status data from the print *European Patent Bulletin* (its online equivalent is *European patent registry*) from 1978; complete specification(s) and claims of published, unexamined applications ('A' documents) from 1986 (full text in the original language of publication); and complete specification(s) and claims of examined, granted patents ('B' documents), if available, from 1991 (full text in English, German and French). Titles are available in all three languages. English abstracts are provided for German and French documents within several weeks of their addition to the database. Claims of 'B' documents are searchable in all three official languages. The approximate breakdown of languages for the full patent specification (text) is 55–60% English, 30–35% German, and 10–15% French. The full text of European patents and applications is obtained from the EPO.

'The TRADEMARKSCAN' databases on Dialog

TRADEMARKSCAN international register and European databases are produced by Compu-Mark. Descriptions of each file are provided in the Sources section on page 2 of the bluesheet. These databases serve principally as preliminary trade-mark-screening tools for checking on the availability of new product and service names. A number of the databases are available through Dialog, covering Austria (file 662), Benelux (file 658), Canada (file 127), Community Trademarks (CTM) (file 227), Denmark (file 659), France (file 657), Germany (file 672), International Register (WIPO) (file 671), Italy (file 673), Liechtenstein (file 677), Monaco (file 663), Spain (file 228), Switzerland (file 661), UK (file 126), US Federal (file 226), and US State (file 246).

Most of these databases feature full records that contain the trade mark, serial number, international class(es), status, goods/services description, current owner, dates and other pertinent information. International Register (Madrid Agreement and Madrid Protocol)/WIPO records are also featured in member countries' national files. Trade-mark words can be searched as phrases (ET=), as whole words or word beginnings in the basic index, or as word fragments or word endings in the rotated index (TR=). Trade-mark designs and logos are referenced in appropriate fields, eg design type (DT=), lining/color claims (PH=) and design phrase (PH=). Records for marks that contain a design include the trade-mark image. Images are available in all files except file 677. Each file can be searched individually or in conjunction with other trade-mark file(s). Special efforts have been made to standardize the search and display fields for all of the databases.

'WIPO/PCT patents fulltext' database on Dialog

This database (Dialog file 349) covers the full text of Patent Cooperation Treaty (PCT) published applications issued under the auspices of the World Intellectual Property Organization (WIPO) since 1983. At present, 171 member states participate in the PCT system. A single PCT application can be designated as valid in any or all of the member states, so it is essentially equivalent to having filed with each designated national and regional patent office. The *WIPO/PCT patents fulltext* database is produced by Micropatent, LLC. The data are searchable online approximately 10 to 14 days after publication of the document. Records in the database contain the searchable text of the complete document, including the specification and claims, titles and abstracts in French and English, patent applicant/assignees and inventors, and patent and priority application data. The complete text is available only for documents in English (71%), French (5%), German (15%) and Spanish (0.05%). Text originally provided to WIPO in non-Latin characters (8.5%), ie Greek, Chinese, etc is not included. Patent and application numbers are standardized on the Dialog service, so they can easily be searched in other patent databases. The MAP command can be used to capture the published application numbers (prefix PN=) or priority application numbers (prefix AN=). The resulting saved strategy can then be executed in another file using the EXS command to obtain additional information about the original invention. For example, file 345, *Inpadoc*, contains legal status actions pertaining to PCT patents and patent family information.

Summary

In this chapter we have discussed the basic features of standards and patents. For standards, the standard number, the status of the standard (for example new, withdrawn or superseded) as well as the date are important search criteria. In the case of patents, the patent number, the country granting the patent, as well as the time are important, in addition to subject keywords and phrases. Users can select advanced search features to search on fields that are specific to patent documents (for example, the inventor, the patent assignee, patent claims, patent examiners, country reference, and so on). Thus, for efficient searching of standard and patent information sources, users should have some acquaintance with standards and patents themselves, as this will help them choose the appropriate search fields. Familiarity with the features of the specific search system, eg the BS online catalogues, the IBM patent search system or Dialog, is also helpful.

Chapter 14

Government, institutional and miscellaneous information sources

Introduction

In Chapters 8 to 12 we discussed the features of electronic information sources covering specific subjects, and in Chapter 13 we considered standard and patent information sources. In the present chapter we shall look at some of the many other types of information sources, such as those generated and published by various government, regional and international organizations and institutions. Such sources contain a variety of information from the factual and statistical to research and reports in numeric, textual and multimedia format; they may not fit any specific subject category, but they are very widely used. We shall also consider sports and leisure information sources, which are sought after by a broad range of users. A list of electronic information sources related to this chapter appears in Appendix 7.

Government, regional, international and institutional information

Side by side with commercial publication sources, a large number of information sources are published by institutions, government, regional and international organizations. Such information sources can cover any subject and range in content from factual and statistical to full-text and multimedia information reporting research, policies, regulations, and so on. Many of these publications are available on CD-ROM as well as online. As we have already seen, searching these information sources requires an understanding of the nature, content and organization of a given source, as well as an acquaintance with the search interface and search and retrieval facilities, which vary significantly from one product to another.

Bekiares and Mallory (1995) comment that government information sources are authoritative, comprehensive and inexpensive, and they are used by the public, statisticians, social workers, students, teachers, politicians, parents, scientists – in short, by people from all walks of society. Katz (1997) suggests that government documents can be classified (1) in terms of the issuing agencies, such as Congress, the judiciary, ministries and executive branches, or (2) in terms of document types, such as records of government administrations, research documents, reports and statistics, and popular sources of information. Pruett (1986) mentions that access to government documents has always been an issue for librarians. Government publications encompass many different kinds of subject matter aimed at diverse audiences. Unique classification systems have been developed for certain types of government publications: the Superintendent of Documents Classification System, developed for US government documents, is an example (Bekiares and Mallory, 1995).

A number of national, regional and international organizations, including research institutions, non-government organizations (NGOs), and United Nations bodies and subsidiaries (such as UNECA, the United Nations Economic Commission for Africa, ESCAP, the Economic and Social Commission for Asia and the Pacific, the World Health Organization, the Food and Agriculture Organization, UNESCO and so on) publish information sources. These are often similar to government publications and include research and project reports, statistics, policy documents, minutes and proceedings of meetings and conferences, and so on.

How to search government, regional, international and institutional information sources

A significant portion of these sources contain statistical information. Statistical and financial information sources are used not only by people in the business and finance sectors but by students, teachers, researchers, professionals, politicians and policy makers, and so on. Techniques for searching such information sources depend on the nature and content of the documents as well as the producers of those documents. The basic search mechanisms are the same as those we have discussed in previous chapters. Most government and institutional publications, including those from the UN and its subsidiaries, carry a unique publication number, which is a useful additional search key.

Government publications are available increasingly in electronic format, on CD-ROM and online. Government agencies in the developed countries, and in many developing countries, have websites that give users access to a number of information sources. This may allow some users to bypass libraries for their information search, though there are many other users who do not have direct access to the Internet who still depend on libraries. Many government, regional and international agencies, like the UN, UNESCO, WHO, IAEA, and so on, publish information on the Internet.

GPO access

The Government Printing Office (GPO) is part of the legislative branch of the US federal government. Created primarily to satisfy the printing needs of the US Congress, the GPO today is the focal point for printing, binding, and information dissemination for the entire federal community. In addition to Congress, approximately 130 federal departments and agencies rely on the GPO's services. Congressional documents, federal regulations and reports, IRS tax forms and US passports are all produced by or through the GPO. Through *GPO access* (**www.access.gpo.gov**) the GPO is at the forefront in providing government information in a wide range of formats, including printing, microfiche, CD-ROM and online technology.

Figure 14.1 shows the search screen of *GPO access*. Here the user can search the GPO website by entering one or more search terms in the 'Search for' box. By clicking on 'Access to Government Information Products' users can search the collection by browsing through a hierarchical list (shown in Figure 14.2). Users can click on any category to go directly to the appropriate collection/web page. The main search page (Figure 14.1) also contains links to some basic information on the GPO. Figure 14.3 shows the output of a search on *GPO access*: brief information is given on the search records, which are arranged in order of relevance (shown by the number of squares on the left of the serial number of the record). The file size, date of creation, etc are shown, as is the total number of hits; the user can move from one output screen to another by

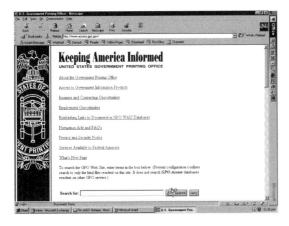

Fig. 14.1 *'GPO access' web page*

Fig. 14.2 *'GPO access' subject categories of government documents*

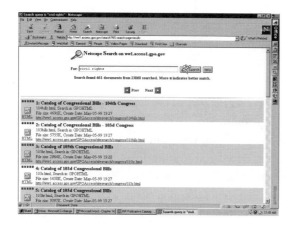

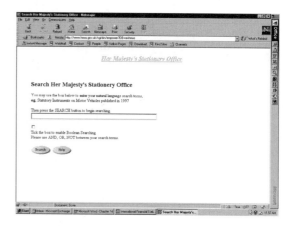

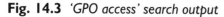

Fig. 14.3 *'GPO access' search output*   **Fig. 14.4** *HMSO search screen*

using the 'Prev' and 'Next' buttons. Users can select one or more records to see the complete HTML file.

HMSO

Her Majesty's Stationery Office (HMSO) is a primary source of government information in the UK: it has been the official publisher to parliament for more than 200 years and is now the largest UK publisher by volume (**http://www. hmso.gov.uk**). The Stationery Office was created when the trading elements of HMSO were privatized in 1996. Figure 14.4 shows the search screen of HMSO. Users can type a query in the search text box using natural language words and phrases. Search terms can be combined using the Boolean AND, OR and NOT operators. Search terms can be nested with Boolean operators to create complex search expressions. Users can use the plus symbol (+) to indicate that a search term must appear in the results, and minus symbol (–) to indicate that a search term must not appear. Figure 14.5 shows the output of a simple search.

Search results are arranged in order of relevance. Results can be refined by selecting any category from the list appearing at the top of the output screen (Figure 14.5) and clicking on the 'improve' button.

The Stationery Office Ltd, UK, has recently developed a portal (see Chapter 15), called ukstate.com (**http://www.ukstate.com/portal.asp**). There are three major categories in this gateway: Your Life, Your Business and Your Government (Figure 14.6).

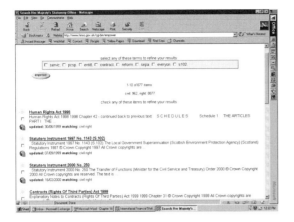

Fig. 14.5 *HMSO search output*

Fig. 14.6 *The UKstate portal*

- 'Your Life' is a guide to official information that affects daily lives. It contains answers to a number of frequently asked questions, as well as links to government sites, key pieces of legislation and the latest news from the best current affairs sources on the web. Information is organized under various categories, such as Education, Family, Finance, Housing, Local Services, Travel, etc.
- 'Your Business' is focused on the needs of business managers. Information is organized under various categories, such as Setting up a company, Trading abroad, Closing a business, etc.
- 'Your Government' is designed to provide information on the business of the UK Parliament and Government. Users can read source documents, UK legal news, European news, and so on. Information is organized under various categories, such as 'What is government?' 'Legislation', 'Parliamentary Tours', 'Parliamentary Business', etc.

Miscellaneous information sources

In this book we have discussed the features of a number of electronic information sources that are either general reference sources or belong to a specific subject area. However, many information sources do not fall into either of these categories. Of these miscellaneous sources we shall discuss only two types: academic/research (theses and dissertations information) and leisure information resources.

ProQuest Digital Dissertations

There are many databases that cover information on theses and dissertations, such as the *ProQuest dissertation abstracts* (University Microfilm International), *Dissertation abstracts* (available from SilverPlatter Information Ltd and Ovid Technologies Inc). Here we shall discuss the features of the online *ProQuest digital dissertations* (**http://wwwlib.umi.com/dissertations/gateway**). With more than 1.5 million entries, it is an authoritative source of information on theses and dissertations. The database includes citations for materials ranging from the first US dissertation, accepted in 1861, to those accepted recently. Of all the titles listed, full text is available for about 1 million items. The database contains works from over 1000 North American graduate schools and European universities and around 47,000 new dissertations and 12,000 new theses are added each year.

There are two interfaces for searching *ProQuest digital dissertations* – the basic search (Figure 14.7) and Advanced Search (Figure 14.8). Both the interfaces provide good search facilities including field-specific and Boolean (and, or, not) search. In the basic search interface, a search can also be limited by date. Using the advanced search interface users can also conduct proximity searches, can combine a search expression with a previous search set, and so on. Users can enter search terms into the search entry window and select the 'Search' button (see Figures 14.7 and 14.8). In the basic search interface users can enter search term(s) in one or more specified boxes, while in the advanced search interface, users can enter search terms, with appropriate search commands, in the search box; or can enter the search term(s) in the boxes below (see Figure 14.8) and then click 'add' which will automatically put the search terms in the search box above. Figure 14.9 shows the results of a simple search – the same output is obtained no matter whether the search is conducted using the basic or the

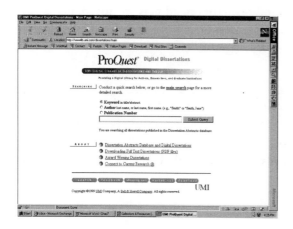

Fig. 14.7 *'ProQuest Digital Dissertations'*
basic search screen

Fig. 14.8 *'ProQuest Digital Dissertations'*
advanced search screen

advanced search interface. Further details of records can be obtained by clicking on the various icons in the output screen (Figure 14.9). Figure 14.10 shows the advanced search screen that displays the search history and here users can conduct a completely new search or can combine a search expression with a previous search set.

By default, the system will display result sets after each search. Users can select a specific search set for viewing the results. When a search is conducted without specifying a field, the retrieval software automatically searches the default field (the keyword or basic index field) which contains all words in the title and abstract fields of a record. However, a field search can be conducted to specify which field should be searched for occurrences of the keyword or phrase. Boolean operators may be used to narrow or broaden a search. For example, title (biology and plants); title (apples or oranges); title (biology) and not school (michigan state university). Parentheses can be used to nest terms for more complex searches. For example, keyword ((cross country or scandinavian) and skiing).

The following proximity operators can be used to specify the order and/or closeness of words. Note that n must be specified as the number of characters, not words:

W/n – the first term is within n characters of the second (without any specified order)

PRE/n– the first term is n characters to the left of the second (here the order of terms is specified).

Fig. 14.9 *Search results for 'Digital libraries' in the title field*

Fig. 14.10 *The advanced search screen showing the search history and the search box*

For example:

information W/1 systems

will find 'information systems' and 'systems information'

Digital PRE/1 instruments

will find only 'digital instruments'.

Phrases are entered naturally as a sequence of words separated by space. For example:

title (web search engines)

will return documents with the exact phrase 'web search engines'.

A question mark (?) at the end of a word is used as a wildcard to find variations and plurals. For example:

keyword (librar?)

will return library, libraries, librarian, librarians and librarianship.

In the advanced search mode, users can conduct a subject search by clicking on the 'Subject Tree' button, or can go to the 'School Index' and browse by the name of Universities. Users can click on the 'Browse' button appearing at the top of both the search interfaces to browse the dissertations by subject. This is the same as using the 'Subject Tree' from the 'Advanced Search' interface.

Features of some leisure information sources

There are now scores of travel companies and tour operators, hotels, tourism departments of governments and companies related to the tourism sector that publish information on the web. Many of these publications are basically marketing tools or publicity materials, but they contain a lot of useful information for travellers and tourists. Other leisure activities, such as sport or cinema, are also well represented online. Some of the search and retrieval features of three leisure information sources are considered below.

SportsLine

This is an excellent online news resource covering different types of sports in the US, Europe and other parts of the world (**http://www.sportsline.com/**). Users can enter a search term or phrase in the search text box or choose a particular sport or country to search. For example, users can select 'Euro Sports' and then search by a specific country, a specific sport, and so on.

Lonely Planet

Lonely Planet is one of the most popular information sources, both printed and electronic, for travel and tourism. Figure 14.11 shows the *Lonely Planet* home page. There are various options for obtaining travel and related information from the search interface (Figure 14.11). Users can enter a search term or phrase from the simple search screen (shown in Figure 14.12); the advanced search screen (shown in Figure 14.13) offers various search options. By clicking on the 'Destinations' option, the user can choose a particular continent, country or destination from a world map (see Figure 14.14). From the home page (Figure 14.11), users can find related health information, useful travel information and tips, and so on. There is also the unique 'theme guides' option, which divides the world into a number of thematic zones and thus allows users to choose a place accordingly, for example, the twilight zone, music and beaches. Users can select any one of these zones to see lists of various countries and places belonging to the chosen category. Associated with each place, users will get a lot of useful local, travel, accommodation and sightseeing information provided, along with various other tips and items of interest.

Fodors.com

The *Fodor* series of guidebooks are very useful information sources on travel and tourism. The information they contain is now available on the web (**http://www.fodors.com/**). As well as providing catalogue and other informa-

Fig. 14.11 *'Lonely Planet' home page*

Fig. 14.12 *'Lonely planet' search screen (Simple Search)*

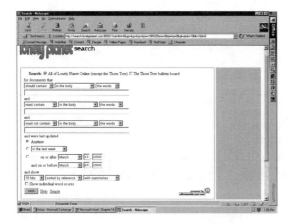

Fig. 14.13 *'Lonely Planet' search screen (Advanced Search)*

Fig. 14.14 *'Lonely Planet' Destinations*

tion on Fodor publications, this site gives information on various aspects of travel and tourism, including useful tips for learning languages. To obtain travel information the user starts from the Planning Center option. He or she then selects a country, state or city, and the information on the chosen place will appear as the search output.

Summary

In this chapter we have discussed the features of three different types of information sources. The two web-based government information sources – *GPO access* and *HMSO* – allow users to search by words or phrases as well as by various categories. These are different from the subject categories used to categorize bibliographic information sources (see Figures 14.2 and 14.6). If users need to search by these, it is helpful if they have some acquaintance with the various categories and subcategories devised by the publisher to classify these particular information sources.

The discussion of the *ProQuest digital dissertations* database indicates that users can conduct a simple or a complex search. However, for the latter, users need to know the various search operators and techniques. In some respects these are similar to those used with many other databases, but the proximity search operators and the corresponding syntax are specific to this database.

Each of the three leisure information sources considered allows users to enter search terms or select a search parameter through browsing. The *Lonely Planet* search interface is more elaborate than the others. Each has its own search and retrieval features which require some sort of training or practice to enable users to conduct successful searches.

Chapter 15

Trends in the electronic information sources and searching environment

Introduction

This book set out to discuss the features of CD-ROM and online information sources with a view to identifying the nature of such electronic information sources, and to pointing out some information search and retrieval techniques that need to be learnt in order to make the best use of these information resources. Considering the fact that an information search may often begin with a search on an OPAC, we have discussed the general features of OPACs and have highlighted the various search and retrieval features of ten selected OPAC systems. Through a description of the general nature and search and retrieval features of various CD-ROM databases and online search services, we have identified those points that need to be considered while conducting a CD-ROM or an online search.

Because the search and retrieval features of CD-ROM and online information sources depend to a large extent on their nature and content, we have discussed the features of selected information sources on specific subjects. While doing so, we have not only chosen examples of databases that are available in CD-ROM format and/or are available through the online search services, we have also chosen many sources that are available on the web. We have done so because many information sources are now available on the web and very many of them are free. Through these examples, we have tried to highlight the various search and retrieval skills that a searcher would need to acquire in order to become an expert searcher. We have also noted that some significant changes are taking place in the information industry, particularly in the area of web-based information sources. For example, the same information source which is sold commercially, either in print or in electronic form, can now be searched free on the web (eg *Britannica online* and the *BSI Standards Catalogue* and *ISO Cata-*

logue). This shows a shift in the information business as well as a shift of responsibilities from information intermediaries – library and information professionals – to the end-users. Many other changes have taken place recently that also have a significant impact on the nature of information services and the information search process. Some of these issues are addressed below. A separate book on information sources and the world wide web, to work as a companion to the present one, is now under preparation and will be published soon by Library Association Publishing.

Information services online

Current awareness and selective dissemination of information (SDI) services have long been regarded as important in the library or information centre. It is now possible to create and manage automated current awareness and SDI services on the basis of locally mounted databases using software supplied by the principal database publishers, such as SilverPlatter and Ovid (Hanson, 1998a, b). Current awareness and SDI services are also available from a number of publishers, companies and organizations through the Internet; some of these services are free. Examples are discussed below.

Contents page services are available free from commercial publishers. They include Elsevier's Contents Direct Service (**http://www.elsevier.com**), *IDEAL Alert* from Academic Press (**http://www.europe.idealibrary.com**), and *Email News* (books) and *Table of Contents e-mailing service* (journals) from Oxford University Press (**http://www.oup.co.uk**). Users register with the publisher or service concerned to obtain the contents pages of journals, as soon as they are published, through e-mail.

Information on new books is also available free from publishers, such as the *Wiley Book Notification Service* (**http://www.permissionplus.net/wiley-wbns/wbns. asp**), and vendors, such as Amazon.com (**http://www.amazon.com**). Again, users need to register to have notification of new titles sent to their e-mail address.

SDI services are available from online search service providers, such as Dialog. *Dialog Alerts* is a variably charged service that allows users to set up profiles to obtain relevant information as soon as it is published. The information may be obtained daily, weekly, bi-weekly or monthly, and delivered by e-mail, fax or post. There are different types of alert services: Guided Search Alerts, Command Search Alerts, Guided Search Interactive Alerts and Command Search Interactive Alerts. These services allow a user to conduct a search which will be saved and run automatically as and when new records are added to the chosen database(s), and the search output will be sent to the user concerned. In the case of the other alert services, *DialogWeb* sends an e-mail message with a listing of article titles from the latest issue of a journal publication. The recipient reviews the list and then sends a reply to have the full text of any of the articles sent directly to their e-mail address. The response is processed and the full text of the article sent to the requester in minutes.

The Institute for Scientific Information (**http://www.isinet.com**) publishes *Current Contents*, which provides information in the fields of science, social science, technology, and arts and humanities. Published weekly in seven editions, it displays the tables of contents from the world's most influential scholarly journals, and provides bibliographic data for journal articles, reviews, editorials, corrections and conference proceedings. It is available in various formats: web (Current Contents Connect); FTP/diskette (Current Contents Desktop, Current Contents on Diskette, and FTP Delivery); CD-ROM (Current Contents on CD-ROM); print (Current Contents Print) and online/FTP (Current Contents Search).

The ISI also provides alerting services, a range of SDI services that deliver up-to-the-minute bibliographic information and full-length author abstracts via the web or e-mail. They draw on the ISI's multidisciplinary database of recently published science, technology, social sciences and arts and humanities journals (including electronic journals), books, and conference proceedings. Each alerting service is unique in its customization, service and content. All are either based on profiles that the user develops independently or designed with the help of information experts at the ISI. There are three alerting services from the ISI, viz *Discovery Agent*, *Personal Alert* and *Research Alert*.

Discovery Agent is an ISI web-based alerting service that delivers customized information to individuals or throughout an entire organization. It uses a specially designed web interface to enable subscribers to create, manage and edit their own personal profiles on an as-needed basis. *Discovery Agent* allows users to test their profile results while they create, update or refine it. It filters its profiles against the ISI *Current contents* database. Alerts are delivered weekly on the web and also by e-mail if the user selects that option: each week, a user may access his or her personal web page to find the latest results for any profile created. Thus the user can potentially have access to his or her personal profile from anywhere in the world, at any time. *Personal Alert* is a service that keeps users up to date with the exact research they need by providing highly customized profile-based alerting and expert consulting. It is delivered directly over the Internet via e-mail and provides complete bibliographic data and author abstracts from the latest research information.

Personal Alert covers over 16,000 science, technology and social sciences journals, books, and conference proceedings from the ISI database. When a user subscribes to *Personal Alert*, he or she works with an ISI information specialist to develop a profile unique to the user's work. Keywords, author names, journal titles and cited references relevant to the user's research interests are run against the ISI database using a proprietary search and retrieval engine. The results are sent directly to the user via e-mail either daily or weekly. The user can modify his/her profile at any time. *Personal Alert* also provides cited reference searching, a unique feature that enables users to expand their search results. It works by uncovering links between author, title and journal references in the footnotes of articles. By building cited reference searching into the user's profile, additional, more recent papers relevant to the user's interests can be found, even if the original papers have no title words or keywords in common. Another ISI service is *Research Alert*, a print-based alerting service that delivers complete bibliographic information. Research Alert is available in two versions: *Customized Research Alerts* is based on personalized profiles developed for the user, and *Research Alert Topics* offers 200 predefined search profiles created by ISI information specialists. Both versions use a proprietary search and retrieval engine, with results delivered as printed weekly reports.

Subject directories, gateways and virtual libraries

As we have already seen, many information sources are now available on the web. In order to locate these sources, users can go directly to the relevant URL (uniform resource locator; or web page address) or, if the user does not know the URL, (1) search the web using a search engine like *AltaVista* or *InfoSeek*, or (2) browse through a subject directory, such as *Yahoo!*, for the category that may contain the information source being sought. As with any search interface, users of both search engines and subject directories need to learn the search and retrieval facilities available in order to search efficiently. Often the results produced by search engines are unhelpful, as a large number of irrelevant records may be retrieved. Subject directories can be time-consuming to use, because users may have to go several steps down the hierarchy to obtain the required information sources, and sometimes it is not easy for a user to decide which category a search topic belongs to. Both search engines and subject directories can retrieve an unmanageable number of hits, sometimes in millions, to sieve through.

Virtual libraries or subject gateways have been developed to help solve these problems. Bradley (1999) has identified the following characteristics of these libraries or gateways:

- they use the expertise of information professionals and subject experts in collecting and organizing web information resources
- information is checked for authority
- emphasis is on the content of an information source rather than its location, and
- the information is current and sometimes value-added.

A portal is a service on the web that offers a broad array of resources and services. The first web portals were separate applications that provided access to the web but by now most of the traditional search engines have transformed themselves into web portals to attract and keep a larger audience. An example is **http://library.dialog.com/bluesheets/bl0126.html**.

There are many examples of virtual libraries, such as the *WWW virtual library* (**http://www.vlib.org/**), the oldest catalogue of the web; *BUBL link* (**http://www.bubl.ac.uk/link/**), a catalogue of Internet resources; *Biz/ed* (**http://www.bized.ac.uk/**), a unique business and economics service for students, teachers and lecturers; and *SOSIG* (**http://www.sosig.ac.uk/**), the social science information gateway.

Development of e-journals and digital libraries

Two relatively recent developments, triggered by the introduction and proliferation of the Internet and web technologies, have brought significant changes in the way end-users look for and use information. The first of these is the development of electronic journals, which are published on the web and/or are made accessible through the web. There are some journals that are only published on the web, such as *D-Lib Magazine* and *Ariadne*; these can be searched directly by end-users. Other electronic journals have their printed counterparts and are made available by aggregators (vendors that provide access to a number of electronic journals published by different publishers) to end-users. The availability of electronic journals on the web has reduced the responsibility of library and information specialists, who have traditionally played the role of acquiring, organizing and providing access to printed journals, current as well as back issues. However, the onus is now on the end-user to select and search the appropriate information from the electronic journals, so it is the users who have to learn the various search and retrieval techniques appropriate to the search interfaces of the publishers and/or aggregators of electronic journals.

The second major development is the setting up of various digital or electronic libraries; these terms are used interchangeably in the literature, though the second is more popular in the UK (Chowdhury and Chowdhury, 1999). Borgman (1999) has analysed the various definitions and connotations of digital libraries that have been proposed. She argues that the research community's definition of digital libraries has evolved from a narrower view emphasizing enabling technologies to one that encompasses the social, behavioural and economic contexts in which digital libraries are used. In her opinion, the views of the library community are reflected in the definition given by the Digital Library Federation (DLF), as reported by Waters (1998) which says that 'Digital libraries are organizations that provide the resources, including the specialized staff, to select, structure, offer intellectual access to, interpret, distribute, preserve the integrity of, and ensure the persistence over time of collections of digital works so that they are readily and economically available for use by a defined community or set of communities.'

A new concept, the hybrid library, has emerged recently (Pinfield et al, 1998; Rusbridge, 1998; Oppenheim and Smithson, 1999). Rusbridge (1998) suggests that a hybrid library is designed to bring a range of technologies from different sources together in the context of a working library, and it integrates systems and services in both the electronic and print environments. He further argues that the term hybrid library is intended to reflect the transitional state of the library, which today can neither be fully dependent on print nor fully digital. Pinfield et al (1998) agree that the hybrid library is on the continuum between the conventional and digital library.

Research in different areas of digital libraries has gained in importance over the past few years. Considerable amounts of money have been allocated to digital library research, and a large number of researchers are working in the field all over the world. In the United States over $68 million has been awarded for digital library research, over $24 million in 1994 as part of the first Digital Library Initiative (DLI-1) and about $44 million for the second phase (DLI-2) (Fox, 1999; Griffin, 1999). Lesk (1999) refers to several other American research projects on digital libraries outside the DLI funding. Research on digital libraries in the United Kingdom has largely been funded by the Electronic Libraries (*eLib*) programme (**http://www.ukoln.ac.uk/services/elib/**). The first two phases of the *eLib* programme cost £15 million over three years (1995–1997); in this period the Joint Information Systems Committee (a joint committee of the Higher Education Funding Councils, and the funding agency for the *eLib* programme) spent about £24 million on data services and probably £50 million on networks (Rusbridge, 1998). The third phase of the *eLib* programme, which is currently ongoing, has sponsored five hybrid library research projects (Pinfield et al, 1998; Rusbridge, 1998; Oppenheim and Smithson, 1999).

Several other digital library research projects have been undertaken in different parts of the world (Chowdhury and Chowdhury, 1999, 2000). These research activities have given rise to a number of research publications. Chowdhury and Chowdhury (1999) have recently reviewed digital library research around the world, and trends in research and development in digital libraries have been reported in a special issue of *Information Processing and Management* (Marchionini and Fox, 1999). Regular research on digital libraries is reported in online journals like *D-Lib Magazine* (**http://www.dlib.org**) and *Ariadne* (**http://www.ariadne.ac.uk**), in various professional journals, at a number of conferences, such as the ACM, European and Asian digital library conferences, and also in a number of institutional and personal websites.

Whether we call them digital or hybrid, the basic objective of these libraries, to enable the retrieval of digital information by or for end-users, remains unchanged. However, as Rowlands and Bawden (1999) mention, 'although more detailed typologies of searching and browsing are described in the information retrieval literature they do not seem to have been studied systematically in the context of the digital library'. Meyyappan and Chowdhury (2000) have recently reviewed the status of 20 working digital libraries around the world, and have shown that they differ significantly as far as their information search and retrieval features are concerned. The same sort of findings have been reported by Chowdhury and Chowdhury (2000), who have compared and contrasted the information retrieval features of 20 working digital libraries.

The changing nature of reference and information services

With the introduction of the Internet and world wide web, the nature of reference and information services has changed drastically. Many reference and information services are now available on the web, either free or for a small fee. These services allow users to enter their search queries and retrieve the answer from an appropriate information source – as with AskJeeves (**http://www.askjeeves. com/**), Ask a Librarian or Internet Public Library (discussed below) – or they may direct the user to an information source at another location on the web. The latter type of service is available from Britannica.com, Infoplease.com, Internet Public Library, and so on.

Ask a Librarian (**http://www.earl.org.uk/ask/**) is a web-based reference service, primarily designed for UK residents, provided by the EARL Consortium for Public Library Networking in the UK (**http://www.earl.org.uk/index.html**). A user has to put the query through an enquiry page which is automatically routed to one of the participating reference libraries which receives it as an e-mail message. The library will send the user, within two days, an e-mail message with their response to the enquiry.

The Internet Public Library (**http://www.ipl.org**) is a prominent example of a reference and information service on the web. The mission statement of the IPL states that:

The Internet Public Library is the first public library of the Internet. As librarians, we are committed to providing valuable services to that world. We do so for many reasons: to provide library services to the Internet community, to learn and teach what librarians have to contribute in a digital environment, to promote librarianship and the importance of libraries, and to share interesting ideas and techniques with other librarians.

There are many such services on the web that are free even from commercial publishers. A good example is *Britannica online* (**http://www.britannica.com/**). Users can search in not only the web version of *Encyclopaedia Britannica*, but also a number of other resources on the web, including books, journals, and personal and institutional web pages. The various websites retrieved in response to a search expression are rated by the editorial team of Britannica.

The future

Library and information services have always been considered as personalized services. However, the recent developments in the CD-ROM and online information world, coupled with developments in e-journals, digital and hybrid libraries, have reduced the involvement of information intermediaries, and now end-users are expected to interact directly with computers for all their information needs. This situation raises an obvious question: will librarians continue to exist, and if so what will be their roles? Matson and Bonski (1997) discuss the effects of the new technology of digital libraries on librarians, and Sutton (1996) discusses the role of reference librarians in digital libraries. Heckert (1998) points out that, as the infrastructure of a digital library takes shape, human help in user interactions will disappear and in future we shall see an almost total reliance on machine help. Griffin (1997) comments that library managers are in the middle of a technology flux which can be compared with the invention and use of the printing press. He suggests that librarians in a digital library environment should learn new vocabularies to understand and use the technology fully; encourage interaction among staff coming from the traditional library and from a technology background; carefully match technologies and users; reach out and educate users and staff; be prepared to lose control over materials that have so long been the library's property; and connect and communicate with local, national and international professional events and work groups.

Ferguson and Bunge (1997) argue that librarians must retain the timeless service values of equity of access, personal service and services tailored to the needs of individuals, and at the same time explore new values, such as integrating technologies, maintaining holistic computing environments, delivering core services through the network, making technology work for all and collaborating across administrative lines. Steele (1997) suggests that in future the head librarian or information officer may well play the role of a chief executive officer (CEO) with responsibilities and vision allied to more devolved structures. Steele further argues that knowledge managers will need to be constantly flexible, and should realize stated goals within an ever-broadening environment of delivery.

Davenport et al (1997) discuss the nature of reference work and the role of reference librarians in digital libraries, where many users serve themselves by means of free-at-point-of-use information services. They consider how the concept of the 'reference desk' can be defined where points of presence for both users and librarians are distributed. They report the results of research undertaken in Edinburgh that explores these issues in the context of the enhanced regional communications available through EaStMAN (the Edinburgh and Stirling Metropolitan Area Network). The project involved the *BIOSIS Abstracts* service hosted by the EDINA (Edinburgh Data and Information Access) consortium, and linked three university libraries (Edinburgh University, Heriot-Watt University and Napier University). The project investigated the experiences of users and the work patterns of librarians, and related these to the design rationale of a prototype web-based network reference consultation support system.

Smith (1996) argues that the important interactions between librarians and users that occur in meta-information environments (those that comprise information about information, such as library catalogues, classification, and so on) in a traditional library may be lost with the automated information access in a digital library. It is therefore important to design special meta-information environments for digital libraries that can compensate for such loss. Hutingford (1998) and Walton and Edwards (1997) report on the IMPEL (Impact on People of Electronic Libraries) study conducted in the UK as part of the eLib's supporting studies segment. IMPEL1 (1993–95) focused on the changing role of qualified librarians in the higher education sector; IMPEL2 (1996–97) (**http://www.unn.ac.uk/~lit8/impel2/impel2.html**) placed emphasis on both the library staff and users in the context of the changing library environment. The IMPEL study supports the proposition that the limiting factors for digital libraries are human and organizational rather than technological.

It is evident that digital libraries will require new or specially trained personnel to develop and run them effectively and efficiently. Tennat (1998) provides a list of skills, experience and qualification requirements of digital librarians. He further argues that it may be more productive if we choose staff who can evolve as the needs of the organization change. Finally, as Cronin (1998) suggests, successful educational programmes geared to the needs of the digital age should be inclusive and tolerant of diverse perspectives, promoting interaction between disciplines and subfields in an effort to create discourse richness, experimentation and innovation.

Appendices

Brief descriptions of the information products appearing in the Appendices have been collected from various primary and secondary sources. Primary sources include the database producers and/or suppliers, and in such cases we have often used their words to describe the products. The secondary sources include *Walford's guide to reference material*, *Gale directory of databases* and *Multimedia and CD-ROM directory*. Databases which have been described in detail in the book do not appear in the Appendices.

Database formats – CD-ROM or online – have not been differentiated, since a particular database may be available in more than one format. However, we have indicated the name of the database producer or vendor immediately after the database name, which will give a clue regarding the format; eg where names of online services such as Dialog (with file number), Ovid, OCLC, etc – or a URL – appear after the database name, the database is available online. In other cases, the database is on CD-ROM. Where databases are available in more than one format, this has been indicated in the description.

Appendix 1
Selected CD-ROM and online information sources on science and technology

Abstracts in new technologies and engineering (ANTE) (Dialog file 238), formerly *Current technology database*, is an abstracting and indexing service covering approximately 350 journals from the UK and the US in technology, engineering and allied subject areas. The file corresponds to the printed products *Abstracts in New Technologies and Engineering* (*ANTE*, formerly *Current Technology Index*) and *Catchword and Trade Name Index*. Abstracts are available from January 1993 to the present.

Academic Press encyclopedia of physical science and technology (**KR OnDisc:** Dialog Corporation, Dialog OnDisc): this title features over 700 articles, including 10,000 illustrations and tables and 6500 bibliographic entries. It covers critical science and technology areas, including physical sciences, mathematics and engineering, and has subject indexing and cross-referencing, plus a table of contents.

AESIS (Australia's geoscience, minerals, and petroleum database) (Dialog file 105) provides a complete index to all available Australian information both published and unpublished in the subject areas. The database covers materials written by an Australian or about Australia or Papua New Guinea. The database indexes in excess of 650 journal titles and also covers conference papers, books, maps, field guides, university theses and unpublished company exploration reports from all the Mines Departments around Australia.

AGRICOLA (AGRICultural OnLine Access) (Dialog file 10) is an extensive bibliographic database covering journal articles, monographs, theses, patents, translations, microforms, audiovisuals, software and technical reports. Available since 1970, *AGRICOLA* serves as a document locator and bibliographic access and control system for the National Agricultural Library (NAL) collection, but since 1984 the database has also included some records produced by cooperating institutions for documents not held by NAL. This extensive database has been maintained since 1970 to provide selective worldwide coverage of primary information sources in agriculture and related fields. Since 1985 the CAB thesaurus has been utilized to select controlled vocabulary terms for subject indexing. Library of Congress subject headings are used as controlled vocabulary for cataloguing records. *AGRICOLA* is also available from other sources, for example, online through STN and on CD-ROM from SilverPlattter Information Ltd.

AGRIS (SilverPlatter Information Ltd, UK) provides worldwide bibliographic coverage of agricultural science and technology literature. Assembled by the AGRIS Co-ordinating Centre of the Food and Agriculture Organization (FAO) of the United Nations, AGRIS offers an international perspective on agricultural research. Different aspects of agriculture, including forestry, animal husbandry, aquatic sciences and fisheries, and human nutrition from over 135 countries are covered.

AGRIS international (Dialog file 203) serves as a comprehensive inventory of worldwide agricultural literature which reflects research results, food production and rural development to help users identify problems involved in all aspects of world food supply. The emphasis is non-US. This file corresponds in part to the printed publication, *Agrindex*, published monthly by FAO. *AGRIS* is a cooperative, decentralized system in which over 100 national and multinational centres take part. It collects and makes available current information on the agricultural literature of the world appearing in journals, books, reports and conference papers. Each country which participates in AGRIS does so by submitting information about documents published within its own territories.

All about science (Queue Inc) contains 48 interactive programs covering intermediate science topics in a high-interest, low readability format, for grades 5 to 9. It contains Elementary Science II and packages on 'Investigating our world', 'Investigating matter and energy' and 'Science of living things'.

American men & women of science (SilverPlatter Information Ltd, UK) includes portraits of over 126,000 American and Canadian scientists and engineers from Bowker's resource book of the same name. Ranging across 10 major disciplines and 180 National Science Foundation subdisciplines, it identifies and profiles leading experts in all physical, biological and related sciences.

Applied science & technology abstracts (OCLC FirstSearch) covers over 350 periodicals on subjects such as chemistry, computer technology, data processing, energy-related disciplines, engineering, mathematics and physics. The database is available from various vendors. That produced by H W Wilson covers abstracting and indexing of 400 core English-language scientific and technical publications.

Applied science & technology index (Ovid Technologies Inc and H W Wilson) is a source of bibliographic references to articles in key science, trade and technology periodicals pertaining to a wide range of scientific and technical topics including aeronautics and space science, chemistry, computer technology, civil, electrical and mechanical engineering, environmental engineering and waste management, food, geology and oceanography.

Aquatic sciences and fisheries abstracts (ASFA) (Dialog file 44) is a comprehensive database on the science, technology and management of marine, brackish-water and freshwater environments and resources. The database covers over 5000 primary journals and a wide variety of other source documents, including books, monographic series, conference proceedings and technical research reports. *Aquatic Sciences and Fisheries* is a collaborative effort of the FAO (Rome), the Intergovernmental Oceanographic Commission of UNESCO (Paris), the Division for Ocean Affairs and the Law of the Sea of the United Nations (New York), the Ocean and Coastal Areas Programme Activity Centre of the United Nations Environment Programme (Nairobi), the International Center for Living Aquatic Resources Management (Manila), the International Council for the Exploration of the Sea (Copenhagen), the World Conservation Union, and national agencies in 23 countries.

Architecture database (Dialog file 179) is the online version of the print publication *Architectural Periodicals Index* (*API*), supplemented with the catalogue records for other materials collected by the British Architectural Library at the Royal Institute of British Architects. The literature indexed includes articles, interviews, obituaries and biographies in more than 400 current periodicals from over 45 countries, as well as some 2000 catalogued items from all over the world, including monographs, conference proceedings, exhibition catalogues, pamphlets and some technical literature.

The Australian – technology and science on CD-ROM (Quarrion Consultancy) contains items on science and technology from one year's issues of *The Australian* newspaper. It is available for 1994 or 1992–4 or 1987–94. Cumulative editions can be purchased and records accessed via password.

The BEST DISC (Cartermill International Ltd): *BEST* (British Expertise in Science and Technology) *Great Britain, BEST Europe* and *BEST North America* provide CV-style records of researchers and engineers working in universities and polytechnics. Information is collected from the individual, and includes details of current research interests, industrial applications, research funding, patents, key publications and previous levels of experience.

Biological & agricultural index (Ovid Technologies Inc and H W Wilson) offers indexing of 258 periodicals, for coverage of all areas of biology and agriculture agricultural chemicals to zoology.

BIOSIS previews (Dialog files 5 and 55) contains citations from *Biological Abstracts (BA)*, and *Biological Abstracts/Reports, Reviews, and Meetings (BA/RRM)* (formerly *BioResearch Index*), the major publications of BIOSIS. Together these publications constitute the major English-language service providing comprehensive worldwide coverage of research in the biological and biomedical sciences. *Biological Abstracts* includes approximately 350,000 accounts of original research yearly from nearly 6000 primary journal and monograph titles.

BIOSIS previews on compact disc (SilverPlatter Information Ltd, UK) contains the references to journal literature from *Biological Abstracts*, and includes references to meetings, books, reports, review articles, books and monographs. Nearly 6000 life science journals and 1500 international meetings are monitored for inclusion.

Biotechnology abstracts on CD-ROM (SilverPlatter Information Ltd, UK) provides coverage of publications describing research in the field of biotechnology, with emphasis on commercial and industrial applications. It covers all aspects of the field, including genetic engineering, biochemical engineering, fermentation, cell culture and waste disposal as reported in over 1100 scientific journals and in the patents literature.

CAB abstracts (Dialog file 50) is a comprehensive file of agricultural information containing all the records in the more than 50 abstract journals published by CAB International (CABI), which has long been recognized as a leading scientific information service in agriculture and related sciences. Of particular note are sections in the database comprehensively covering literature in the fields of veterinary medicine, human nutrition, developing countries, leisure, recreation and tourism. Over 14,000 serial journals in over 50 languages are scanned, as well as books, reports and other publications. About 150,000 items per year are selected for inclusion in *CAB abstracts*; over 95% of the literature is abstracted, while less important works are reported with bibliographic details only. An online thesaurus is available as an aid in locating broader, narrower and related subject terms. File 250, *ONTAP CAB abstracts*, is available for ONline Training And Practice; it contains approximately 38,000 *CAB abstracts* records from early 1993.

CA on CD (Chemical Abstracts Service, CAS) contains complete CAS citations with associated abstracts, structure diagrams, issue keyword indexes and *CA* volume indexes.

CA SEARCH: chemical abstracts (Dialog files 308–314, 399) includes over 13 million citations to the worldwide literature of chemistry and its applications from 1967 onwards. *CA SEARCH* corresponds to the bibliographic information and complete indexing found in the print *Chemical Abstracts* published by CAS. The controlled vocabulary *CA* general subject index headings, related general subject terminology from the *CA* index guide, and CAS registry numbers, each with its modifying phrase are included. Chemical substances are represented by CAS Registry Numbers, unique numbers assigned to each specific chemical compound: corresponding substance information may be searched in the Dialog chemical substance files such as *CHEMSEARCHTM* (file 398). All records from the 8th collective index period forward are contained in file 399; files 308–314 contain records from the individual collective index (CI) periods as indicated in the file data.

Cambridge environmental science & pollution management abstracts (Ovid Technologies Inc) provides access to environmental information. It combines information on scientific research and government policies. Conference proceedings and documents are included, along with information from primary journals in the field.

China's who's who in science and technology (English edition) (HUWEI Consultants) includes information on 4000 Chinese scientists, engineers and persons in charge of S&T policy-making and management, with personal information, education and job history.

Compendex (KR OnDisc) provides comprehensive coverage of the world's significant engineering and technical journal and conference literature. This database is also available online, through Ovid Online, for example, and on the web (Ei CompendexWeb); see also **Ei Compendex** (below).

Computer select (Information Access Co) scans business and computer technology publications for information on computer-related products and topics and industry reviews. It contains full-text articles, product specifications and industry profiles.

Concise engineering and technology index (Ovid Technologies Inc) covers 425 engineering journals and conference proceedings, all with abstracts.

Current contents on CD-ROM – engineering, computing & technology (Institute for Scientific Information, USA) provides access to full bibliographic data on articles contained in 1030 journals in a broad range of disciplines, including aerospace engineering, chemical engineering, electrical and electronics engineering, environment, materials science, metallurgy and more.

Current contents on CD-ROM – physical, chemical & earth sciences (Institute for Scientific Information, USA) provides access to full bibliographic data on the articles contained in 925 journals in a broad range of disciplines, including analytical chemistry, applied physics, chemistry, earth sciences, mathematics, organic chemistry, physics, space science and more.

Current contents search (Dialog file 440) is the online version of ISI's *Current Contents* series of publications. *Current contents* is a weekly service that reproduces the tables of contents from current issues of leading journals in the sciences, social sciences, and arts and humanities. *Current contents search* consists of seven subsets based on *Current contents* editions: clinical medicine; life sciences; engineering, technology and applied sciences; agriculture, biology and environmental sciences; physical, chemical and earth sciences; social and behavioural sciences; and arts and humanities. In addition to providing access to the tables of contents of the journals covered, *Current contents search* provides complete bibliographic records for each item. These items include articles, reviews, letters, notes and editorials.

Derwent biotechnology abstracts (Dialog file 357, produced by Derwent Information Ltd) provides comprehensive coverage of publications describing research in the field of biotechnology. It covers all aspects of biotechnology, including genetic engineering, biochemical engineering, fermentation, cell culture and waste disposal, as reported in scientific journals and in the patents literature. Each month data from 1000 to 1200 documents are added to the file. Each record in the database contains bibliographic information and abstract of up to 200 words, together with controlled-language indexing. Approximately 27% of the records are patent records and patent documents that include patent number, patentee and publication details.

Derwent drug file (Dialog files 376, 377, 912, 913, produced by Derwent Information Ltd) is a complete information package specifically designed for the pharmaceutical industry. It provides references from the worldwide pharmaceutical literature going back to 1964. The database covers all aspects of drug synthesis, development, evaluation, manufacture and use. The combination of biological and chemical information enables searchers to find data on all types of structure–activity relationships.

Dictionary of organic compounds on CD-ROM (Chapman & Hall) is designed as a first point of reference for chemical information on organic compounds. The database supplies identifying information, numerical physical data, descriptive information and reference and structural information. The software allows the user to make joint text and substructure searches.

Dictionary of science and technology CD-ROM (Academic Press Inc) covers 124 fields acoustics to zoology. It offers 130,000 entries, 350 illustrations, 3500 spoken pronunciations, bookmarking and annotating, sophisticated Boolean search options and custom spelling dictionaries, which can be loaded into a word processor.

Ei Compendex (Dialog file 8) provides worldwide coverage of approximately 4500 journals and selected government reports and books. Subjects covered include civil, energy, environmental, geological and biological engineering; electrical, electronics and control engineering; chemical, mining, metals and fuel engineering; mechanical, automotive, nuclear and aerospace engineering; and computers, robotics, and industrial robots. In addition to journal literature, over 480,000 records of significant published proceedings of engineering and technical conferences formerly indexed in *Ei Engineering Meetings* are included in file 8. The *Ei Compendex* database is also available on CD-ROM (SilverPlatter Information Ltd).

Encyclopedia of physical science and technology (Academic Press Inc) contains 700 articles, including 10,000 illustrations and tables, 6500 bibliographic entries, 8700 glossary entries and search tools.

Energyline (Dialog file 69) is the online version of *Energy Information Abstracts*, and also includes 8000 energy- and environment-related records dating back to 1971 from the *Energy Index*. *Energyline* provides a primary source for information relating specifically to energy. Its data are drawn from many conventional discipline-oriented fields such as chemistry or engineering, but are incorporated into *Energyline* only as they relate to energy issues and problems. Its coverage includes books, journals, congressional committee prints, conference proceedings, speeches and statistics.

Engineering & applied science (RMIT Publishing) contains 11 Australian databases covering engineering, road design, road safety, road economics, transport systems and planning, water and waste water utilization, wetlands ecology, building and construction engineering.

Enviroline (Dialog file 40) covers more than 1000 international primary and secondary publications reporting on all aspects of the environment. These publications highlight such fields as management, technology, planning, law, political science, economics, geology, biology and chemistry as they relate to environmental issues. *Enviroline* corresponds to the print *Environment Abstracts*. The *Environment Abstracts* document delivery service (DIALORDER EIC) can supply about 55% of the documents referenced in the database.

Fluidex (Fluid Engineering Abstracts) (Dialog file 96, produced by Elsevier Science) is a specialized bibliographic database of the global literature in the use, control and management of fluids for engineering applications. The content ranges from flow theory to reviews of the latest pipeline or pump technology, to discussion of the environmental impact of reservoir construction or waste-water treatment. By bringing together both the trade and scientific literature, it provides a unique source of information for scientists and engineering professionals. *Fluidex* contains references to articles from 550 international scientific and technical journals, plus reports, conference proceedings and books.

Food science and technology abstracts (FSTA) (Dialog file 51) provides comprehensive coverage of research and development literature in areas related to food science and technology. It corresponds to the printed publication *Food Science and Technology Abstracts*, and includes abstracts from over 1800 journals published in over 90 countries. Additional sources of information include: patents (5%), reviews, poster presentations, abstracts of theses, technical sessions, reports, symposia, books, conference proceedings, legislation, standards, lectures, yearbooks and special workshops. An online thesaurus is included in the file.

General science abstracts (H W Wilson) contains coverage of 150 popular and professional science periodicals, plus the science section of the *New York Times*. There are 19 specialities to tap into, with abstracting from March 1993 and indexing from May 1984.

General science index (H W Wilson) covers 150 of today's most popular periodicals in science, from general interest publications, such as *Discover* and *Sierra*, to the specialized, such as *Journal of the American Chemical Society*, from May 1984. It offers easy search features, content-clarifying title enhancements, complete bibliographic data and more.

GeoArchive (Dialog file 58) indexes over 100,000 references each year, including journals, books, conferences, dissertations and technical reports. Subjects covered are geology, geochemistry, geophysics, mathematical geology, engineering geology, hydrology, water resources, the environment, conservation, etc.

Geobase (Dialog file 292, also available on OCLC FirstSearch) is a bibliographic database covering worldwide research literature in physical and human geography, earth and environmental sciences, ecology and related disciplines. It has unique coverage of non-English-language and less readily available publications. Over 2000 journals are fully covered, with an additional 3000 having partial coverage; over 2000 books, monographs, conference proceedings and reports are also included.

GeoRef (available on OCLC FirstSearch), the database of the American Geological Institute, covers worldwide technical literature on geology and geophysics. It indexes papers from over 13,000 serials and other publications representative of the interests of the 29 geological and earth science societies that are members of the AGI.

Hutchinson science library (Helicon Publishing Ltd) is published in association with the Science Museum, London. The *Science Library* brings together science titles from the Helicon reference range. Users can check formulae, answer 800 quiz questions, learn about the latest developments in every field from genetics to quantum theory and trace their development over the centuries.

Information science abstracts (Dialog file 202) provides references and abstracts in the fields of information science and library science. The database indexes and abstracts articles from over 300 journals, as well as from books, research reports, conference proceedings and patents. Each record includes the bibliographic citation and abstract as well as descriptors drawn from a controlled vocabulary. This database is also available on CD-ROM, from SilverPlatter Information Ltd (UK).

INSPEC (The Database for Physics, Electronics and Computing) (Dialog file 213) corresponds to the three *Science Abstracts* print publications: *Physics Abstracts*, *Electrical and Electronics Abstracts*, and *Computer and Control Abstracts*. The *Science Abstracts* family began publication in 1898. Approximately 16% of the database's source publications are in languages other than English, but all articles are abstracted and indexed in English. The database utilizes controlled vocabulary from the *INSPEC* thesaurus. A single classification scheme is used for all records from 1969 to the present. The special Dialog online thesaurus feature is available to assist searchers in determining appropriate subject terms and codes. Beginning in January 1987, *INSPEC* records also include chemical substance indexing and numerical index terms. The CD-ROM version of this database, *INSPEC ondisc*, is available from SilverPlatter.

Interactive science encyclopedia (Andromeda Interactive Ltd) contains almost 3000 articles covering all aspects of science, together with over 3000 photos and pieces of artwork, 50 video clips, 50 animations, 134 ProActivities (various pre-defined activities, 20 of which are interactive), 75 sound effects, and 8 narrated slide shows explaining the main science topics.

MathSci (American Mathematical Society) contains information from *Mathematical Reviews* and *Current Mathematical Publications*. There are more than 1 million records in the database and about 60,000 are added every year. Information is provided on mathematics and its applications in related fields, such as statistics, computer science and operations research.

McGraw-Hill CD-ROM science and technical reference set 3.0 (McGraw-Hill Publishing Company) is the third edition of the *McGraw-Hill concise encyclopedia of science and technology*. It contains 98,500 terms, 115,000 definitions taken from the *McGraw-Hill dictionary of scientific and technical terms*, 1700 illustrations, 30 video clips and biographical profiles of hundreds of scientists.

McGraw-Hill multimedia encyclopedia of science & technology (McGraw-

Hill Publishing Company) combines the print edition with multimedia technology, search capabilities, and a user-friendly interface. It features 7300 articles written by 3000 international scientists, 122,600 definitions, over 550 high-resolution colour graphics, photos, maps, charts, tables and 39 animation sequences.

Merck index online (Dialog file 304) is the online version of the monographs in the printed 12th Edition of *The Merck index* (Whitehouse Station, NJ, USA), an internationally recognized one-volume encyclopedia of chemicals, drugs and biologicals. Each monograph in the encyclopedia (each record in the database) discusses a single chemical entity or a small group of very closely related compounds. Updates contain material not yet available in print. Records contain molecular formulas and weights, systematic chemical names (including CAS names), generic and trivial names, brand names and their associated companies, company codes, CAS registry numbers, physical and toxicity data, therapeutic and commercial uses, and bibliographic citations to the chemical, biomedical and patent literature.

METADEX (Metals Science database) (Dialog file 32), produced by Cambridge Scientific Abstracts, provides comprehensive coverage of international metals literature. It corresponds to the printed publications *Review of Metal Literature* (1966–67), *Metals Abstracts* (1968 to the present), *Alloys Index* (1974 to the present), *Steels Supplement* (1983–84) and *Steels Alert* (January–June 1985). The *Metals Abstracts* portion of the file includes references to about 1200 primary journal sources. *Alloys Index* supplements *Metals Abstracts* by providing access to the records through commercial, numerical and compositional alloy designations, specific metallic systems and intermetallic compounds found within these systems. Informative abstracts are included for most records since 1979.

Microcomputer abstracts (Dialog file 233) contains abstracts and citations for literature on the use of microcomputers in business, industry, education, libraries and the home. Over 90 publications are covered, including widely read mass-market computer publications, as well as those focusing on specific topics, such as hardware platforms, operating systems (Windows, DOS, UNIX, Macintosh, etc.), online systems, management, networks, and electronic publishing. Informative abstracts summarize software, hardware and book reviews, feature articles, news, columns, program listings, product announcements and buyer/vendor guides. A controlled vocabulary of descriptors is used for indexing. The database is produced by Information Today, Inc and corresponds to the quarterly print publication *Microcomputer Abstracts*.

MicroComputer abstracts (available via OCLC FirstSearch) covers popular magazines and professional journals on microcomputing for business, education, industry and the home.

NTIS: national technical information service (Dialog file 6) consists of summaries of US-government-sponsored research, development and engineering, plus analyses prepared by federal agencies, their contractors, or grantees. It is the means through which unclassified, publicly available, unlimited distribution reports are made available for sale from agencies such as NASA, Department of Defense (DOD), Department of Energy (DOE), Housing and Urban Development (HUD), Department of Transportation (DOT), Department of Commerce, and some 240 other agencies. Additionally, some state and local government agencies now contribute summaries of their reports to the database. NTIS also provides access to the results of government-sponsored research and development from countries outside the USA. Organizations that currently contribute to the NTIS database include: the Japan Ministry of International Trade and Industry (MITI), laboratories administered by the United Kingdom Department of Industry, the German Federal Ministry of Research and Technology (BMFT), the French National Centre for Scientific Research (CNRS) and many more. This database is also available through other vendors, such as Ovid, and is also available on the web.

Nuclear science abstracts (**KR OnDisc:** Dialog Corporation, Dialog OnDisc) covers worldwide nuclear science and technology literature. It contains 1 million records selected from 33 volumes of the print *Nuclear Science Abstracts*, which provides abstracts and citations for a range of unclassified documents that include scientific/technical reports from the US Atomic Energy Commission and the US Energy Research and Development Administration.

Pollution abstracts (Dialog file 41) is a resource for references to environmentally related literature on pollution, its sources and its control. Subjects covered are air pollution, environmental quality, noise pollution, pesticides, radiation, solid wastes and water pollution.

Polymer online (Dialog file 322) is the online version of the second edition of the *Encyclopedia of polymer science and engineering*, published by John Wiley and Sons, Inc. The database provides coverage of polymer science and engineering, including materials, methods and the latest advances in macromolecular science. Natural and synthetic polymers, plastics, fibers, elastomers and processing are all covered.

SciSearch: a cited reference science database (Dialog file 434) is an international multidisciplinary index to the literature of science, technology, biomedicine, and related disciplines produced by the Institute for Scientific

Information (ISI). *SciSearch* contains all of the records published in the *Science Citation Index* (*SCI*), plus additional records from Current Contents publications. *SciSearch* is distinguished by some important and unique characteristics. First, journals indexed are selected on the basis of several criteria, including citation analysis, which results in coverage of the most significant publications in the scientific, technical and biomedical literature. Second, in addition to the more conventional retrieval methods, *SciSearch* offers citation indexing, which permits searching by cited references. *SciSearch* indexes approximately 4500 major scientific and technical journals; some 3800 of these are further indexed by the references cited within each article, allowing for citation searching. An additional 700 journals indexed have been drawn from the *ISI Current Contents* series.

Transport (SilverPlatter Information Ltd, UK) contains the OECD's *International Road Research Documentation* (*IRRD*), *ECMT TRANSDOC* database, and the *TRB Transportation Research Information Services*. It includes over 650,000 records on research in transportation systems and their components – highways, traffic, transport, road safety, and the economics and social sciences of transportation; another 12,000 records are added each year.

TOXLINE (Dialog file 156) covers the toxicological, pharmacological, biochemical and physiological effects of drugs and other chemicals. It is composed of a number of subfiles, several of which are unique to *TOXLINE*. About 45% of the approximately 120,000 records added per year are from the *TOXBIB* subfile, which is derived from *MEDLINE*. The *TOXBIB* and *BIOSIS* (since August 1985) subfiles may be searched using the US National Library of Medicine's medical subject headings (MeSH). The records in these two subfiles are updated annually with the current version of MeSH. An online thesaurus is available to aid in locating MeSH descriptors.

TULSA (Petroleum Abstracts) (Dialog file 87), produced by *Petroleum Abstracts*, contains bibliographic references with abstracts to scientific articles, patents, meeting papers and government reports of interest to geologists, geophysicists, petroleum engineers, and other technical professionals and managers in the oil and gas exploration and production industry.

WasteInfo (SilverPlatter Information Ltd, UK) contains information on recycling, waste treatment and disposal, waste minimization, environmental legislation and policy, and other associated environmental issues. It is compiled by the Waste Management Information Bureau and has over 105,000 records, to which are added about 5000 to 6000 every year.

Wilson applied science & technology abstracts (Dialog file 99) provides comprehensive abstracting and indexing of more than 400 core English-language scientific and technical publications. Non-English-language periodicals are indexed if English abstracts are provided. Periodical coverage includes trade and industrial publications, journals issued by professional and technical societies, and specialized subject periodicals, as well as special issues such as buyers' guides, directories and conference proceedings. Types of material indexed include feature articles, interviews, obituaries, biographies, speeches and product evaluations. *Wilson Applied Science & Technology Abstracts* is the equivalent of H W Wilson's *Applied Science & Technology Index* (*AST*) and H W Wilson's *Applied Science & Technology Abstracts* (*ASA*). This database is also available on CD-ROM from SilverPlatter.

Wilson biological & agricultural index (Dialog file 143) provides indexing of 258 widely used periodicals, including a wide range of scientific journals; from popular to professional, that pertain to biology and agriculture. About 45% of the focus is on agriculture. Types of material indexed include feature articles, biographical sketches, reports of symposia and conferences, review articles, abstracts and summaries of papers, selected letters to the editor, special issues or monographic supplements, and book reviews.

Wilson general science abstracts full text (H W Wilson) is a database created for students and non-specialists. It provides access to 150 professional English-language science periodicals as well as the science section of the *New York Times*. Full-text articles are provided from 36 select periodicals.

Wilson general science index (SilverPlatter Information Ltd, UK) is a guide to current information in 139 English-language periodicals in the physical, life and health sciences. It indexes feature articles and other material from journals. Subjects covered include: astronomy, atmospheric science, biology, botany, chemistry, earth science, ecology, food and nutrition, genetics, geology, mathematics, medicine and health, microbiology, oceanography, physics, physiology and zoology.

Zoological record online (Dialog file 185) produced by *BIOSIS*, provides extensive coverage of the world's zoological literature, with particular emphasis on systematic/taxonomic information. The database corresponds closely to the printed index *Zoological Record*. The database includes thorough subject indexing in both controlled- and natural-language format. It indexes articles from over 6000 international serial publications; theses, monographs, conference proceedings and special reports are also scanned for relevant information.

Selected CD-ROM and online information sources on social sciences and humanities

Abortion & reproductive rights: a comprehensive guide to medicine, ethics and the law (Oryx Press) contains information on the medical, legal and ethical issues surrounding abortion and reproductive rights. With over 20,000 pages of text, the unabridged audio of the US court case Roe *v*. Wade, 500 graphics, ultrasound video and over 5000 hyperlinks, it provides a global perspective through contributions by authorities and politicians.

Africa news service (Dialog files 606 and 806) is an international news database covering political, economic and social developments in Africa. Contributors include the Panafrican News Agency, headquartered in Dakar, with more than 30 correspondents throughout Africa providing daily coverage and specialized features, and the Nairobi-based All Africa Press Service. Publications covered include some of Africa's best-known independent periodicals, among them the *Post* of Zambia, the *Mail* and *Guardian* of Johannesburg, the Addis *Tribune*, the Sudan *Democratic Gazette*, and Nigeria's *Newswatch* and *The Week*. The service also provides a selection of key speeches and comments on Africa and US–Africa relations. *Africa news* is contained in two databases: file 606 contains current data, beginning in June 1999; file 806 contains archive data from July 1996 to May 1999.

AgeLine (Dialog file 163) is produced by the American Association of Retired Persons (AARP) and provides bibliograpic coverage of social gerontology – the study of aging in social, psychological, health-related and economic contexts. The delivery of health care for the older population and its associated costs and policies are particularly well covered, as are public policy, employment and consumer issues. The literature covered is of interest to researchers, health professionals, service planners, policy-makers, employers, older adults, and their families and consumer advocates. Journal citations make up roughly two-thirds of the database, with the rest devoted to citations from books, book chapters and reports.

Annotated bibliography for English studies (ABES) (http://abes.swets.nl) covers secondary literature in English studies in four main subject areas: language and linguistics, cultural studies, literary studies and film studies. Publication types include books, journals, newspaper articles, videos, web pages, etc.

Anthropological index online (http://lucy.ukc.ac.uk/AIO.html) is provided by the Royal Anthropological Institute of Great Britain and Ireland. Topics include anthropology, archaeology, ethnography and linguistics.

Applied social sciences index and abstracts (ASSIA) (Dialog file 232) is a comprehensive reference database on modern society and its problems. Aspects of law, business, national politics and, in particular, local government are included. The database provides strong emphasis on the applied aspects of social sciences. About 40% of the coverage is on the United Kingdom, 45% on North America, and 15% on the rest of the world. All documents contain a short informative abstract, full bibliographic details, and index terms that facilitate both general and subject-specific searches. Approximately 680 worldwide English-language journals and newspapers, representing 16 countries, are routinely scanned, with about 80% abstracted cover to cover and 20% selectively.

Art abstracts (Dialog file 435) is a bibliographic database that cites articles from more than 300 periodicals published throughout the world. Coverage includes periodicals, yearbooks and museum bulletins published in English and other languages. In addition to articles, reproductions of works of art that appear in cited periodicals are indexed. For example, if a painting appears in an advertisement, *Art Abstracts* provides the artist's name, the title of the work, and a full bibliographic citation.

Art literature international (Dialog file 191) abstracts and indexes current publications in the history of art. The database is produced by RILA, the International Repertory of the Literature of Art (a bibliographic service of the Getty Art History Information Program of the J. Paul Getty Trust), and corresponds to the printed publication *RILA*. It is sponsored by the College Art Association of America and the Art Libraries Society of North America. More than half of the records contain informative abstracts.

Arts & humanities citation index (Institute for Scientific Information, USA) covers more than 1150 arts and humanities journals. It also covers individually selected items from over 5000 science and social science journals in areas such as archaeology, art, dance, language, literature, music, poetry and more.

Arts & humanities search (Dialog file 439) is a multidisciplinary database that corresponds to the *Arts & humanities citation index*. The database covers 1300 of the world's leading arts and humanities journals, plus relevant social and natural science journals, and has additional records from the *Current Contents* series of publications.

AUSTROM – Australian social science, law and education databases (RMIT Publishing) contains 12 Australian bibliographic databases covering a range of subject areas in social sciences, humanities, education, architecture, sport, criminology, and leisure and recreation. It includes *APAIS* (Australian Public Affairs Information Service), produced by the National Library of Australia.

British education index (BEI) (Dialog file 121) contains the subject descriptions of, and bibliographic references to, significant journal literature relating to education and the teaching of curricular subjects. The files form part of *ERIC international*, a cluster of educational databases comprising the British, Australian, and Canadian education indexes. The database covers all aspects and fields of education from preschool to adult and higher education, normally qualified by age or educational levels. The range of interest within indexed journals results in broad subject and geographical coverage.

Child abuse and neglect (National Clearinghouse on Child Abuse and Neglect Information in collaboration with the National Information Services Corporation, USA) is a CD-ROM database aimed at researchers, practitioners, policy-makers and others working to identify, treat and prevent child abuse and neglect. The online version of this database (**http://www.nisc.com**) contains over 18,000 bibliographic citations and abstracts of professional literature, primarily of US origin. Publication types include books, journals, government reports, conference papers, state annual reports, curricula and unpublished papers.

CobuildDirect (**http://titania.cobuild.collins.co.uk**) is an online service for accessing a 50 million word database of modern English. It consists of hundreds of different texts from a wide range of sources: books, magazines, newspapers, personal letters, leaflets, together with 10 million words of transcribed natural spoken English. The data are part of the 300 million word Bank of English. It enables retrieval of concordances (screens of text centred on chosen word, set of words, or phrase) and collocation lists (statistically ordered lists showing the other words with which the chosen word or phrase is most commonly associated).

Cross-cultural CD (SilverPlatter Information Ltd, UK) is a series of full-text files containing text from the Human Relations Area Files (HRAF), exploring the social and behavioural sciences and humanities in 60 different societies around the world in the 19th and 20th centuries. The five volumes cover human sexuality and marriage; family, crime and social problems; old age, death and dying; childhood and adolescence, socialization and education; and religious beliefs and religious practices.

Current contents on CD-ROM – arts & humanities (Institute for Scientific Information, USA), provides access to full bibliographic data on the articles contained in more than 1120 journals in a broad range of disciplines, including art and architecture, history, literature, philosophy and more.

Current contents on CD-ROM – social & behavioural sciences (Institute for Scientific Information, USA), provides access to full bibliographic data on the articles in more than 1570 journals in a broad range of disciplines, including anthropology, business, economics, law, management, psychology, sociology and more.

DISCovering world history (Gale Research Inc) offers access to information on people, events and social movements that shaped history. Users can search by name, keyword, place, era or subject.

Dissertation abstracts (http://gateway.ovid.com/autologin.html) contains information about dissertations and master's theses produced in North American colleges and universities from 1861 to the present, and from around the world since 1988. The database covers various subjects, such as literature, chemistry, psychology, business, economics, biology, history, philosophy, sociology and information science. Abstracts are available for dissertations from 1980 to the present, and for master's theses from 1988 to the present.

Dissertation abstracts online (Dialog file 35) is a subject, title and author guide to virtually every American dissertation accepted at an accredited institution since 1861. Selected master's theses have been included since 1962. In addition, since 1988 the database has included citations for dissertations from 50 British universities that have been collected by and filmed at the British Library's Document Supply Centre. Beginning with *DAI* (*Dissertation Abstracts International*) (spring 1988), citations and abstracts from *Worldwide dissertations* (formerly *European dissertations*), are included in the file. Abstracts are included for doctoral records from July 1980 (*Dissertation Abstracts International*, volume 41) to the present, and for master's theses from spring 1988 (*Master's Abstracts*, volume 26) to the present.

EconLit (http://gateway.ovid.com/autologin.html) includes citations and abstracts of the international literature in the field of economics. The database covers journal articles, dissertations, books, conference proceedings, etc. Topics include economic theory and history, labour economics, international, regional and urban economics, and other related subjects. *EconLit* is also available on Dialog (file 139).

Education abstracts (Dialog file 437) is a bibliographic database that cites every article of at least one column in length in more than 400 English-language periodicals and yearbooks published in the United States and elsewhere. English-language books related to education published in 1995 or later are also indexed. The database offers well-written, detailed abstracts describing the content and scope of the source periodical articles. Abstracts, available in approximately 67% of records since abstracting began in 1994, range from 50 to 150 words each.

Education PlusText (1994-present) (**http://www.umi.com/proquest/global. html**) contains references from over 400 education titles. Full text/image coverage is available for over 160 titles. Subjects covered include adult education, comparative education, educational technology, special education, teacher education, etc. The database is accessible via ProQuest Direct, a web-based information retrieval system. Display options include citation/abstract, text only (HTML), full scanned images (PDF), or text+graphics (HTML and PDF). Retrieval options include print, save and e-mail.

ERIC (Educational Resources Information Center) on Ovid Online (**http://gateway.ovid.com/autologin.html**) contains over 900,000 citations and abstracts of primary documents and journal articles. It includes all entries from *Resources in Education* (*RIE*) and *Current Index to Journals in Education* (*CIJE*). Publication types include books, journal articles, conference papers and unpublished papers. This database is also available on CD-ROM through different vendors, such as SilverPlatter, and through other online vendors, such as Dialog (file 1).

Humanities abstracts (H W Wilson) provides abstracts for book reviews, indexing and full bibliographical information on the history of ideas, comparative religion, popular culture, and more, with coverage of 14 major disciplines in the humanities from 400 periodicals. Abstracting coverage begins with March 1994, indexing with February 1984.

Humanities index (H W Wilson) is a resource featuring indexing of 400 periodicals from 14 major disciplines. More than 2500 new entries are added monthly, providing students and scholars with searchable up-to-date coverage and full bibliographic information. Publications are indexed from February 1984 to the present.

Humanities index (Ovid Technologies Inc) is a collection of references pertaining to periodical articles on numerous subjects in the arts and humanities. Disciplines covered include classical studies, area studies, dance, drama, journalism, music and the performing arts. The database features indexes to reviews of current books in the humanities and original works of fiction, short stories, poetry and drama.

Library literature (Dialog file 438) is a bibliographic database that indexes more than 200 key library and information science periodicals, along with books, chapters within books, library school theses and pamphlets. Types of periodical materials covered are feature articles, obituaries, interviews, notices of appointments and awards, regularly appearing columns, special theme issues, editorials (of reference value), letters to the editor (of reference value) and book reviews

Linguistics and language behaviour abstracts (*LLBA*) (Dialog file 36) provides current selective access to the world's literature on linguistics and language behavior as a service to all researchers and practitioners in disciplines concerned with the nature and use of language. Articles abstracted in *LLBA* are drawn from approximately 1200 regularly scanned domestic and international journals. The CD-ROM version is available from SilverPlatter.

LISA (*Library and information science abstracts*) (Dialog file 61) corresponds to the printed abstracting service of the same name produced by Bowker-Saur. The database covers the field of librarianship and information science, and includes many related areas, such as publishing, and specific applications of information technology in such fields as medicine and agriculture. *LISA* on Dialog consists of two subfiles: *LISA* records that cite published works and *CRLIS* records corresponding to the printed *Current Research in Library and Information Science*, which provides international coverage of in-progress or recently completed research projects. Abstracts are provided for all *LISA* records from 1976 to the present and for all *CRLIS* records. *LISA* is now available on the web (**http://www.lisanet.co.uk**).

LIterature ONline (LION) (**http://lion.chadwyck.com**) is a library of more than 260,000 works of English and American poetry, drama and prose, plus biographies, bibliographies and key secondary sources.

Map art world geopolitical deluxe (Cartesia Software) comprises editable maps for graphic designers, containing everything from standard *World geopolitcal*, plus an additional CD of country maps in high detail. All maps are saved as *Adobe illustrator 5* files, with each group of features in a separate layer for easy editing.

MLA international bibliography (SilverPlatter Information Ltd, UK) is an analytical bibliography of scholarship in literature, language, linguistics and folklore, produced by the Modern Language Association of America. The bibliography includes published critical writings on literature transmitted orally, in print, or in audiovisual media, and on human language, including natural languages and invented languages (eg sign languages for the deaf and Esperanto).

Music search (MUSE) (NISC, National Information Services Corporation, USA) features two essential databases on music literature from 1969 to the present on one CD-ROM: *RILM* (Répertoire International de Littérature Musicale) *abstracts of music literature* and the music catalogue of the US Library of Congress. *MUSE* provides more than 177,000 RILM abstracts, plus the RILM thesaurus and over 161,000 records from the Library of Congress. In addition to the music catalogue, there are records from the Library of Congress on disciplines related to music, such as dance, linguistics, religion and archaeology. Both databases can be searched together or individually.

PAIS (Public Affairs Information Service) international (http://gateway.ovid. com/autologin.html) is an index of books, directories, conference proceedings, articles, and other materials relating to public affairs, as well as public and social policy, covering economic, political and social issues. The database contains references to journal articles, statistical yearbooks, pamphlets, reports, government documents and microfiche worldwide. *PAIS international* is also available on Dialog (file 49), which is the online version of the print publications *PAIS Bulletin* (1976–90), *PAIS Foreign Language Index* (1972–90), and *PAIS International in Print* (1991–present).

Periodical abstracts research II (http://www.umi.com/proquest) provides abstracts and indexes to approximately 1650 journals. Articles are available in abstracts, full-text and image formats. Abstracted materials are available from 1971, while full-text and image material is available from 1987. The subjects covered include behavioural sciences, chemistry, current affairs, health, history, geography, language, mathematics, psychology, science and sports.

Philosopher's index (KR-ONDisc) is a major source of information in the areas of aesthetics, epistemology, ethics, logic and metaphysics. The database also contains materials on the philosophy of various disciplines, such as education, history, law, religion and science.

Population information online (POPLINE) (SilverPlatter Information Ltd, UK) provides comprehensive coverage on population, family planning and related health issues. More than 213,000 citations with abstracts are drawn from published and unpublished sources from all over the world. *POPLINE* is supported by the United States Agency for International Development and the United Nations Population Fund. Sources for materials include the US government, international agencies, family planning organizations and databases on sociology, clinical medicine and health. Publication types include government reports, books, journals, technical reports, court decisions, dissertations, conference papers, unpublished reports and training manuals.

ProQuest dissertation abstracts humanities & social sciences (UMI) includes primary research material. It contains over 587,000 citations to doctoral dissertations and master's theses. All fields are fully searchable.

ProQuest social science index/full text (UMI) covers social science from anthropology to urban studies. It combines abstracts and indexing from the H W Wilson Company's *Social Science Index* of over 400 titles.

PsycINFO (Ovid Online) is a database providing bibliographic access to the international literature in psychology, as well as the related behavioural and social sciences. The database includes information from empirical and case studies, surveys, bibliographies, literature reviews and discussion articles from over 1300 journals, as well as conference reports and dissertations. The *PsycINFO* database on Dialog (file 11) provides access to the international literature in psychology and related behavioural and social sciences, including psychiatry, sociology, anthropology, education, pharmacology and linguistics. The records from 1967 to the present are indexed using controlled vocabulary from the thesaurus of *Psychological Index* terms. An online thesaurus is available in *PsycINFO* to assist in locating items from the thesaurus.

PsycLIT (SilverPlatter Information Ltd, UK) provides summaries of the international literature in psychology and related fields compiled from the *PsycINFO* database. It covers journals and monographic series from approximately 45 countries, in more than 30 languages. *PsycLIT* from Ovid Technologies Inc offers access to over 632,000 bibliographic references from literature published worldwide in the areas of psychology and related disciplines. Both journal literature and English language books and chapters are indexed in this database. *PsycLIT/EBSCO* CD-ROM (EBSCO Publishing) provides access to over 600,000 records. The database is contained on 2 CD-ROMs. It indexes and abstracts journal articles dating back to 1974, and books and book chapters from 1987 to the present.

Quotations database (Dialog file 175) contains literary, political and other quotations of note. It consists of material from the *Oxford dictionary of quotations (ODQ)*, published by Oxford University Press. The database presents brief quotations accompanied by the author's name, birth and death dates, and the source of the quote. Material is drawn from poets, novelists, playwrights, politicians, public figures, the Bible, Vulgate, the Book of Common Prayer, the Latin Mass, ballads, Greek and Latin classics, modern European language classics and so on.

SIRS researcher (http://sks.sirs.com) is a general reference database with thousands of full-text articles on social, scientific, historic, economic, political and global issues. Sources include more than 1200 US and international newspapers, magazines, journals and government publications.

Social SciSearch (Dialog file 7) is the citation index database produced by the

Institute of Scientific Information (ISI). It indexes all significant items (articles, reports of meetings, letters, editorials, correction notices, etc.) from more than 1500 of the most important worldwide social science journals. Additional articles relevant to the social sciences are selected from over 2400 journals in the natural, physical and biomedical sciences. The database offers some unique information retrieval techniques.

Social science source (EBSCO Publishing) provides keyword access to comprehensive abstract and index coverage of over 500 journals from the areas of political science, international relations, economics, public policy, sociology and psychology. The searchable full text of 79 important journals is accompanied by pertinent tables and charts.

Social sciences abstracts (H W Wilson) is an abstracting database used for research at undergraduate, graduate and professional level on the latest concepts, trends, opinions, theories and methodologies in all areas of the social sciences. It provides abstracting and indexing of over 400 core periodicals, in 18 specialities.

Social sciences citation index (Institute for Scientific Information, USA) provides coverage of over 1700 social science journals by title, cited author, cited work and author address. It also covers selected items from over 3300 other scientific and technical journals in areas such as anthropology, communication, economics, geography, history, law, psychiatry, social work, sociology and more. This database is available online as well as on CD-ROM from several vendors.

Sociological abstracts (SA) (Dialog file 37) covers the world's literature in sociology and related disciplines in the social and behavioural sciences. Over 1600 journals and other serial publications are scanned each year to provide coverage of original research, reviews, discussions, monographic publications, panel discussions, and case studies. Conference papers and dissertations are also indexed.

SPORT discus (Ovid Online) is a database from the Sport Information Resource Centre, Ontario, Canada. It covers all aspects of sports, fitness and recreation. It includes both practical and scientific information, and corresponds to the print publications *Sport Bibliography*, *Sociology of Leisure* and *Sport Abstracts: a Review of Social Science Literature* and its successor, *Sport & Leisure: a Journal of Social Science Abstracts*. In addition, it also includes the *HERACLES* database (1975–1992), which is the largest French language sports database in the world and contains bibliographic information on sports, physical activities and leisure. About 30% of the records contain abstracts.

UNBIS plus on CD-ROM (Chadwyck-Healey Inc) comprises 11 bibliographic, factual, authority and textual files covering UN documents and publications, as well as citations to publications of governments, international organizations, agencies and commercial publishers acquired by the UN Dag Hammarskjold Library. In addition, *UNBIS* includes citations to UN agendas, speeches, voting records, etc.

UnCover (http://uncweb.carl.org) indexes over 5 million articles from over 18,000 journals; over 4000 current citations are added daily. It covers titles in the arts, humanities, science, medicine and social sciences. Users may search for articles, verify citations or view tables of contents in journals.

United Nations master treaty index (William S Hein & Co Inc) contains a cumulative index to all treaties and agreements published in the *United Nations Treaty Series*. The disc includes two releases of the *Current United Nations treaty index* (paper guide) and two releases of the *United Nations master treaty index on CD-ROM.*

United Nations statistical yearbook (DSI Data Service & Information GmbH) contains about 1 million entries relating to data for all countries and areas. It represents a description of the world economy, its structure, major trends and recent performance; 140 table systems are included, covering world and region summaries, population and social statistics, economic activity and international economic relations.

Wilson humanities abstracts (SilverPlatter Information Ltd, UK) provides indexing of 350 English-language periodicals covering archaeology, classical studies, art, performing arts, philosophy, history, music, linguistics, literature and religion. It is a resource for graduate students, professionals and librarians looking for answers to specific questions and for help in research projects in the humanities subject area.

Wilson humanities abstracts full text (H W Wilson) is a reference tool for research in the humanities, covering 14 disciplines from 400 periodicals. Full-text articles are provided from 96 publications. A similar database, *Humanities abstracts full text*, available on Dialog (file 436), cites articles from some 400 English-language periodicals covering a wide range of disciplines in the humanities. Periodical coverage includes some of the best-known scholarly journals and numerous lesser known but important specialized magazines. Types of materials include feature articles, interviews, obituaries, bibliographies, reviews, and original works of fiction, drama and poetry. The database offers well-written detailed abstracts describing the content and scope of the source articles for approximately 80% of the records. Full-text articles are included for records from more than 97 journals from January 1995 onwards.

Wilson humanities index (SilverPlatter Information Ltd, UK) indexes 345

English-language periodicals. Students, teachers, researchers and librarians can use the index for information in the following areas: art, archaeology and classical studies, dance, drama, film, folklore, history, journalism and communications, language and literature, music, performing arts, philosophy, religion and theology.

Wilson social sciences abstracts (SilverPlatter Information Ltd, UK) provides abstracting and indexing of over 415 English-language periodicals in the areas of anthropology, criminology, economics, law, geography, policy studies, psychology, sociology, social work and urban studies.

Wilson social sciences abstracts full text (H W Wilson) covers 415 English-language periodicals on social sciences. Full-text articles are provided from 112 select publications. *Wilson social sciences abstracts* on Dialog (file 142) provides abstracting and indexing of more than 415 core English-language periodicals published in the United States and elsewhere. Types of materials indexed include feature articles, interviews, obituaries, biographies and book reviews.

Wilson social sciences index (SilverPlatter Information Ltd, UK) offers indexing of over 340 key English-language periodicals in the social sciences, providing up-to-date coverage of this multifaceted, interdisciplinary field. Coverage includes anthropology, area studies, community health and medical care, economics, ethnic studies, geography, international relations, law, criminology, minority studies, planning, public administration and more.

World bank data CD (PEMD Education Group Ltd) provides economic and social data in over 700 data series for over 200 countries, going back to at least 1970. The data can be used directly with any analysis or charting program. The PEMD *Discovery* graphing program is included.

World geopolitical deluxe (Image Club Graphics Inc) is a two-CD set with 39 world maps and globes, 10 detailed world maps with countries, rivers and cities, 58 maps of continents and regions, 31 country maps plus detailed maps of every country in the world.

World history – 20th century (MultiEducator Inc) contains more than 50 historic news reels, hundreds of photos, maps and graphs of the 20th century. Users can search for data chronologically, by name, or through the almanac entry of any particular country.

Appendix 3

Selected CD-ROM and online business information sources

1.4 million female executives and business owners (American Business Information Inc) is a tool for anyone selling a product or service that has particular appeal to affluent female consumers. The disc can be searched by executive/company name, type of business, number of employees and sales volume within any geographic area.

10 million US businesses on CD-ROM (American Business Information Inc) is a marketing tool that gives information on 10 million US businesses, including company name, full address, contact name and title, number of employees, sales volume, standard industrial classification (SIC) code and credit score. Applications include market research, statistical analysis, direct marketing, sales territory assignment and lead generation (leading companies).

1998 EEM CD-ROM (Hearst Business Communications Inc) provides access to *EEM/Electronic master* database by product or manufacturer. It includes 4400 product data pages from over 1000 manufacturers, and also contains vendor information.

ABC direct marketing CD-ROM (ABC voor handel en industrie CV) contains information on more than 100,000 companies from Benelux and northern France, for direct marketing purposes. The disc can be searched by company name, collective headings of products/services, brand names and foreign representatives.

ABI/INFORM Global (SilverPlatter Information Ltd, UK) provides citations and abstracts for articles in over 1000 journals published worldwide. This database includes the full text for over 500 periodicals in the following business areas: accounting/auditing, banking and finance, data processing/information management, economics, government, healthcare, human resources, insurance, law and taxation, telecommunications, marketing, transportation and more. This database is also available from UMI.

Accounting & tax database (Dialog file 485) provides comprehensive indexing and informative abstracts of articles in prominent accounting, taxation and financial management publications from the United States and other countries. In addition to the bibliographic citation and indexing, most records contain 25 to 150 word abstracts.

African business intelligence (Dialog Corporation – Dialog OnDisc) contains data and analysis from Economist Intelligence Unit (EIU) publications, including *Country Reports and Profiles, Financing Foreign Operations, Investing, Licensing and Trading Conditions Abroad, Crossborder Monitor Newsletter, Country Risk Service* and *Country Forecasts*.

American Banker – KR OnDisc (Dialog Corporation – Dialog OnDisc) includes all articles from *American Banker*, the newspaper of record for the banking community, with in-depth analyses of issues affecting the banking and financial services industry. It also includes regulations affecting the industry, and articles and speeches by industry luminaries.

American business disc (American Business Information Inc) is compiled from 5000 nationwide *Yellow Pages* directories, *Business White Pages*, annual reports, press releases, city directories, the *NASDAQ Fact Book* and others. It contains information, searchable by various fields, on over 10 million US and Canadian businesses and organizations on one CD-ROM.

AND export (AND Electronic Publishing BV) contains a road planner for Benelux, France and Germany, together with a translation program for English, French and German business correspondence.

AP News (Dialog files 258 and 858) provides the full text of Associated Press's coverage of national, international and business news, as well as sports and financial information. *AP News* is available 24 hours after the data are transmitted on its high-speed DataStream service. The Associated Press is the largest supplier of general-interest news to the media worldwide, serving more than 15,000 newspaper and broadcast outlets in 115 countries. *AP News* is compiled by more than 1100 journalists in 141 United States news bureaus and 83 overseas news bureaus. In addition, as a US news cooperative, the AP has access to the news compiled by approximately 1500 newspaper members and 6000 radio–television members in the United States.

Asia-Pacific Business Intelligence on disc (Economist Intelligence Unit) contains country profiles; reports on financial conditions, investing, licensing and trading; country forecasts; a country risk service; a crossborder monitor and a global outlook. Volume 1 covers the economic situation in Australia, Cambodia, China, Hong Kong, Japan, North and South Korea, Laos,

Macau, Mongolia, New Zealand, Pacific Islands, Vietnam and Taiwan, and Volume 2 covers the economic situation in Afghanistan, Bangladesh, Brunei, India, Indonesia, Malaysia, Myanmar (Burma), Nepal, Pakistan, the Philippines, Singapore, Sri Lanka and Thailand.

Asia's 7,500 largest companies (William Snyder Publishing Associates) provides financial and marketing data on public and privately owned companies in the Philippines, Indonesia, Taiwan, Japan, Hong Kong, Korea, Singapore, Thailand, China and Malaysia.

Asian-Pacific kompass disc (Editus Nederland BV) provides information on 420,000 Asian–Pacific companies, including name, address, product list, directors and management, turnover and employment.

Australian business compendium (United Directory Systems) contains the names, addresses and phone numbers of 7600 companies in Australia. The disc also contains company data, such as turnover, number of employees, SIC/ASIC codes and job titles etc.

Australian business index (United Directory Systems), featuring more than 970,000 current records, provides a profile of Australia's business sector. The records contain information from a variety of statistical sources, and they can be sorted according to field, such as company name, category of operation, size, number of employees and location.

Authority business law library (Matthew Bender & Co Inc) provides information on US business law, including the following titles: *Current legal forms, Warren's forms of agreements, Antitrust counselling & litigation techniques, Commercial damages, Business organizations, Cable TV law* and more.

Bankers' almanac (Bankbase, Bowker-Saur) is a source of reference on all the world's banks.

BCC market research (Business Communications Company) includes market research reports that provide comprehensive information on market segmentation, industry structure, production and consumption statistics, marketing strategies, new technologies and their applications, market penetration, major company profiles, distribution networks and pricing. Tables and figures depict market trends, with projections. Approximately 80% of the studies deal with US market data, while the remaining 20% cover world markets as well.

Bookscope business (Primary Source Media and Gale Research) is a bibliographic database that enables users to search tables of contents, title information since 1989 for over 100 business publishers, book reviews, book summaries, author biographies and affiliations, and conference proceedings.

Business & commerce (Digital Stock Corporation) is a collection of royalty-free stock photography for advertising, graphic design, pre-press, multimedia and publishing.

Business dateline (Bell & Howell Information and Learning) provides the full text of major news and feature stories from 550 regional business publications from throughout the United States and Canada. The regional perspectives reported in the business press make *Business Dateline* an excellent source of in-depth business information with a local point of view. Virtually every aspect of regional business activities and trends is covered in the file, with particular emphasis on economic conditions in selected cities, states, or regions, as well as mergers, acquisitions, company executives, new products and competitive intelligence.

Business-facts on CD (National Decision Systems) contains business statistics by SIC code, number of employees, sales volume and daytime population counts. Available for US states, county, MSA (Michigan Statutes Annotated), zip, census tract and block geography levels. Can be used alone or downloaded for use with other software packages.

Business search UK (Thomson Directories) contains the complete Thomson Directories database of over 2.1 million business listings.

Business source (EBSCO Publishing) offers full text of over 530 business-related journals, including *Forbes*, *Fortune*, *The Economist* and more than 40 regional publications.

Business source plus (EBSCO Publishing) offers indexing and abstracts for 600 general business, trade, accounting, finance, economics, marketing, human resources and technology periodicals, and the searchable full text of 200 of those titles.

Business Week interactive guide to world business and economics (McGraw-Hill Publishing Company) contains statistical information on more than 226 countries. Areas covered include world of information guides, country maps, key facts, industry investment and companies, labour force, export and import, agriculture, armed forces, communications and media, energy, education, population and welfare, sex and age, economics, transport and natural resources.

Business wire (Dialog files 610 and 810) contains the full text of news releases issued by approximately 10,000 corporations, universities, research institutes, hospitals and other organizations. The file primarily covers US industries and organizations, although some information on international events is included. Records in *Business wire* vary in length, but typically contain fewer than 500 words. News releases are available in the *Business wire* database on the day of receipt.

Butterworths company law service on CD-ROM (Butterworths) is a reference library, bringing together legislation from *Butterworths company law handbook*, the full text of *Butterworths company law service*, commentary from

Halsbury's laws of England, the full text of cases from *Butterworths company law cases* and case summaries from *The Digest*.

Butterworths corporate finance & banking 'books on screen' (Butterworths) provide access to the legislation, rules and regulations in corporate finance. Included are listing rules of the London Stock Exchange, rules of the London Stock Exchange, *Butterworths company law handbook*, *City code on takeovers and mergers*, Bank of England materials, Securities and Futures Authority regulations, and *Butterworths banking law handbook*.

Butterworths financial regulations services on CD-ROM (Butterworths) enables users to search on changes in financial services rules and regulations. It includes the Securities and Investments Board rulebook, the Personal Investment Authority rulebook, the Investment Management Regulatory Organization rulebook, Securities and Futures Authority regulations, *Butterworths financial services law handbook* and *Butterworths company law handbook*.

Canadian business and current affairs (SilverPlatter Information Ltd, UK) combines an indexing and abstracting database with direct access to the full-text content of the articles indexed. It contains the full text of over 130 Canadian periodicals and sources of current affairs information, and indexes over 600 periodicals and 9 daily new sources.

Canadian business & current affairs (CBCA) – KR OnDisc (Dialog Corporation – Dialog OnDisc) provides access to information on Canadian national/local activities and news, business, politics, education, social issues, arts, sport and leisure. Each year Micromedia indexes 220,000 articles from 200 business periodicals, 340 magazines, and 10 newspapers.

Chemical business NewsBase – KR OnDisc (Dialog Corporation – Dialog OnDisc) provides company, product and market information on the chemical industry and its end-users worldwide. Raw materials, bulk chemicals, fine and specialty chemicals are covered. Information is drawn from 600 journals, newspapers, publisher and company literature sources.

Chinese business intelligence (Dialog Corporation – Dialog OnDisc) includes data and analysis from the EIU reference publications, such as *Country Reports and Profiles*, *Financing Foreign Operations*, *Investing, Licensing and Trading Conditions Abroad*. Topics include acquisitions and alliances, business regulations, capital and alliances, business regulations, capital markets, financial management, intellectual property, labour developments and so on.

D&B business locator (Dun & Bradstreet Corporation) provides instant access to over 10 million company listings, along with a step-up linkage that allows users to view higher levels on the corporate family tree, all the way to the 'ultimate parent'. It is of use to marketing, credit, corporate research, purchasing or legal decision-makers.

D&B principal international business disc basic (Dun & Bradstreet Corporation) provides access to key marketing information on 70,000 leading international companies. It also provides the names of each company's top decision-makers.

Delphes European business is the leading French database on markets, products and companies. It contains bibliographic citations and informative abstracts on virtually every aspect of European business. It includes some areas of particular significance from the European perspective: French national and regional economy, European economies and markets, and company information. Geographic coverage is approximately 60% France (country and regions), 25% Europe and European Union, and 15% international (America, Africa, Asia). Abstracts are produced by approximately 60 French chambers of commerce and industry, and a dozen French and foreign specialized organizations under the direction of the Paris Chamber of Commerce and Industry (CCIP) and Assembly of the French Chambers of Commerce and Industry (ACFCI). A comprehensive hierarchical thesaurus in French, English and Spanish (available from the producer) can be used for broad or specific retrieval of subjects or geographic areas. The text of the abstracts is in French. Copies of complete documents abstracted in Delphes can be ordered from the CCIP.

Doing business in Asia (CCH) gives an overview of the system of law and government, the organization of the legal profession, and the laws which regulate the business activities of investors in Australia, China, Hong Kong, India, Indonesia, Japan, Korea, Malaysia, Myanmar, the Philippines, Singapore, Taiwan, Thailand and Vietnam. Topics include land tenure, contract, commercial and company law, taxation, incentives and disincentives, import and export controls, exchange controls, labour and nationality laws, intellectual property, insurance, settlement of disputes, transport and shipping.

Eastern Europe business database (NTIS – National Technical Information Service) contains information on more than 50,000 businesses of varying size both government and privately owned, which together produce 92% of the total economic output in the region. It enables the user to search by product, company name or other criteria.

EIU international business newsletters on disc (SilverPlatter Information Ltd, UK) is a complete collection of all the Economist Intelligence Unit newsletters covering business developments in over 180 major and emerging markets, to keep users in touch with what is happening on all business fronts – economic and political developments, regulatory changes, financial markets, industry trends, labour conditions, corporate strategies and more.

Encyclopedia of banking and finance (McGraw-Hill Inc) includes legal, analytical and statistical information. It contains mathematical formulas, financial-performance ratios, background data on money supply, industry information affecting lending and investment, and other legal and regulatory references.

English for business (University of Wolverhampton) is a language course for business English. It includes six CDs with the following titles: *Managing quality*, *International marketing*, *An introduction to a company*, *Organising change* and *International sales*.

Europa (OneSource Information Services Ltd) contains numerical and textual information on over 135,000 public and private companies throughout Europe. The product features analytical software with flexible searching and reporting capabilities, and transfer of data to a spreadsheet.

Europe's 15,000 largest companies (William Snyder Publishing Associates) provides financial and marketing data on the continent's key public and privately owned companies.

European business ASAP (Information Access Company) includes information about management, trade, industries, human resources, advertising, finance, accounting, banking and marketing.

Finance & accounting (Yorkshire International Thomson Multimedia Ltd) consists of three sections: financial management, theory, and a set of book-keeping exercises and printable accounting templates.

Forbes greatest business stories of all time (Microsoft Corporation) chronicles the economic progress of some of America's leading business figures, past and present. Multimedia business histories are brought to life with text, video, audio and animated charts and graphs, while interactive case studies teach the management lessons that underlie the stories.

French dictionary of business, commerce & finance (Routledge) consists of some 50,000 entries in both French and English, including 4000 abbreviations. Terms are drawn from the whole range of business, commerce and finance terminology.

FT prices on CD-ROM (Financial Times Information) provides cost-effective electronic access to up to 13 years of price information, starting in 1983, from the back pages of the *Financial Times*, including information on UK and European equities, commodities, currencies, indices, interest rates and UK managed funds. You can find a particular price or value on a specific date, or trace it over a period of time and display the results immediately as a graph or table. You can search either by using a global search function to select any price by country and sector, or you can select from commodities, currencies, indices, interest rates, UK managed funds and bonds.

Gale business resources on CD-ROM (Gale Research Inc) contains information on more than 200,000 US businesses; users can search by company name, market share, rankings, essays, industry statistics, associations, number of employees, annual sales and revenues.

German business CD-ROM (M\COMM GmbH und Co. KG) provides information on over 2 million German companies, with details on addresses, phone and fax numbers, business operations and branches.

German dictionary of business & commerce (Routledge) consists of approximately 50,000 entries in both German and English, including 4000 abbreviations. Terms are drawn from the whole range of business, commerce and finance terminology.

Global business provider (OneSource Information Services Ltd) is an integrated source of information on companies globally.

Global development finance 1998 (DSI Data Service & Information GmbH) is a reference guide for economists, bankers, country-risk analysts, financial consultants and others involved in investment lending and capital flows worldwide. It offers statistical tables for regional, income and indebtness groups, and statistical tables for the 136 countries that report public and publically guaranteed debts.

Global market information database (GMID) (Euromonitor International) povides data on countries and markets, and offers historical statistics and forecasts, information sources, brand and company information, plus full-text market analysis. It provides access to the following seven unique information resources: detailed market size data; country marketing parameters; marketing forecast data; brand and company information; business information sources; marketing profiles and full-text market analysis.

GPO on SilverPlatter (SilverPlatter Information Ltd, UK) contains bibliographic citations from 1976 to the present for government publications, such as books, reports, studies, serials and maps, from the *Monthly Catalog* published by the US Government Printing Office. Topics covered include finance, business, demographics, agriculture, medicine, public health and more. The database contains over 400,000 bibliographic records.

Green book 1998 (Singapore) (Promedia Periodicals Pte Ltd) provides 300,000 products and services listings, 100,000 brand name listings, 100,000 company profiles, specific guides including computer, electronic, motoring, etc., and other information such as tourist attractions. It is available in print, on CD-ROM and on the web.

Hong Kong business index (United Directory Systems) is a business-based telephone directory of Hong Kong businesses. It includes an Asian supplement covering additional regional information on Taiwan, Singapore and China. The disc covers the Hong Kong *Yellow Pages*, enhanced with fax numbers, employee numbers, contact names and SIC codes.

Hoover's company profiles on CD-ROM (William Snyder Publishing Associates) includes company profiles on over 2500 major US and international corporations. Each database is fully searchable and the profiles are displayed in an easy-to-read format. Company profiles can be searched by operations, strategies, histories, products and brand names, officers, competitors, locations, financial information etc.

ICC company index (ICC Information Ltd) contains information and financial data on 1.2 million limited companies in Great Britain. It can be used to identify a range of companies matching certain criteria. Balance sheet and performance figures are available on every British limited company.

Information USA 3.5 (InfoBusiness Inc) contains full information on every Federal Domestic Assistance programme available, giving the user access to all federal grants, loans, scholarships, mortage loans, insurance, technical and financial assistance programmes, statistical data, surplus property, government auctions etc.

Inland Revenue internal guidance manuals 'books on screen' (Butterworths) includes all of the UK Inland Revenue's guidance manuals. It includes a facility to search by word, phrase or number. Relevant areas of the text can be printed out. Users can also add their own notes anywhere in the text.

International financial statistics (IFS) (International Monetary Fund) provides statistics on exchange rates, international reserves, banking, balance of payments, government finances, prices, etc., for most countries in the world. Statistics on some data go as far back as 1948.

Investext (Dialog file 545) is the world's largest online database of company and industry research. It provides the full text of 700,000 company, industry and geographic research reports written by analysts at more than 300 leading investment banks, brokerage houses and consulting firms worldwide. It provides in-depth analysis and data on approximately 50,000 publicly traded companies, including sales and earnings forecasts, market-share projections, and research and development expenditures. Other *Investext* reports analyse specific industries/products and businesses in geographic regions. The reports are particularly useful for market research, strategic planning, competitive analysis, and financial forecasting. *Investext* offers the complete text of each research report and abstracts for most reports over four pages in length. Each report is divided into individual text records, one for each page of the report, and has a table of contents record. All records comprising a report are tied together with a common six- or seven-digit report number. All reports are indexed at the page level by company, industry, product(s) and business subject(s).

Kompass CD plus (KRIS) (Microinfo Ltd) covers products, services and company information, financial data, parents and subsidiaries, and industrial trade names.

McGraw-Hill's small business lawyer (McGraw-Hill Publishing Company) is an interactive standalone electronic sourcebook of more than 300 forms and agreements covering thousands of business transactions, including personnel, leases, credit and collections, corporate forms, loans, partnerships and professional services.

Middle Eastern business intelligence (Dialog Corporation – Dialog OnDisc) contains data and analysis from the EIU publications *Country Reports and Profiles, Financing Foreign Operations, Investing, Licensing and Trading Conditions Abroad, Crossborder Monitor Newsletter, Country Risk Service* and *Country Forecasts*.

Moody's company data (Moody's Investors Service) provides access to public companies listed on major American and regional exchanges. This title offers direct access to financial statements in native currencies and full business descriptions. Other information includes statements of cash flows, notes to financials, letters to shareholders, footnotes to financials, analysis by geographic region or product line. Over 11,000 non-US-based public companies in over 100 countries are covered. Comprehensive textual and financial data, featuring Moody's database of public company information including textual descriptions of company history, business and products, long-term debt, properties and more; plus financial statements in their native currencies.

The New Zealand business index (United Directory Systems) is a business directory of New Zealand businesses. It includes addresses, fax and telephone numbers, type of business, employee numbers and contact names.

OECD statistical compendium (DSI Data Service & Information GmbH) is a database on macroeconomic statistics compiled by the Organization for Economic Cooperation and Development on its 25 member countries. More than 280,000 monthly, quarterly and annual time series are presented with complete historical data.

Oxford business shelf (Oxford University Press, Electronic Publishing Department) is aimed at those working and writing in a business environment, and business teachers and students. It contains the *Concise dictionary of business*, the *Concise dictionary of law*, the *Oxford dictionary of abbreviations*, and a world gazetteer.

People in business (Gazelle Studios) contains 200 business-oriented images of men and women at meetings and at work, and a variety of office-related equipment. Photos are stored in 24-bit colour TIFF, 8-bit colour PICT; unlimited reproduction rights are offered if an image is under a quarter of a page, or under 10,000 copies are made.

Pharmaceutical company profiles (IMS World Publications Ltd) offers information for strategic and competitive decisions. It covers around 110 key companies each year, giving details on strategy statements, research pipelines and product portfolios with sales forecasts, research programme analysis, and information on company structure and subsidiaries.

Profiles in business (Digital Vision) is a collection of 100 monochromic images of business professionals shot against a white background.

ProQuest business dateline (UMI) covers regional and business information from throughout the US and Canada. It contains articles from over 450 American business tabloids, magazines, daily newspapers and business-newswire services.

Reuters business briefing is an online database covering a wide range of topics from more than 4000 sources around the world. Coverage includes daily newspapers, journals and newswires. It also provides profiles of over 22,000 companies worldwide, which allows users to keep track of competitors, suppliers, customers and partners. *Reuters Business Briefing* connects the user to one of the world's most powerful business information databases, serving as a single link to global and local newswires, many of the world's leading newspapers, trade publications and business magazines.

Singapore 1000 (Promedia) provides information on the top 1000 companies ranked by sales and 2000 largest corporations in Singapore. Company profiles of the 1000 companies are also available. The companies are also ranked by industry, nationality and net profits. The database was established in 1980 to satisfy market demand in a more comprehensive and user-friendly way.

South American business information (SABI) (Dialog files 617 and 817) is an international news service that covers the South American market. It provides extensive and comprehensive abstracts of articles from the main business publications in five South American countries. This daily newswire service covers newspapers, business and trade journals from Argentina, Brazil, Chile, Paraguay, and Uruguay. File 617 contains current data, from July 1999; file 817 contains archive data from July 1996 to February 1999.

Top 100,000 companies database (CML Data Ltd) provides information on 100,000 companies in the United Kingdom, including names, addresses and telephone numbers, sales volume, number of employees, line of business and SIC codes.

Top finance companies database (CML Data Ltd) provides information on finance companies in the United Kingdom, including names, addresses and telephone numbers, sales volume, number of employees, line of business and SIC codes.

UK Business browser (OneSource Information Services Ltd) contains information gathered from a variety of suppliers and integrated to provide a comprehensive source of information on 360,000 companies.

UK company factfinder – KR OnDisc (Dialog Corporation – Dialog OnDisc) is a comprehensive resource for information about UK quoted companies. It contains analysed financials with up to 10 years of financial history and credit information, full-text annual reports and full-text research reports from approximately 60 respected brokerage houses.

US business reporter – KR OnDisc (Dialog Corporation – Dialog OnDisc) features full-text business news from 16 leading US metropolitan newspapers (including the *LA Times*, *Boston Globe*, *NY Newsday*, *Miami Herald*, *Seattle Times*), plus selected company news releases from *Business Wire*. It is a valuable source of current information on products, markets, companies and industries around the US.

West European business intelligence (Dialog Corporation – Dialog OnDisc) lists EIU information services on the world's market in Western Europe, including full country reports and profiles and information on financing foreign operations and investing, licensing and trading conditions.

Who's Who in European business and industry (Who's Who Edition GmbH) is a directory of 9500 key figures in European business and industry. It also includes 5000 profiles of the largest European organizations and coverage of 40 national markets, cross-referenced and with hyperlinks for quick and convenient access.

Wilson business abstracts (H W Wilson Company) is a database providing abstracts of current bibliographic information from over 345 business journals. It covers accounting, acquisitions and mergers, advertising, building and construction, finance and investments, government regulations, industrial relations, insurance, international business, management, marketing, real estates, taxation etc. It is available from Ovid Technologies Inc.

Wilson business abstracts full text (H W Wilson) covers 400 business periodicals including the *New York Times* and the *Wall Street Journal*. It helps users gather data on industry, financial trends, business alliance and more. Full-text articles are provided from 145 publications.

World database of business information sources (Euromonitor plc) contains information on over 12,000 organizations, 13,000 publications, 2000 exhibitions and 700 online databases. It also includes a mailing-label print option, which allows users to mail either the named contact or the person holding a specific job title.

World marketing data and statistics 1999 on CD-ROM (Euromonitor Plc) is a statistical database on business and marketing information of 1232 different data types covering 209 countries. The data are grouped into 24 different subject areas, including advertising and media, banking and finance, communications, consumer expenditure patterns, consumer market sizes, cultural and economic indicators, and health and living standards. Some of the data go back to 1977.

World reporter is a comprehensive global news source, developed jointly by three of the world's leading information companies: the Dialog Corporation, Financial Times Information, and Dow Jones & Company. It covers the leading newspapers, business magazines and newswires from all regions of the world, including emerging markets. *World Reporter* is an English-language database that includes full-text articles from the majority of the English-language sources; English-language abstracts are provided for non-English-language sources.

Worldwide tax daily (Dialog file 792) is a daily international tax information service from Tax Analysts, which provides comprehensive information on US and international developments, as well as tax news and documents from over 100 countries. News stories, summaries and full-text documents are included in the file. It also contains over 3000 tax treaties, including the complete set of US tax treaties with supporting documents, and tax spanning most of the 20th century in over 180 countries, plus trade and investment agreements and customs materials. All information is updated each weekday. Most documents are in English, although some foreign language documents are included.

Appendix 4

Selected CD-ROM and online legal information sources

All England law reports on CD-ROM (Butterworths) includes over 18,000 case reports, all indexed and with head notes.

American Law Institute restatements of the law (West Group) provides various titles customized for each subscriber. These include 10 currently published restatements of the law: agency, conflict of laws, contracts, foreign relations law of the United States, judgments, property, restitution, security, trusts and unfair competition.

Arbitration database on CD-ROM (LRP Publications) includes published arbitration decisions, dating from 1978 to the present. Information is available on the arbitrator's background, how the arbitrator ruled, and more. Case summaries are linked to the search results for quick access to the full-text version of the case.

Australasian legal literature index (Computer Law Services Pty Ltd) provides indexes on a large number of law journals from Australia, New Zealand, Papua New Guinea and other Pacific Rim countries. It contains 22,000 documents with 120 to 130 new entries added each month. *ALLI* allows users to search by author, title, date, source, case name, act title and jurisdiction.

Authority banking and commercial law library (Matthew Bender & Co Inc) provides information on US banking and commercial law, including the following titles: *Banking law, Goods in transit, A guide to remedies in business litigation, Secured transactions under the UCC, UCC reporter digest, Forms and procedures under the UCC* and more.

Authority California law and practice library (Matthew Bender & Co Inc) provides information on California cases, codes and regulations, including the following titles: *California forms of pleading & practice, California legal forms, California points and authorities, California probate practice, California wills &*

trusts and more.

Authority Florida law and practice library (Matthew Bender & Co Inc) provides information on Florida law, including the following titles: *Southeast transaction guide*, *Florida rules*, *Florida statutes*, *Florida real estate transactions*, *Florida forms of jury instruction*, *Florida civil trial guide*, *Florida family law*, *Florida torts* and more.

Authority insurance law library (Matthew Bender & Co Inc) provides information on US insurance law, including the following titles: *The law of liability insurance*, *Insuring real property*, *Responsibilities of insurance agents and brokers*, *Insurance risk management – state and local governments*, *Insurance bad faith litigations*, *The law of life and health insurance* and more.

Authority intellectual property law library (Matthew Bender & Co Inc) provides information on US intellectual property law, including the following titles: *Nimmer on copyright*, *Patents and trademarks*, *Milgrim on trade secrets*, *World patent law & practice*, *Computer law* and more.

Authority tax and estate planning law library (Matthew Bender & Co Inc) provides information on US tax and estate planning law, including the following titles: *Tax planning for corporations and shareholders*, *Modern estate planning*, *Applying GAAP and GAAS*, *Income taxation of foreign related transactions*, *Murphy's will clauses* and more.

Bibliography of nineteenth-century legal literature (Chadwyck-Healey Ltd) is an author/subject catalogue of law treatises and law-related literature held in 12 legal collections in Britain, Ireland and the USA. It contains 40,000 records and 250,000 items in a subject classification scheme with 1000 headings.

Blue sky laws and regulations on CD-ROM (CCH Inc) contains every blue-sky law and regulation for 50 US states plus Guam, Puerto Rico and District of Columbia. It includes Uniform Securities Acts, report letters, blue-sky legal opinions and no-action letters, selected securities insurance, legal investment laws and regulations, licensing, and disclosure/reporting requirements for issuers, broker-dealers and investment advisors.

British companies legislation 1998 (CCH Editions Ltd) contains the texts of the following seven main statutes: the Companies Act 1985, the Business Names Act 1985, the Companies Consolidation (Consequential Provisions) Act 1985, the Insolvency Act 1986, the Company Directors Disqualification Act 1986; the Financial Services Act 1986 and the Companies Act 1989. In addition, certain ancillary legislation (including the insider dealing provisions in the Criminal Justice Act 1993), the Insolvency Rules 1986 (as amended) and other subordinate legislation relating to company law are reproduced.

British company law library (CCH Editions Ltd) is a comprehensive information service on the law and practice of British company law. It includes detailed commentary, with emphasis on practical guidance; full text of British statutes and statutory instruments on company law, with extensive cross references and history; and other notes and coverage of company law cases.

British standards on CD-ROM (Technical Indexes Ltd) provides complete British standards on CD-ROM. The information is made available by special agreement with the British Standards Institution. It contains full text with images, divided into 12 sections.

British tax library (CCH Editions Ltd) is based on the loose-leaf *British tax reporter*. It aims to provide a reference source incorporating detailed commentary on UK direct taxes.

Brooker's civil procedure library (Brooker's Ltd, Wellington) contains the text of two loose-leaf publications of McGechan on procedure and district court procedure, with the *Procedure reports of New Zealand*.

Brooker's Law Directory (Brooker's Ltd, Wellington) is a legal directory of New Zealand that includes more than 6500 listings of legal practitioners, 2400 firms, government departments, local bodies, associations, conversion tables and complete listings of courts and the judiciary.

Business lawyer (Data Trace Publishing Company) includes the last 15 years of the *Business lawyer* (1981–96), plus a collection of articles.

Butterworths company law service on CD-ROM (Butterworths) is a reference library, bringing together *Butterworths company law handbook*, the full text of *Butterworths company law service*, commentary from *Halsbury's laws of England*, the full text of cases from *Butterworths company law cases* and case summaries from *The Digest*.

Butterworths family and child law library (Butterworths) contains the texts of *Butterworths family law service*, *Rayden and Jackson on divorce and family matters*, Clarke Hall and Morris on All ER and *Family court reporter*.

California law on disc (Michie Company) contains Supreme Court of California decisions since 1883, Court of Appeals of California decisions since 1944, and Appellate Departments of the Superior Court decisions since 1944.

The Canadian tax library (CCH Canadian Ltd) offers four options.
Option 1 contains Income Tax Act and regulations, income tax bulletins, circulars and rulings, *Canadian tax reporter, Dominion tax cases 1997, Dominion tax cases 1920-1996, Window on Canadian tax, Tax window files, Canadian master tax guide* and income tax forms. **Option 2** contains information on Canadian income tax and regulations. **Option 3** contains information on tax acts and regulations and Canadian goods and services tax reports. **Option 4**

contains information on Income Tax Act and regulations and provincial tax reports.

Child abuse & neglect (National Information Services Corporation) contains databases on documents, legal statutes, public awareness materials, audiovisual materials, local-to-international programmes, and the *Child abuse & neglect* thesaurus. It also includes *Public awareness materials for adults and children* database, *National organizations* database and other relevant databases.

Code of federal regulations (CFRs) (National Technical Information Service) is a comprehensive source of all 50 federal regulations titles.

Commonwealth statutes and statutory rules (Computer Law Services Pty Ltd) contains the full text of all the Commonwealth statutes in force, fully consolidated and incorporating all amendments. It contains hypertext links and cross-references. Reprinted and amending statutory rules are also included.

Company law library (Brooker's Electronic) contains commentary on companies acts, financial reporting, receivership, registration, plus over 950 full-text company and securities cases, with Brooker's *Company and Securities Law Reports* included.

Court filings (Dialog file 793), formerly *Court Petitions and Complaints (PETEXT)*, is a weekly tax service from Tax Analysts that provides coverage of tax-related petitions complaints filed in the US federal courts, including the tax court, the federal district courts, the federal courts of appeal, the US bankruptcy court, and the court of federal claims. Petitions and complaints, the legal documents used by tax practitioners to request court review of a tax controversy, are of interest to tax practitioners because they can help identify cases similar to ones they have pending, and can help predict the outcome of a tax filing position. Analytical summaries and selected full-text documents are included in the file. Documents are classified by Internal Revenue Code section, where applicable, in the CF field. Coverage begins in 1992.

Criminal justice periodical index (Dialog file 171) provides indexing of over 100 journals, newsletters and law reports. Subjects covered include: abortion, arrest (police methods), child abuse, commercial crime, computer crime, court reform, crime prevention, drug abuse, due process of law, evidence, family law, fingerprinting, forensic science, jail administration, judges, juvenile offenders, legal aid, narcotics trafficking, negligence, organized crime, parole officers, prisons, recidivism, security forces, victimless crimes, violence and more.

Current legal information (Sweet & Maxwell Ltd) provides access to *Legal journals index*, incorporating articles from 230 journals and 30,000 entries a year; *Financial journals index*; *Daily law reports*, a monthly summary of all cases in the newspapers and *Lloyd's List*; Badger; *Current law monthly digest*; *Current law year books* 1986–94.

Electricity at work – regulations (Instinct Training Ltd) is aimed at employers and managers, and contains information on background and legal aspects, dangers of electricity, safe systems of work, a checklist for users and managers, and earthing and related precautions

Electronic industrial relations law reports (Industrial Relations Services) features the past 25 years of the journal *Industrial Relations Law Reports* on a single CD-ROM. The disc is a source of information on employment case law, and provides search facilities and the ability to annotate cases, highlight points, place bookmarks and create links between cases.

Electronic law reports (eLR) (Context Ltd) is a two-CD set containing all 753 volumes of law reports dating back to 1865. It also includes four modern entries: appeal cases, Chancery, Queen's (or King's) Bench and family.

Encyclopedia of China's laws and regulations (Huwei Consultants) provides the full text of laws and regulations effective in China since 1949. Contains the databases *Laws and regulations of China*, *Laws and regulations of China governing foreign-related matters*, *Explanations of justice of China* and *Judicial precedents in China*.

EPA shadow law (Envires Corporation) includes environmental compliance and enforcement information. The complete text of the documents is in four databases: *Administrative law, appeals and orders*; *Consent decrees*; *Internal policy and guidances* for all program areas and *RODs, Amendments and ESDs*.

ESPACE-LEGAL (European Patent Office) contains the complete text of all the decisions (both published and unpublished) of the Board of Appeals at the EPO. The disc also contains the text of patent conventions, treaties and guidelines as well as facsimile copies of EPO applicants' forms.

EU infodisk (Infonorme London Information) is the official bibliographic database of the European Union containing draft and implemented directives, regulations and decisions from the commission, council, parliament and court, plus abstracted articles concerning the EU from 2000 periodicals. It also contains the official UK Department of Trade and Industry *Spearhead* database on the implementation of EU directives into national law.

Eurolaw (Infonorme London Information) is the full-text legal database of the European Union covering treaties, secondary, supplementary and proposed legislation (directives and regulations), Court of Justice reports, national implementation details and questions raised in the European parliament. Also contains the DTI *Spearhead* database and additional up-to-date court cases.

Family law (Computer Law Services Pty Ltd) contains the full text of a selection of Commonwealth, New South Wales and Victorian acts and regulations, including the Family Law Act, Child Support Act, Family Law Rules, all child support regulations and NSW/Victorian Adoption Acts, decisions of the family court from 1996 and decisions from high and NSW supreme courts.

Federal case law disc 1 – high and federal court decisions (Computer Law Services Pty Ltd) contains the full text of decisions from the high court and federal court on disc 1 and from the family court and administrative appeals tribunal on disc 2. Each court is separately searchable. Both reported and unreported judgments are included.

Federal register (Dialog file 180) provides the full text of the *Federal Register*, a daily publication of the United States government. Published every federal working day, the *Federal Register* provides a uniform system for making available to the public regulations and legal notices issued by federal agencies and the president. The documents are grouped and published in the following categories: Presidential documents, rules and regulations, proposed rules, notices, and Sunshine Act meetings. Corrections, table of contents, and Unified Agenda records are also available online. Daily and weekly current awareness searching allows the user to monitor recent developments.

Florida law on disc (Michie Company) contains Florida statutes (unannotated), Florida Supreme Court decisions since 1886, Florida District Court of Appeals decisions since 1957 and the rules of court service.

Food law in the European Union – the guide to putting EU food legislation into practice (Chapman & Hall) is a product-orientated CD-ROM covering European food law. The emphasis is on interpreting laws from a food industry perspective without prejudicing the accuracy of the information. The database covers pan-European legislation information, recent legislation and policy developments in Brussels, and legislation of member states.

Gale group legal resource index (LRI) (Dialog file 150) is the most comprehensive index available to the legal literature of the English-speaking world. It provides subject, author, case name and statute name access to over 700 journals from the major nations of the common-law tradition. All material of permanent reference value from each journal is indexed. Special article types covered include case notes, book reviews, columns, letters, obituaries and editorials. Non-analytical reports and digests of cases, minor personnel notes, association announcements, and non-essential news items are excluded. The *Index* provides access to valuable information for both the legal professional and all researchers who wish to investigate the legal aspects of any topic. For legal professionals, *LRI* provides access to information on developing legal trends, extensive background information necessary to become acquainted with unfamiliar areas of law, and historical analysis of cases. For the business or general researcher, *LRI* provides access to articles that analyse the legal aspects of mergers and acquisitions, taxation, environmental hazards, and issues such as legal ethics and criminal justice.

Georgia law on disc (Michie Company) contains the Official Code of Georgia (annotated), Georgia rules of court (annotated), Georgia Supreme Court decisions since January 1937, and Georgia Court of Appeals decisions since January 1945, selected federal cases and Georgia attorney-general opinions (July 1994 issue).

Government regulations databank (TES Ltd) is a CD-ROM containing government rules and regulations. *A guide to GATT law and practice*, Vista Inter-Media Corporation, Analysis by WTO of the General Agreement on Tariffs and Trade, with background including history, tables and graphs.

Harvard law review (Data Trace Publishing Company) includes the last 15 years of the *Harvard Law Review* (1981–96), on one fully searchable disc.

HFCA's laws, regulations and manuals (National Technical Information Service) contains all of the legislative and executive authorities that establish the programmes administered by the Health Care Financing Administration. The manuals provide policies and procedures developed for implementation of the mandate given HCFA.

HCFA's laws, regulations, manuals on CD-ROM (Health Care Financing Administration) includes over 20 HCFA programme manuals, related publications and memoranda on Medicare and Medicaid, titles 42 and 45 of the Code of Federal Regulations, and titles 11, 18 and 19 of the Social Security Act.

Health care law and management guide on CD-ROM (CCH Inc) is a guide to state and federal laws and court decisions affecting health-care facilities and attorneys representing them.

HSDB (Health and Safety Database) on CCINFOdisc (Canadian Centre for Occupational Health & Safety) provides information on the toxic effects and environmental health and safety concerns of over 4400 hazardous chemicals. Over 150 different information fields are available; subjects include carcinogenicity and biomedical effects, analytical and monitoring methods, exposure standards and regulations.

Index to foreign legal periodicals (SilverPlatter Information Ltd, UK) is an index to articles appearing in approximately 450 legal journals published worldwide. In-depth coverage is provided of international, comparative and foreign law (Arabic language material excepted). Also analyses the contents of approximately 80 individually published collections of legal essays,

Festschriften and congress reports each year.

Index to legal periodicals (Ovid Technologies Inc) is a collection of current bibliographic information on articles in core legal periodicals in all areas of jurisprudence, including legislation originating in the United States, Puerto Rico, Great Britain, Ireland, Canada, Australia and New Zealand. Features a table of cases, a table of statutes and a listing of book reviews.

LEXDATA plus (Jurinfor) is a companion to *LEXDATA*, a complementary database on Portuguese legislation, and includes the images of all the pages of *Diario De Republica*. Annual discs are currently available from 1980 to 1995.

LEXIS-NEXIS (online), is part of NEXIS, one of the world's largest online libraries of international news and information. It has a collection of full-text databases offering a comprehensive source of electronic information for business, financial, news and market information research. At present there are more than 172 libraries with more than 5600 databases available in NEXIS. *LEXIS* is one of the world's leading online legal research services. It provides access to a comprehensive collection of full-text primary legal source materials. *LEXIS* users have access to millions of pages of law reports, unreported cases and statutory texts, organized in different libraries according to jurisdiction.

New Zealand case law digest (**NZCLD**) (Brooker's Ltd, Wellington), contains a collection of summaries of reported and unreported judgments and decisions of New Zealand courts and tribunals. These are designed to assist in locating and identifying relevant cases.

Ontario family law – electronic (CCH Canadian Ltd) contains commentary on vital family law issues, valuable practice tips, all relevant Ontario and federal statutes and regulations, and rules of court and practice directions. Topics include support, adoption, custody and access, and domestic contracts.

OSHA regulations, documents and technical information on CD-ROM (US Department of Labor) contains the full text of a variety of US Occupational Safety and Health Administration documents, including *Air contaminants* (preamble, standard and Z-tables), *Bloodborne pathogens* (preamble and standard), *Blood lead labs* (OSHA accredited), *Chemical sampling information* and *Consultants* (expert witnesses).

Repertory of Hungarian economic rules of law (HyperMedia Systems Ltd) is an electronic collection of Hungarian regulations. It includes the regulations of business organizations and international relations, including joint venture, financial, banking, taxation, foreign exchange, foreign trade and custom regulations and laws, decrees and regulations concerning official licences and international contracts.

Small business legal pro deluxe CD (Nolo Press) is a reference library for small business owners which contains the complete text of four of Nolo's business books – *The legal guide for starting and running a small business, Tax savvy for small business, The employer's legal handbook* and *Everybody's guide to the Small Claims Court*.

Smart building law (Brooker's Ltd, Wellington) is a database which provides reference material for local authorities and anyone working in the building trade or advising in the building field.

Special education law on CD-ROM (LRP Publications) contains the full text of special education court decisions, SLA decisions, *Education administration online*, OCR letters of findings, OSEP policy rulings, and complete statutes and regulations relating to special education.

Taxation law (Computer Law Services Pty Ltd) contains the *Income Tax Assessment Act 1936 consolidated to date, CLS Australian business taxes, CLS Australian tax transactions, CLS online tax news*, Australian tax office rulings and determinations, Federal and state tax-related case law, Commonwealth and state tax-related legislation and a number of useful indexes.

Tax notes today (TNT) (Dialog file 790) and **State tax today (STT)** (Dialog file 791) are comprehensive daily federal and state tax services published by Tax Analysts. They contain analytical summaries combined with the full text of all important legislative, regulatory, judicial and policy documents regarding US federal and state taxation respectively. All information is updated daily, each business day of the year. Both files provide the most current documents in any specific area of tax law indexed with a controlled list of document types. The news stories contained in both files are written by tax attorneys, tax accountants, public finance economists and journalists on the staff of Tax Analysts. Most documents from the US and state governments appear online within 24 hours of their release.

Tolley's company law link is a database of Great Britain's company law and corporate insolvency information. Expert commentary from *Tolley's company law*'s loose-leaf service on every aspect of company law is combined with the full text of all relevant UK and EU legislation.

US copyrights (Dialog file 120) provides access to registration details for all active copyright and mask-work registrations on file at the US Copyright Office. The database has been designed primarily as a fast screening tool for checking the ownership and registration status of a particular work. It is also useful for checking a particular individual's or entity's portfolio of registered works.

West's legal directory – attorney library (West Group) contains profiles of law firms, branch offices and attorneys from all 50 US states, Puerto Rico, the

Virgin Islands, District of Columbia and Canada. It also includes governmental counsel and corporate counsel, AALS law teachers, international lawyers, *Haver's companion to the bar* and *Simon's European law directory*.

Wilson index to legal periodicals & books (SilverPlatter Information Ltd, UK) indexes articles in 620 leading legal journals, yearbooks, institutes, bar association organs, university publications, law reviews and government publications. It covers banking, constitutional law, criminal law, environmental protection, labour law, landlord/tenant decisions, malpractice suits, public law and politics, securities and antitrust legislation, tax law, estate planning and more.

Wisconsin law on disc (Michie Company) contains Wisconsin statutes, Wisconsin court rules, attorney-general opinions, Wisconsin Supreme Court decisions since 1944, Wisconsin Court of Appeals decisions since August 1978, Wisconsin Supreme Court and Court of Appeals unpublished decisions since 1978 and Wisconsin Acts.

Worldwide tax daily (Dialog file 792) is a daily international tax service from Tax Analysts that provides comprehensive information on US and international developments as well as tax news and documents from over 100 countries. News stories, summaries and full-text documents are included in the file. It also contains over 3000 tax treaties, including the complete set of US tax treaties with supporting documents, and tax spanning most of the 20th century from over 180 countries, plus trade and investment agreements and customs materials. All information is updated each weekday. Most documents are in English, although some foreign language documents are included.

Appendix 5

Selected CD-ROM and online
health information sources

1997 PDR electronic library on CD-ROM (Medical Economics Company) enables users to look up drug-prescribing information by brand name, generic name, manufacturer, therapeutic category, indication or side effect. It includes current editions of *Physicians' desk reference*; *PDR supplements*; *PDR for non-prescription drugs*; *PDR for ophthalmology* and *PDR guide to drug interactions, side effects, indications, contraindications.*

1997 red book – pharmacy's fundamental reference (Medical Economics Company) is the pharmacy's source of product information and prices of prescription drugs. It also offers reference information about patient counselling and clinical information.

ABMS medical specialists plus (Bowker-Saur) lists career and educational histories of over 466,000 specialists in 25 disciplines and 70 sub-specialities. It includes complete career details and contact addresses, and contact information for US and Canadian medical schools.

AIDSLINE (Dialog file 157), produced by the US National Library of Medicine, contains citations to literature covering research, clinical aspects and health policy issues concerning AIDS. The citations are derived from the following databases: *MEDLINE* (file 155), *CANCERLIT* (file 159) and *Health-STAR* (file 151). In addition, the file includes the meeting abstracts from the international conferences on AIDS, the symposia on nonhuman primate modes of AIDS and AIDS-related abstracts from the annual meetings of the American Society of Microbiology. *AIDSLINE* is indexed using NLM controlled vocabulary, MeSH (medical subject headings). Also included in the file is an online thesaurus to aid users in locating MeSH descriptors. Approximately 20,000 records are added per year; over 89% of the articles referred to are in English.

AMA directory of physicians in the United States (American Medical Association) contains listings of US physicians, including non-federal physicians, in military service, government agencies and the US public health service, and those temporarily residing outside the US. Search options include first or last name, city, state, region, type of physician and primary speciality.

AMA family medical guide (Dorling Kindersley Multimedia) is a medical home reference tool with information on today's prominent health issues, such as Alzheimer's disease, AIDS, chronic fatigue syndrome, stress and drug abuse. It features diagnostic symptom charts, and sets of questions to determine the significance of particular symptoms and the level of urgency for medical attention.

Best of diet & health (Rocelco Inc) is a collection of 30 programs, including *Aerobic fitness log*, *Alternative health guide*, *Better diet analyzer*, *Bike pro*, *Deal a meal*, *Diet balancer*, *Diet test*, *Eyesight*, *Fitness log*, *Health stress manager*, *Leaner*, *Managing your food*, *Master meal manager*, *Me & my metabolism*, *MealMate*, *Non medical pain relief*, *Nutrition analyst*, etc.

BiblioMed EMR – essential medical reference (Healthcare Information Services Inc, a division of Lippincott-Raven Publishers) contains the full text of *Physician's GenRx*, the *Merck manual* and *Stedman's dictionary* (25th edition).

Biological abstracts on compact disc (SilverPlatter Information Ltd, UK) contains citations and author-written abstracts to peer-reviewed biological and biomedical research articles published in nearly 6500 journals. It covers basic biological research and field, laboratory, clinical, experimental and theoretical work in every area of the life sciences, including agriculture, biochemistry, biotechnology, ecology, immunology, microbiology, neuroscience, pharmacology, public health and toxicology.

BMA family health encyclopedia (Dorling Kindersley Multimedia) contains information and advice written by doctors and consultants. The disc includes explanations of over 650 diseases and disorders, and guidance on preventive health care. It also features a link to DK's *Online Health Club*.

Body contour – basic health, fitness and body care programme (CD-i) (SPC Group) enables the user to record data including age, weight, gender and heart rate. These figures are stored and interpreted to present users with a graphical representation of their fitness level, and to devise a tailored fitness programme and nutrition from the European perspective, with breakfast, lunch and dinner menus.

Bookscope medical (Primary Source Media and Gale Research) provides bibliographic information in all areas of medical publishing. Chapter headings, contents listings and reviews from specialist journals on English-language medical books may be accessed.

CAB health (SilverPlatter Information Ltd, UK) offers coverage of areas relating to determinants of human health, communicable diseases and their control. Over 11,000 serial sources from 130 countries are scanned for relevant articles. *CAB health* gives in-depth coverage of communicable diseases, tropical diseases, parasitic diseases and parasitology, human nutrition, community and public health, and medicinal and poisonous plants.

CDP-file-health promotion & education database/AIDS school health education database/Cancer prevention & control database (NCCDPHP-CDC) contains chronic disease prevention and health promotion information, records of HIV/AIDS educational materials and educational information on cancer.

ClynPsyc NISC (National Information Services Corporation) is a catalogue of over 780,000 bibliographic records and abstracts of international periodicals on clinical psychology, psychiatry and mental health.

Cumulative index to nursing & allied health literature (CINAHL CD) (SilverPlatter Information Ltd, UK) provides access to virtually all English-language nursing journals. It covers biomedicine, management, behavioural sciences, health sciences librarianship, education and consumer health. It provides references to new books, pamphlets, audiovisuals, dissertations, educational software, selected conference proceedings and standards of professional practice in the nursing and allied health fields.

Cyril & Methodius home encyclopedia of health (Cyril & Methodius) consists of 9 chapters: anatomy, conventional medicine, non-conventional medicine, sexual life, mother and child, health habits, nutrition, hygiene and first aid. It contains over 2500 entries, more than 1500 illustrations and 200 video clips.

Directory of European medical organizations (CBD Research Ltd) contains information about 4100 European medical organizations, including full address, activities, contact names and publications.

DRUGDEX system (Micromedex Inc) provides referenced drug information for health care professionals who prescribe, order, dispense or administer medication. Investigational, international, FDA approved and OTC preparations are included. The system is indexed by US and international brand/trade names, generic names, disease states, dosage, pharmacokinetics, cautions, interactions and clinical applications.

EarthLaw (Information Handling Services Inc) is a complete collection of US environmental and safety regulatory information. It provides access to regulatory and compliance information from the Environmental Protection Agency, Occupational Safety and Health Administration, Public Laws and Regulations, Department of Transportation regulations, Federal Register and

Federal Coast Guard regulations. It also contains states' environmental regulations.

EMBASE (Dialog files 72 and 73) has long been recognized as an important comprehensive index of the world's literature on human medicine and related disciplines. About 400,000 records are added annually, in recent years over 80% of which contain abstracts. Each record is classified and indexed by medical research specialists who assign terms and codes in accordance with EMTREE, a highly developed classification schedule and controlled vocabulary, consisting of over 39,000 terms and nearly 170,000 synonyms. In recent years *EMBASE* has provided access to periodical articles from more than 3300 primary journals from approximately 70 countries. An additional 450 journals are screened for drug articles. File 73 contains records from January 1974 to the present, and file 72 contains records from 1993 to the present. The *EMBASE* database is used to produce 41 print abstract bulletins and one print drug literature bibliography. All journal articles are added to the database within 15 days of the journal's receipt, and all records appear online with complete indexing.

EMBASE alert CD (Elsevier Science BV/Secondary Publishing Division) is a current awareness file on CD-ROM providing access to pharmacological and biomedical literature. *EMBASE alert* emphasizes drugs and pharmacology, toxicology, human medicine, biological sciences relevant to human medicine, psychiatry, public, occupational and environmental health, health policy and management, substance dependence and abuse, forensic science, and biomedical engineering and instrumentation. A CD-ROM version of *EMBASE*, called *EMBASE Alert CD*, is available from Elsevier Science BV.

Environmental chemistry, health and safety – KR OnDisc (Dialog Corporation – Dialog OnDisc) contains information on chemicals that cause actual or potential harm to humans or the environment. Business and legal issues are covered in addition to scientific and technical information.

European Union medical devices library (Information Handling Services Inc) contains all of the documents issued by the European Union relating to the registration and regulation of medical devices.

Family health tracker (Memorex-N-TK, Entertainment Technology, Inc) is a program designed to record the user's medical charts, including prescriptions, blood tests, insurance, dental visits and health, diet and exercise information.

Harvard guide to women's health (Harvard Business School Publishing) is a multimedia title which illustrates health-related issues.

Hazard: health & safety in the workplace (3V Multimedia Computersysteme GmbH) is designed as a modular package which can be used for training, reference and practical activities tailored to the needs of each individual workplace. The trainee is asked to identify potential health risk situations.

Health & drug information library (SilverPlatter Information Ltd, UK) is a collection of full-text patient information covering over 6000 topics. It includes information on infant, child and adolescent health, women's health, adult health and medications, and a number of illustrations to augment the text.

Health & safety/risk abstracts (National Information Services Corporation) includes *Health & Safety Science Abstracts* (1981–present), with regard to aspects of pollution, waste, radiation, pesticides and epidemics, and *Risk Abstracts* (1990–present), encompassing risks arising from industrial, technological, environmental and other sources. Interdisciplinary coverage includes public/environmental health, social issues and psychological aspects.

Health and psychosocial instruments (HaPI) database (Behavioral Measurement Database Services) is a multidisciplinary database on measurement instruments, covering questionnaires, rating scales, interview forms, checklists, vignettes/scenarios, indexes, coding schemes, projective techniques, tests and more. It offers abstracts from journals covering nursing, medicine, public health, psychology, social work, sociology, communication, organizational behaviour, library and information science, and education.

Health care (Educational Activities Inc) is a guide to understanding medical terminology, hospital and home care, safety and emergency procedures, doctors' orders and counselling instructions.

Health source plus (EBSCO Publishing) provides indexing and abstracting for nearly 500 consumer health, nutrition and professional titles, 210 of which are in full text. Coverage was expected to grow to 255 by 1997 along with the full text of five books. The full text of over 500 health pamphlets is included.

Medical devices (Derwent Information Ltd) provides industry-specific engineering information from the world's patent-issuing authorities.

Medical library (TechPool Studios) is a collection of high-resolution photographs of hospitals, patients, doctors, nurses and children in health-care settings (volume 1) and of health-care technology, covering surgery, prescriptions, instruments and procedures (Volume 2).

Medical research centres on CD-ROM (FT Healthcare) includes details on over 8500 medical research centres worldwide. It features full contact details including address, telephone and fax numbers, and current research and development activities.

Medical terminology – the language of health care (Waverly Europe Ltd/Williams & Wilkins Europe Ltd) provides medical students with an interactive terminology database. The courseware is based on the textbook of the same name by Margie E Willis.

MEDLINE (Ovid Technologies Inc, also available through Dialog files 154 and 155), produced by the US National Library of Medicine, is one of the major sources for biomedical literature. *MEDLINE* corresponds to three print indexes: *Index Medicus*, *Index to Dental Literature* and *International Nursing Index*. Additional materials not published in *Index Medicus* are included in the areas of communication disorders, and population and reproductive biology. MEDLINE is indexed using NLM's controlled vocabulary, MeSH. An online thesaurus is available to aid in locating MeSH descriptors. Approximately 400,000 records are added per year, of which more than 85% are in English.

MEDLINE – KR OnDisc (Dialog Corporation – Dialog OnDisc) is a databases of biomedical literature, covering the broad field of biomedicine. *MEDLINE* provides data on toxicology, nutrition, pharmacology, medicine, veterinary medicine, psychiatry, medical engineering and pathology. It includes the current year plus the previous six years, subject contents, indexes and the MesH thesaurus.

Merriam-Webster's medical dictionary (CMC Research Inc) is a guide to health-care terms, abbreviations, medication names and more. Entries include written pronunciations and examples showing how words are used in contemporary medical literature, covering topics from all major fields of medical research and practice, including AIDS research, biochemistry, obstetrics, pharmacology and geriatric medicine.

MICROMEDEX healthcare series (MICROMEDEX Inc) is a library of toxicology, drug therapy, and emergency medicine which comprises the following databases: *POISINDEX* (emergency poison identification and management information), *IDENTIDEX* (tablet and capsule identification), *EMERGINDEX* (emergency and acute care information), *DRUGDEX* (referenced drug information), *TOMES* (industrial medical and hazard information), and *Martindale: the extra pharmacopoeia*.

Mosby's medical abbreviations guide – abbreviations, acronyms, prefixes and suffixes, Greek alphabet, metric system (Mosby-Year Book Inc) contains over 22,000 abbreviations covering medical conditions, drug weights, biological, physical and chemical terms, associations, institutions, and other medical and health-care terms. It also includes approximately 4000 acronyms, 1700 prefixes and suffixes, and over 250 chemical and physical symbols.

Mosby's medical encyclopedia (The Learning Company Inc) provides access to nearly 20,000 medical terms and 1200 illustrations, allowing the user to research symptoms, diseases and treatments. Includes video clips of medical procedures. Features a detailed atlas of human anatomy and a complete guide to prescription and over-the-counter drugs.

National Institute for Occupational Safety and Health (NIOSHTIC), (SilverPlatter Information Ltd, UK) contains citations and abstracts to occupational health and safety literature from more than 400 journals, monographs and technical reports. It covers toxicology, epidemiology, pathology and histology, occupational medicine, health physics, behavioural sciences and hazardous waste.

National Institute for Occupational Safety and Health (NIOSH) pocket guide (MICROMEDEX Inc) contains critical data for approximately 400 chemicals. The information presented includes exposure limits, IDLH concentrations, incompatibilities and reactivities, personal protection and recommendations for respirator selection.

New England journal of medicine (Dialog file 444) contains full-text articles from the print version of the journal (excluding meeting notices, 'Books Received' and advertising content). Founded in 1812, the *NEJM* is the oldest continuously published medical journal in the world. It maintains the largest voluntarily-paid circulation of any peer-reviewed scientific journal, reaching physicians and other health-care professionals in more than 120 countries.

Occupational safety and health (NIOSH) (Dialog file 161) is produced by the Clearinghouse for Occupational Safety and Health, a division of the National Institute for Occupational Safety and Health. It includes citations to more than 400 journal titles, as well as over 70,000 monographs and technical reports, and covers all aspects of occupational safety and health, including such topics as hazardous agents, unsafe workplace environments and toxicology.

OECD health data 1997 (OECD Electronic Editions) is a systematic collation of data on key aspects of the health systems of 29 OECD member countries. The data include approximately 700 series (300,00 statistics) and are accessible interactively.

Pharmaceutical news index (PNI) (Dialog file 42) is the online source of current news about pharmaceuticals, cosmetics, medical devices and related health fields. *PNI* cites and indexes all articles from publications on the following topics: drugs, corporation and industry sales, mergers and acquisitions, and government legislation, regulations and court action. It covers requests for proposals, research grant applications, industry speeches, press releases and other news items.

ProQuest medical library (UMI) is designed for pre-med and nursing schools as well as for health-care professionals. It contains information from all major health-care fields including nursing, paediatrics, neurology, pharmacology, cardiology and physical therapy.

QMR – quick medical reference (First DataBank) is a consultation program providing diagnostic assistance on three levels. It functions as an electronic textbook with over 630 internal-medicine disorders, the diagnostic implications of combinations of diseases, and diagnostic decision-making expertise.

Safety (CD-i) (Mediavision BV) includes games to assist the user to learn about safety in general and safe practices to be employed in industry, at school and at home.

Stedman's concise medical and allied health dictionary (Waverly Europe Ltd/Williams & Wilkins Europe Ltd) features 40,000 entries and over 380 illustrations. It includes all the terms and definitions, a full colour 32-page ADAM anatomy insert and an additional 16-page insert of diagnostic images.

Tobacco & health abstracts (National Information Services Corporation) is a comprehensive overview of tobacco related literature.

TOM health & science (Information Access Company) contains 27 health titles, 29 science titles and the full text from over 20 of the indexed titles taken from a selection of 60 publications.

TOXLINE on CCINFOdisc (Canadian Centre for Occupational Health & Safety) is a set of three CD-ROMs containing over 800,000 references to published material and research in progress in the areas of environmental pollution, reproductive effects of chemicals, food and water contamination, occupational hazards and more.

UK occupational health & safety information service (Information Handling Services Inc) is a compilation of key UK health and safety legislation and regulations. It contains material from the UK Health and Safety Commission, Health and Safety Executive, and Health Education Authority plus relevant British standards, codes of practice, and guidance materials for a range of industrial groups.

Appendix 6

Selected CD-ROM and online standard and patent information sources

ACEL standards index plus (IHS Australia Pty Ltd) is a reference database of all Australian and ASTM standards. Includes title, document history, abstract, referenced documents, scope paragraph, equivalent standards, etc.

APIPAT (American Petroleum Institute Patent Abstracts) (Dialog file 353) provides comprehensive coverage of patents related to the petroleum, petrochemicals, natural gas and energy industries. It corresponds to the following print bulletins of *Patent Abstracts: Petroleum Processes, Petroleum & Specialty Products, Chemical Products, Environment, Transport & Storage, Petroleum Substitutes, Catalysts/Zeolites, Tribology, Reformulated Fuels* and *Oilfield Chemicals*. Coverage is worldwide. Before 1982, coverage was limited to patents issued by the United States, Belgium, Canada, France, West Germany, Great Britain, the Netherlands, Japan, South Africa, the European Patent Office and the World Intellectual Property Organization.

ASME boiler & pressure vessel code (Information Handling Services Inc) contains the full text and graphics of the 1995 *Boiler & pressure vessel code* of the American Society of Mechanical Engineers, including all code sections, tables, charts, equations, code cases, interpretations and referenced ASME standards.

ASTM standards source (American Society for Testing and Materials), contains 10,000 standards for testing methods, definitions, practices and classifications. Coverage includes metals, construction, petroleum products, textiles, paints, plastics, rubber, electrical insulation and electronics, energy sources and medical devices.

Automotive patents profiles on CD-ROM (Derwent Information Ltd) features abstracts of newly patented developments in the automotive industry.

Abstracts, with drawings and diagrams, cover automotive technologies from major manufacturing countries worldwide.

British Standards on CD-ROM (Technical Indexes Ltd) provides complete British Standards on CD-ROM, by special agreement with the BSI. Contains full text with images, divided into 12 sections.

Canadian enviro OSH legislation plus standards (Canadian Centre for Occupational Health & Safety) contains the national edition plus those standards referenced in the legislation.

Chinese patent abstracts in English (Dialog file 344) is produced by the European Patent Office in cooperation with the Patent Documentation Service Centre of the People's Republic of China. The file includes all patents published in the People's Republic of China since the opening of the Chinese Patent Office on 1 April, 1985. Records contain bibliographic information as well as English-language titles and abstracts.

CLAIMS/CITATION (Dialog files 220, 221 and 222) is designed to answer the question of which later patents cite another patent. The files reference over 5 million patent numbers cited in US patents since 1947. Each record includes a US patent number plus patent numbers (both US and non-US) cited to that patent by other US patents. Each quarterly addition to the files also updates the content of the earlier patents. The files can be used as companion files to the other IFI/CLAIMS patent files (see below), since *CLAIMS* patent file records include citation counts giving the number of patents cited. After using the CLAIMS patent file, the *CLAIMS/CITATION* file may be used to retrieve the full list of citing patent numbers. File 222 covers 1971 to the present, file 221 covers 1947 to 1970 and file 220 covers up to 1947.

CLAIMS/US PATENTS (Dialog files 340, 341 and 942), produced by the IFI CLAIMS Patent Services, provides access to over 2.9 million US patents issued by the US Patent and Trademark Office (USPTO) since 1950. The database contains all granted US chemical patents from 1950; mechanical and electrical patents, reissues, defensive publications and statutory invention registrations (SIRs) are included from 1963; design and plant patents are available from December 1976; and from 1971 the *CLAIMS* records include all information found on the front page of US patent documents plus exemplary and non-exemplary claims. Earlier records contain basic bibliographic data and the exemplary claims only. Provisional application data, extracted by Dialog from the full text of US patents, is also included. The *CLAIMS* database is offered in three versions. The basic version (file 340) contains the patent records described above. *CLAIMS/UNITERM* (file 341) and *CLAIMS/COMPREHENSIVE* (file 942) contain the same patent records, but also include in-depth controlled indexing for chemical and chemically significant patents from 1950. File 942 provides enhanced search capabilities. There are several companion files: *CLAIMS/CURRENT PATENT LEGAL STATUS (CLS)* (file 123) covers patent post-issue actions, such as reassignments, extensions, re-examinations and disclaimers; *CLAIMS/REFERENCE* (file 124) contains an online version of the USPTO manual of classification and the general term indexing thesaurus used with files 341 and 942; *CLAIMS/CITATION* (files 220, 221 and 222) provides examiner cited and citing patent numbers; and *CLAIMS/COMPOUND REGISTRY* (file 242) is a dictionary of IFI's chemical compound vocabulary.

Communications standards & architectures (DataPro Information Services Group) presents specifications and analysis of open and proprietary communications standards and architectures.

Derwent world patents index (DWPI) (Dialog files 350, 351, 352 and 280), produced by Derwent Information, provides access to information from more than 18 million patent documents, giving details of over 9 million inventions. Each week approximately 20,000 documents from 40 patent-issuing authorities are added.

Devices standards library (IHS Nordic A/S) contains ISO standards for the medical device industry.

Directory of safety standards, literature and services (Van Nostrand Reinhold) is a resource of state and federal safety standards, emergency contact information and related services.

ENFLEX standards (IHS Environmental Information Inc) contains a graphic image database of environmental, health and safety standards from the American National Standards Institute, American Society of Mechanical Engineers, American Society for Testing and Materials, American Welding Society, Society of Automative Engineers and Underwriters' Laboratories. The user can search by table of contents, society acronym, document number and publication date. Viewing features include zoom, pan, rotate, fit to screen and adjust image.

ESPACE Series on CD-ROM (European Patent Office) provides information on European and other patents. Titles in the series include the following:

ESPACE-Access A: contains bibliographic data taken from the front page of EPO and PCT patent applications, including in the majority of cases an abstract in English. Cross-references are provided to other discs in the *ESPACE* series.

ESPACE-Access B: contains bibliographic data of all granted European patents from 1980 to date, and first claims and citations from 1991 to date.

ESPACE-AT: contains information on all recently published Austrian patent applications.

ESPACE-Benelux: contains patent publications from Belgium, the Netherlands and Luxembourg.

ESPACE-Bulletin: contains legal status data on all European patent applications filed since 1978. Searches can be performed in up to 70 different bibliographic and legal-status data items. It includes cross-references to *ESPACE-EP* and *First*.

ESPACE-CH: contains patent publications from Switzerland.

ESPACE-DK: contains patent publications from Denmark.

ESPACE-EP A Documents: contains, in approximately 1000 entries, facsimile images of the entire European Patent applications and bibliographic data taken from the first page of each document (stored in text format).

ESPACE-EP B Documents: contains all granted European patents from 1980 onwards, with some 1000 complete patent documents in facsimile format including bibliographic data, texts and figures. Searches can be performed in 13 different bibliographic data elements (including International Patent Classification or IPC and document title words).

ESPACE-ES: contains patent publications from Spain.

ESPACE-First: contains some 10,000 first pages of published European patent applications and published PCT international applications, in facsimile format, including bibliographic data, texts and figures. Searches can be performed in 13 different bibliographic data elements (including IPC and document title words).

ESPACE-IT: contains patent publications from Italy.

ESPACE-Legal: contains the complete text of all the decisions (both published and unpublished) of the board of appeals at the EPO. The disc also contains the text of patent conventions, treaties and guidelines as well as facsimile copies of the EPO applicants' forms.

ESPACE-World: contains all published international patent applications filed under the PCT from 1978 onwards, with some 1000 complete applications in facsimile format, including bibliographic data, text and figures. Searches can be performed in 13 different bibliographic data elements (including IPC and document title words).

Eurofile (European legislation & standards) on CD-ROM (Technical Indexes Ltd) is the reference source to all documentation required for 1992 and beyond. Eurofile provides full-text information vital for companies producing or marketing goods within Europe.

European patents fulltext (Dialog file 348) covers all European patent applications and granted European patents published since the opening of the European Patent Office (EPO) in 1978, and bibliographic records for PCT (Patent Cooperation Treaty) applications transferred to the EPO.

French patents (Dialog file 371) covers all French patent applications and granted French patents published by the Institut national de la propriété industrielle (INPI). All patents published in France since 1966, as well as all special pharmaceutical patents (*brevets spéciaux médicaments*) published between 1961 and 1978, are included. Records include bibliographic, administrative and legal status data for each patent. Abstracts and descriptors are also available since 1978. All records are in French, but English descriptors are available from 1987. Several display formats provide field labels in English.

IHS communications standards library (Information Handling Services Inc) is a collection of technical standards for defining and regulating the communications industries. It is indexed and cross-referenced.

INPADOC/family and legal status database (Dialog file 345), produced by the European Patent Office, contains a listing of patents issued in 66 countries and patenting organizations. The International Patent Documentation Center (INPADOC) was formed in 1972 with the support of the World Intellectual Property Organization to provide a centralized bibliographic source for patent documents. INPADOC is now part of the European Patent Information and Documentation System operated by the EPO. The Dialog version of the INPADOC database is unique in that it brings together patent families, ie all equivalent patents that share common priorities for a particular invention. The patent families contain information on over 40 million patents and 42 million legal status actions. Each family record contains bibliographic data consisting of title, inventor and assignee for most patents, patent and application data, and legal-status information, if available. The database brings together information on priority application numbers, countries and dates. Legal-status information is provided for 22 countries.

JAPIO database (Dialog file 347), provided by the Japan Patent Information Organization, represents the most comprehensive English-language access to Japanese unexamined patent applications (Kokai Tokkyo Koho) published since October 1976. All technologies are covered. Application records include both Japanese and non-Japanese priorities. Abstracts are provided only for applications originating in Japan, but are available for most records. Images of front page drawings, when available for a given patent, are also included.

Patents ASSIGN (US Patent & Trademark Office) includes assignments recorded at the USPTO from August 1980 to the present. The entire assignment record for a patent may be searched, including assignments made before and after the patent was issued.

Patents ASSIST (US Patent & Trademark Office) includes a patentee-assignee file showing assignments at time of issue for utility patents since 1969, for other types of patents since 1977 and for inventors since 1975. It also includes the attorney roster file, an index to the US patent classification *Manual of classification*, *Manual of patent examining procedure* and other search tools.

Patents BIB (US Patent & Trademark Office) contains bibliographic information for utility patents issued from 1969 to the present, and for other patent documents issued from 1977. It includes the year of issue, the state/country of the inventor's residence, the assignee at the time of issue, and title, status and abstracts for the last 25 years.

Patents international (IMSWorld Publications Ltd) is a reference source for drug patents giving an evaluated analysis of the patent position for more than 1100 drugs. Analysis of a company's patent portfolio, a country, a therapy class or a drug are all possible. It includes details of SPCs, CCPs, drug status and marketing exclusivity.

Patents preview + specifications (Derwent Information Ltd) covers new drugs made public for the first time through the patent offices in France, Germany, Japan, USA and the UK, and the Patent Cooperation Treaty and European Patent Office. Users can search on enhanced title, bibliographic data, structure, abstract and pharmaceutical data fields.

PatentScan (Derwent Information Ltd) contains all patents issued by the USPTO between 1974 and 1994. It contains US and non-US patent and journal citations from the PTO examiners' search report.

PatentView (Derwent Information Ltd) provides complete United States patents available in full chemical, electrical and general/mechanical engineering versions.

PATOS text (1980–1990) (Wila Verlag Wilh. Lampl GmbH) contains bibliographic information and main claims of German patent applications, patents granted since 1980 and utility models since 1983.

SAE publications & standards database on CD-ROM (SAE International Electronic Publishing) contains bibliographic references of all texts published by the Society of Automotive Engineers between 1906 and 1996. Also provides information on articles published in SAE magazines (*Automotive Engineering*, *Truck Engineering* and *Aerospace Engineering*) from 1990 to 1995).

Standards CD-ROM (InfoMagic Inc) is a collection of domestic and international communications standards and documentation. It covers CCITT/ITU networking, telecommunications and data communications standards including the ISO X series, ISDN, SS7 and modem character encoding. Internet materials include complete IENs and RFCs, Netinfo directories and templates, network resource guide, IETF and IESG minutes and charters.

Telecomm standards collection (Information Handling Services Inc) contains standards from ANSI, IEEE, ISO, EIA and ITU (CCITT/CCIR) for telecommunications professionals involved in signal transmission, plant construction, network design and equipment manufacturing.

UK defence standards (IHS Nordic A/S) includes coverage of all unclassified MoD documents since 1992. The CD-ROM is produced in agreement with the British Ministry of Defence.

US patents fulltext (Dialog files 652, 653 and 654) provides access to the complete text of all patents issued by the USPTO since 1974, with partial coverage of selected technologies from 1971 to 1973. Each record contains all front-page information, including title, author(s), assignee(s), related applications, classification data, cited references and abstract. The complete text of the original patent usually includes a description of drawings (but not the actual drawings), the background/field of invention, a brief summary of the invention, the detailed description/embodiment of the invention, examples and all claims. Additional post-issuance legal-status information is supplied by IFI/Plenum Data Corporation for patents that have been reassigned, re-examined, granted an extension beyond the normal 17/20-year period, expired prior to the normal 17/20-year period, or reinstated after late payment of the maintenance fee.

US PatentSearch (MicroPatent LLC, USA) contains three or more years of patents on each CD-ROM, searchable by patent number, abstract, title, exemplary claim, date of issue, inventor, application number and others.

USAPat (US Patent & Trademark Office) includes facsimile images of patents issued weekly from the USPTO. The database is searchable by patent number only.

Worldwide standards service (Information Handling Services Inc) provides information on over 290,000 standards from approximately 440 standards-developing bodies from around the world; it contains a comprehensive summary of every document included in the service, as well as full-text standards from many organizations.

Some Internet sites with standards information

AFNOR (*Association française de normalization*): **http://www.afnor.fr/english/welcome.htm**

ANSI (American National Standards Institute): **http://www.ansi.org**

ASTM (American Society for Testing and Materials): **http://www.astm.org**

BSI (British Standards Institution) and its electronic standards catalogue: **http://www.bsi.org.uk**

CEN (European Committee for Standardization): **http://www.cenorm.be/)**

DIN (*Deutsches Institut für Normung*) catalogue and order-placement: **http://www.din.de**

ETSI (European Telecommunications Standards Institute): **http://www.esti.fr/**

IEC (International Electrotechnical Commission): **http://www.iec.ch**

IEEE (Institute of Electrical and Electronics Engineers) standards products catalogue: **http://standards.ieee.org/catalog/index.html**

ISO (International Organization for Standardization) and the ISO catalogue: **http://www.iso.ch**

ITU (International Telecommunication Union): **http://www.itu.int**

NEMA (National Electrical Manufacturers Association): **http://www.nema.org**

NSSN: A National Resource for Global Standards offers a free basic search and enhanced search subscription: **http://www. Nssn.org**

SAE (Society of Automotive Engineers): **http://www.sae.org**

SCC (Standards Council of Canada) national standards search system: **http://www.scc.ca/search-front/index.html**

WSSN (World Standards Service Network): **http://www.wssn.net/wssn/**

Some patent information on the Internet

Canadian trade-marks database: **http://strategis.ic.gc/**

CIPO's Canadian patent database: access to over 75 years of patent descriptions and images from more than 1.4 million patent documents **http://patents1.ic.gc.ca/intro-e.html**

Esp@cenet via the European Patent Office: **http://ep/espacenet.com/** (see p. 213).

IBMs patent server: **http://www.patents.ibm.com/** (see p. 211)

Registered patents and trade-marks agents (Canadian Intellectual Property Office): **http://napoleon.ic.gc.ca/cipo/agentdb.nsf/**

USPTO patent database provides full-text and bibliographic patent information for patents granted since 1976: **http://patents.uspto.gov/**

USPTO trademark database: **http://www.uspto.gov/tmdb/index.html**

Appendix 7

Government, regional, international, statistical and leisure information sources

African studies on CD-ROM (National Information Services Corporation) is an anthology of 5 CD-ROM databases providing access to multidisciplinary information on Africa. It includes: *Africa Institute*, *The Southern African database*, *School of Oriental and African Studies*, *Bibliography on contemporary African politics and development* and *International library of African music*.

American housing survey – national core and supplement 1989, 1991 and 1993 (US Bureau of the Census, MC1921) provides data on the year, structure, type and number of living quarters, occupancy status, access, number of rooms, property value, kitchen and plumbing facilities, type of heating fuel used, source of water, sewage property, housing expenses and government assistance for heating and cooling costs or other energy-related services.

Commonwealth (Government of Australia) managers' toolbox (Australian Department of Finance) is a consolidated library of procedural and legislative manuals commonly used in the daily operations of the Australian public service, covering personnel management, finance, security, asset management, and so on.

Dissertation abstracts online (Dialog file 35) is a definitive subject, title and author guide to virtually every American dissertation accepted at an accredited institution since 1861. Selected master's theses have been included since 1962. Since 1988 the database has included citations for dissertations from 50 British universities that have been collected and filmed by the British Library Document Supply Centre.

Enviroline (Dialog file 40) (Congressional Information Service Inc) covers the world's environmental information. It provides indexing and abstracting coverage of more than 1000 international primary and secondary publications reporting on all aspects of the environment. These publications highlight such fields as management, technology, planning, law, political science, economics, geology, biology and chemistry as they relate to environmental issues.

Foodline: international market data (Dialog file 54) (Leatherhead Food Research Association) gives detailed analyses of international food and drink markets, identifying key market players, highlighting new-product launches, assessing consumer attitudes and retail trends, and tracking company news. The database serves as an ideal quick reference source for key market and company data, such as market values and volumes, market shares, advertising expenditures, production and trade figures, and retailing and packaging trends. It has extensive coverage of international markets, including the United Kingdom, mainland Europe, North America, Australia, and the Pacific Rim, as well as emerging markets in South America, Eastern Europe, and the Far East. All food and drink product groups are covered, including both branded and own label products, as well as reports on speciality food sectors, alcoholic beverages, pet foods, fresh produce, and food additives.

Government contracts library (West Group) gives details of federal statutes and regulations, federal administrative agency rulings, judicial decisions and treatise materials.

Government regulations databank (TES Ltd) is a CD-ROM containing government rules and regulations.

GPO access is a service of the US Government Printing Office that provides free electronic access to a wealth of important information products produced by the federal government. The information provided on this site is the official published version, and the information retrieved can be used without restriction, unless otherwise noted.

GPO monthly catalog of US government publications (MoCat) (USGPO) contains cataloguing and indexing records for US federal publications, subscriptions, posters, maps and electronic products from all three branches of the federal government, independent agencies, government corporations, boards, commissions and committees. It identifies publications distributed through the Federal Depository Library Program as well as government publications submitted to the GPO.

The GPO (Government Printing Office) publications reference file (Dialog file 166) indexes GPO public documents currently for sale, as well as forthcoming and recently out-of-print publications. These publications are produced by the legislative and executive branches of the US federal government. This file is used to identify, verify, or select GPO publications for purchase. The information provided includes availability, price and stock number.

International financial statistics (IFS) (International Monetary Fund) is a standard source of international statistics on all aspects of international and domestic finance, published monthly. It reports, for most countries of the world, current data needed in the analysis of problems of international payments and of inflation and deflation, ie data on exchange rates, international liquidity, international banking, interest rates, prices, production, international transactions, government accounts, and national accounts. Information is presented in country tables and in tables of area and world aggregates.

ITU-T recommendations (CCITT) (International Telecommunications Union) contains fully searchable indexed ITU-T recommendations, which constitute the basis for international telecommunication standards. Developed by the Telecommunication Standardization Sector, these are the results of studies on technical, operating and tariff questions with the objective of standardizing telecommunications on a worldwide basis.

Occupational safety and health (NIOSH) (Dialog file 161), produced by the Clearinghouse for Occupational Safety and Health, a division of the National Institute for Occupational Safety and Health, includes citations to more than 400 journal titles, and over 70,000 monographs and technical reports. *NIOSH* covers all aspects of occupational safety and health, including such topics as hazardous agents, unsafe workplace environment and toxicology.

OECD international trade by commodities statistics (OECD Electronic Editions) presents the imports and exports of OECD member countries (in US$ and volume), broken down by commodity and by partner country.

Rubicon – Canadian federal government profiles (Canadian Government Publishing) provides access to the 1996 federal government telephone directories for the National Capital and Pacific regions and National Defence updated to May 15, 1996, the most recent 1995 version for the Ontario, Central, Quebec and Atlantic regions, the entire Open Bidding Service subscriber database and information for over 28,000 companies.

Singapore trade connection (Singapore Trade Development Board) includes external trade statistics and a monthly digest of statistics. Data are available on over 6000 companies in various industries and sectors. It also provides useful economic and trade-related information on various countries.

Statistical yearbook (United Nations Statistics Division, 43rd issue, 1999) provides economic and social statistics for over 200 countries and areas around the world. The content of the *SYB-CD* CD-ROM is largely based on the print version of the yearbook. It contains series covering, in general, 1980 to

1996 or 1997, and presents the statistics available to the Statistics Division up to 30 September 1998. Main areas covered include: population and social statistics; national accounts; finance; labour force, wages and prices; agriculture, mining and manufacturing; transport and communications; energy, environment and land use; science and technology; international trade and tourism; balance of payments; and development assistance.

TREND (Time series retrieval and dissemination) (Department of Statistics, Singapore) is a time series database that covers a wide range of statistics on the economic, demographic and social characteristics of Singapore. Data are included on Singapore's national accounts, balance of payments, labour, public finance, business expectations, and housing and construction.

US Census Bureau (http://www.census.gov). This site is an excellent provider of timely, relevant and quality data about the people and economy of the United States.

US Government: – the first 200 years (CLEARVUE/eav) is a two-disc exploration, with interactive multimedia programs, of the changes in US government through its first 200 years. Users can learn about the relative power of each branch of government, and how these relationships have shifted over time.

World competitiveness yearbook 1999 (International Institute for Management Development) is a CD-ROM version of the book *World competitiveness yearbook*. 'It ranks nations' environments and analyzes their ability to provide an environment in which enterprises can compete.' Altogether 47 economies are covered, using 288 different criteria. Two-thirds of the data in this title are taken from international, regional and country statistics, and the rest from an executive survey of 4160 respondents.

World data 1995: World Bank indicators on CD-ROM is the most comprehensive package of statistics and analyses the World Bank has ever produced, with the convenience of being on CD-ROM. It provides economic indicators on 209 countries. Economic information on each country can be searched from the *Time series* database and *Country report* database.

World factbook 1996 & handbook of international economic statistics 1996 (NTIS) (Microinfo Ltd) is a reference service for 267 nations and other entities; it includes maps. The *Handbook of international economic statistics* 1996 provides basic worldwide statistics for comparing the economic performance of major countries and regions.

World trade analyzer (1980–1996) (International Trade Division of Statistics, Canada) provides detailed annual information about imports and exports amongst all the major trading countries in the world.

Worldwide government & defense directory (Dialog Corporation – Dialog

OnDisc) is a complete guide to members of government in 195 countries. It provides names and contact details of key personnel in the legislative branches of government and the diplomatic community, as well as in the military and defence establishments. It includes biographies of heads of state and ministers in every government.

Yearbook of international organizations plus (K G Saur Verlag GmbH & Co) combines both the *Yearbook of international organizations* and *Who's who in international organizations*, including information about the range, activities and key personnel of more than 32,000 international organizations active in over 225 countries.

Leisure and entertainment information sources

Best of sports games (Rocelco Inc) is a collection of over 30 games including 1994 pool, 3 point basketball, 4D boxing, body blow, caddieshack golf, defense football, darts, digital downs, digital league baseball, epic baseball, NHL hockey, PGA tour golf, shooting gallery, tennis 3D and others.

FIFA football rules (Scottish Council for Educational Technology) provides a guide to the rules and regulations of football.

Film index international (Chadwyck-Healey Ltd) is a resource for information on entertainment films and movie personalities. It contains key details of over 90,000 films released up until the end of 1991. Search options include title, date, director and content. The product includes references to thousands of periodical articles.

Fodors.com previously *Fodor's travel online*, makes the information in Fodor's guides available on the web (**http://www.fodors.com/**), and provides users with travel tips and links (see p. 225).

Fodor's interactive sports and adventure vacations (Ledge Multimedia) is an interactive travel-planner guide which includes 500 holidays to choose from, with 30 different sports and adventure categories, 30 minutes of action video, more than 1000 colour photographs and over 500 maps covering the USA (including Alaska and Hawaii).

Lonely Planet online (**http://www.lonelyplanet.com/**): see p. 225.

Magill's survey of cinema (Dialog file 299) contains comprehensive full-text articles on over 1800 notable films, as well as brief entries, consisting of an abstract and credit listing for hundreds of other films. It is the online version of Salem Press's annual, multi-volume print reference set. The full-text listings include film title, release date, country of origin, extensive cast and credit listings, colour/black and white indicator, abstract, critical essay, citations to noteworthy reviews, list of significant awards, qualitative rating and running time.

Olympia: 2800 years of athletic games (Finatec SA) covers extensively the Olympic Games and sports in Ancient Greece, and follows the history of athleticism from prehistory to the modern revival of the Games in Paris in 1896. The last chapter looks briefly at the modern Olympic Games.

Result – the BBC sports quiz (BBC Multimedia) features over 3000 questions.

Sports illustrated almanac (Memorex-N-TK, Entertainment Technology Inc) in its 1995 edition uses 30 minutes of video, colour photographs and reporting to look at the year's sporting action. It also has 500 trivia questions.

Sport & leisure (Digital Stock Corporation) is a collection of royalty-free stock photography for advertising, graphic design, pre-press use, multimedia and publishing.

SPORTDiscus (Dialog file 48) is a bibliographic database, international in scope, covering all aspects of sport, fitness, recreation and related fields. Articles from more than 2000 sport-related journals, monographs, articles on books, theses and CD-ROMs in English, French and other languages are indexed for inclusion. The Sport Information Resource Centre (SIRC), the database provider, is the largest resource centre in the world collecting and disseminating information in the area of sport, physical education, physical fitness and sports medicine.

SportsLine.com (**http://www.sportsline.com/**). The company SportsLine.com was established in 1994, and since then has become a unique online information provider for all types of sporting activities.

Travel & Leisure's guide to the great cities of Europe (The Learning Company Inc, HQ) is a travel guide exploring 15 European cities. It is connected electronically to up-to-date information.

References

Aitchison, J (1992) Indexing languages and indexing. In Dossett, P (ed) *Handbook of special librarianship and information work*, 6th edn, Aslib, 191–233.

Aitchison, J and Gilchrist, A (1997) *Thesaurus construction and use: a practical manual*, 3rd edn, Aslib.

Allott, A M (1992) Standards, technical regulations and codes of practice: an overview. In Dossett, P (ed) *Handbook of special librarianship and information work*, 6th edn, Aslib, 95–122.

American Library Association (1989) *American Library Association Presidential Committee on Information Literacy: final report*, American Library Association.

Anderson, C R (1998) Proactive reference, *Reference & User Services Quarterly*, **38** (2), 139–40.

Anderson, S (1998) A new horizon: an evaluation of a library online public access catalogue, *Library and Information Research News*, **22** (72), 15–24.

Ashton, J (1998) Development of the British Library's OPAC 97: the value of a user-centred approach, *Program*, **32** (1), 1–24.

Balay, R (1996) *Guide to reference books*, 11th edn, American Library Association.

Bekiares, S E and Mallory, M (1995) Government documents and statistics sources. In Bopp, R E and Smith, L C (eds), *Reference and information services: an introduction*, 2nd edn, Libraries Unlimited, 556–605.

Blunt, A (1980) *Law librarianship*, K G Saur.

Booker, D (ed) (1995) *The learning link: information literacy in practice*, Auslib Press.

Books in print on disc. CD-ROM. New Providence, USA, R R Bowker. Annual.

Booth, A and Walton, G (2000) *Managing knowledge in health services*, Library Association Publishing.

Bopp, R E (1995) History and varieties of reference services. In Bopp, R E and Smith, L C (eds), *Reference and information services: an introduction*, 2nd edn, Libraries Unlimited, 3–35.

Bopp, R E and Smith, L C (eds) (1995) *Reference and information services: an introduction*, 2nd edn, Libraries Unlimited.

Borgman, C (1996) Why are online catalogs still hard to use? *Journal of the American Society for Information Science*, **47** (7), 493–503.

Borgman, C (1999) What are digital libraries? Competing visions, *Information Processing and Management*, **35**, 227–43.

Bradley, P (1999) *The advanced Internet searcher's handbook*, Library Association Publishing.

Braun, E E (ed) (1998) *Gale directory of databases*, vol 1, Online databases; Vol 2, CD-ROM, diskette, magnetic tape, handheld, and batch access database products, Gale.

British Standards Institution (1985) *Guidelines for the establishment and development of multilingual thesauri*, BS 6723.

British Standards Institution (1987) *Guidelines for the establishment and development of monolingual thesauri*, BS 5723.

Bruce, C S (1997) *The seven faces of information literacy*, Auslib Press.

Burke, M E and Hall, H (1998) *Navigating business information sources: a practical guide for information managers*, Library Association Publishing.

Burtler, F P (1999) *Business research sources: a reference navigator*, McGraw-Hill.

California Media and Library Educators Association (1994) *From library skills to information literacy: a handbook for the 21st century*, Hi Willow Research and Publishing.

Carter, C E and Bordeianu, S (1999) The real world of integrating electronic resources into a web OPAC, *Serials Librarian,* **36** (3/4), 455–60.

Chalcraft, A, Prytherch, R and Willis, S (1998) *Walford's guide to reference material*, 7th edn, Vol 3, Generalia, language and literature, the arts, Library Association Publishing.

Childers, T (1983) Information and referral: public libraries, Ablex.

Chowdhury, G G (1999a) Internet and information retrieval research, *Journal of Documentation*, **55** (2), 209–25.

Chowdhury, G G (1999b) *Introduction to modern information retrieval*, Library Association Publishing.

Chowdhury, G G and Chowdhury, S (1999) Digital library research: major issues and trends, *Journal of Documentation*, **55** (4), 409–48.

Chowdhury, G G and Chowdhury, S (2000) An overview of the information retrieval features of twenty digital libraries, *Program*, **34** (4), 341–73.

Commonwealth Universities Yearbook, Association of Commonwealth Universities, 1958 – Annual.

Cousins, S (1999) Virtual OPACs versus union database: two models of union catalogue provision, *Electronic Library,* **17** (2), 97–103.

Cronin, B (1998) Information professionals in the digital age, *International Information and Library Review*, **30** (1), 37–50.

Daniells, L M (1993) *Business information*, 3rd edn, University of California Press.

Davenport, E, Goldenberg, A and Procter, R (1997) Distributed expertise: remote reference service on a metropolitan area network, *Electronic Library,* **15** (4), 271–8.

Day, A and Walsh, M (2000) *Walford's guide to reference material*, 8th edn, Vol 2, Social and historical sciences, philosophy and religion, Library Association Publishing.

Dewey for Windows: the CD-ROM version of the Dewey Decimal Classification, 21st edn, OCLC, 1996.

Diaz, K R (ed) (1997) *Reference sources on the Internet: off the shelf and onto the Web*, Haworth Press.

Dunsire, G (1999) Bringing it all back home: retrieval and access for the global information society, *International Cataloguing and Bibliographic Control,* **28** (1), 13–14.

Eisenberg, M B, Berkowitz, R E (1990) *Information problem-solving: the big six skills approach to library and information skills instruction*, Ablex.

Encyclopedias, atlases and dictionaries (1995) Bowker.

Europa world year book (1989–) Europa.

Ferguson, C D and Bunge, C A (1997) The shape of services to come: values-based versus reference service for the largely digital library, *College & Research Libraries,* **58** (3), 252–65.

Forrester, W H. and Rowlands, J L (1999) *The online searcher's companion*, Library Association Publishing.

Fox, E A (1999) Digital libraries initiative (DLI) projects 1994–1999, *Bulletin of the American Society for Information Science*, 7–11.

Griffin, S M (1997) Digital libraries and the NSF/DARPA/NASA Digital Libraries Initiative. In Raitt, D (ed) *Libraries for the new millennium: implications for managers*, Library Association Publishing, 124–47.

Griffin, S M (1999) Digital Libraries Initiative – phase 2: fiscal year 1999 awards, *D-Lib Magazine*, **5** (7/8), available at
http://www.dlib.org/dlib/july999/07griffin.html [visited 3.12.99].

Grogan, D (1979) *Practical reference work*, Clive Bingley.

Hanson, T (1998a) Managing current awareness services. In Hanson, T and Day, J (eds), *Managing the electronic library: a practical guide for information professionals*, Bowker-Saur, 623–37.

Hanson, T (1998b) Overview: managing reference and information services. In Hanson, T and Day, J (eds), *Managing the electronic library: a practical guide for information professionals*, Bowker-Saur, 335–56.

Hanson, T and Day, J (eds) (1994) *CD-ROM in libraries: management issues*, Bowker.

Heartsill, Y (ed) (1983) *The ALA glossary of library and information science*, American Library Association.

Heckert, R J (1998) Machine help and human help in the emerging digital library, *College & Research Libraries*, **59** (3), 250–9.

Hildreth, C R (1988) Online library catalogues as IR systems: what can we learn from research? In Yates Mercer, P A (ed) *Future trends in information science and technology*, Taylor Graham, 9–25.

Holm, L A (1999) ONE project – results and experiences, *International Cataloguing and Bibliographic Control,* **28** (1), 29–33.

Hoskisson, T (1997) Making the right assumptions: know your user and improve the reference interview, *Reference Librarian*, **59**, 67–75.

Hutingford, J (1998) The impact of IMPEL, *Ariadne*, **13**, available at **http://www.ariadne.ac.uk/issue13/impel** [visited 10.12.98].

INNOVAcorp, *Standards information*, available at **http://www.innovacorp.ns.ca/infosvcs/stand.htm**

International Organization for Standardization (1985) *Guidelines for the establishment and development of multilingual thesauri*, ISO 5964.

International Organization for Standardization (1986) *Guidelines for the establishment and development of monolingual thesauri*, ISO 2788.

Jahoda, G and Braunagel, J S (1980) *The librarian and reference queries: a systematic approach*, Academic Press.

Jennerich, E Z and Jennerich, E J (1997) *The reference interview as a creative art*, 2nd edn, Libraries Unlimited.

Katz, W A (1997) *Introduction to reference work, 7th edn, Vol 1: Basic reference sources; Vol 2: Reference services and reference processes*, McGraw-Hill.

Kennedy, S D (1998) *Best bet Internet: reference and research when you don't have time to mess around*, American Library Association.

Kister, K F (1994) *Kister's best encyclopedias*, 2nd edn, Oryx Press.

Kopak, R W and Cherry, J M (1998) Bibliographic displays and web catalogues: user evaluations of three prototype displays, *Electronic Library,* **16** (5), 309–23.

Kumar, L (1999) *Gale directory of databases*, Vol 1, Online databases; Vol 2, CD-ROM, diskette, magnetic tape, handheld, and batch access databases products, Gale.

Large, A and Behesti, J (1997) OPACS: a research review, *Library and Information Science Research*, **19**, 111–33.

Large, A, Tedd, L A and Hartley, R J (1999) *Information seeking in the online age:*

principles and practice, Bowker-Saur.

Lea, P W and Day, J (eds) (1996) *The reference sources handbook*, 4th edn, Library Association Publishing.

Lesk, M (1999) Perspectives on DLI-2: growing the field, *D-Lib Magazine*, **5** (7/8), available at
http://www.dlib.org/dlib/july99/07lesk.html [visited 3.12.99].

Library of Congress (1998) *Subject headings list*, 21st edn, Library of Congress.

Mambretti, C (1998) CD-*ROM technology: a manual for librarians and educators*, McFarland & Company.

Marcaccio, K Y (ed) (1989) *Computer-readable databases: a directory and data-sourcebook*, 5th edn, Gale Research.

Marchionini, G and Fox, E (1999) Editorial: Progress toward digital libraries: augmentation through integration, *Information Processing and Management*, **35**, 219–25.

Marland, M (ed) (1981) *Information skills in the secondary curriculum: the recommendations of a working group sponsored by the British Library and the Schools Council*, Methuen Educational.

Matson, L D and Bonski, D J (1997) Do digital libraries need librarians?, *Online*, **21** (6), 87–92.

Meyyappan, N and Chowdhury, G G (2000) A review of the status of twenty digital libraries, *Journal of Information Science*, **26** (5), 331–48.

Mullay, M and Schlicke, P (1999) *Walford's guide to reference material*, 8th edn, Vol 1, Science and technology, Library Association Publishing.

Multimedia and CD-ROM directory on CD-ROM (1998) 20th edn, Waterlow New Media Information.

Neelameghan, A and Tocatlian, J (1987) Egypt: national information policy: establishment of a national information policy and strategy for its implementation, UNESCO, (FMR/PGI/103).

Oppenheim, C and Smithson, D (1999) What is the hybrid library?, *Journal of Information Science*, **25** (2), 97–112.

Pillow, L (1997) Patent resources on the Internet: a reference librarian's guide. In Diaz, K R (ed) *Reference sources on the Internet: off the shelf and onto the Web*, Haworth Press, 45–9.

Pinfield, S, Eaton, J, Edwards, C, Russell, R, Wissenburg, A and Wynne, P (1998) Realizing the hybrid library, *D-Lib Magazine*, October, available at
http://www.dlib.org/dlib/october98/10pinfield.html [visited 3.12.99].

Poulter, A, Tseng, G and Sargent, G (1999) *The library and information professional's guide to the world wide web*, Library Association Publishing.

Pruett, N J (1986) *Scientific and technical libraries*, Vol 2, Special formats and subject area, Academic Press.

Prytherch, R (1995) *Harrod's librarians' glossary*, 8th edn, Gower.

Rader, H R (1995) User education and information literacy for the next decade: an international perspective. 61st IFLA General Conference, Istanbul, August 20–25, 1995.

Rasmussen, E (1999) Libraries and bibliographical systems. In Baeza-Yates, R and Ribeiro-Neto, B, *Modern information retrieval*, ACM Press, 397–413.

Rothstein, S (1953) The development of the concept of reference service in American libraries, 1850–1900, *Library Quarterly*, **23**, 7–8.

Rowlands, I and Bawden, D (1999) Building the digital library on solid research foundations. *Aslib Proceedings*, **51** (8), 275–82.

Rowley, J (1992) *Organizing knowledge: an introduction to information retrieval*, 2nd edn, Gower.

Rowley, J (1997) The evaluation of interface design on CD-ROMs, *Online and CD-ROM Review*, **21** (1), 3–11.

Rowley, J (1998) The changing face of current awareness services, *Journal of Librarianship and Information Science,* **30** (3), 177–83.

Rowley, J (1999) *The electronic library*, 4th edn, Library Association Publishing.

Rusbridge, C (1998) Towards the hybrid library, *D-Lib Magazine*, July/August, available at
http://www.dlib.org/dlib/july98/rusbridge/07rusbridge.html [visited 3.12.99].

Saffady, W (1992) *Optical storage technology 1992: a state of the art review*, Meckler.

Schnell, E H (1997) Health and medicine. In Diaz, K (ed) *Reference sources on the Internet: off the shelf and onto the Web*, Haworth Press, 215–22.

Scott, J and Wootliff, V (1992) Business and commercial information. In Dossett, P (ed) *Handbook of special librarianship and information work*, 6th edn, Aslib.

Shelfer, K M (ed) (1997) *Business reference services and sources: how end users and librarians work together*, Haworth Press.

Sibley, J (1992) Patents and trade marks. In Dossett, P (ed) *Handbook of special librarianship and information work*, 6th edn, Aslib, 65–94.

Smith, L (1995) Selection and evaluation of reference sources. In Bopp, R E and Smith, L C (eds) *Reference and information services: an introduction*, Libraries Unlimited, 293–314.

Smith, T R (1996) The meta-information environment of digital libraries, *D-Lib Magazine*, July/August, available at
http://www.dlib.org/dlib/july96/new/07smith.html [visited 8.12.98].

Spitzer, K L, Eisenberg, M B and Lowe, C A (1998) *Information literacy: essential skills for the information age*, ERIC Clearinghouse on Information Technology, Syracuse University.

Statesman's yearbook, Macmillan Press, Annual, 1864–

Steele, C (1997) Managing change in digital structures. In Raitt, D (ed) *Libraries for the new millennium: implications for managers*, Library Association, 148–68.

Su, S-F (1994) Dialogue with an OPAC: how visionary was Swanson in 1964?, *Library Quarterly*, **64**, 130–61.

Sutton, E D and Holt, L E (1995) The reference interview. In Bopp, R E and Smith, L C (eds) *Reference and information services: an introduction*, 2nd edn, Libraries Unlimited, 36–54.

Sutton, S A (1996) Future service models and the convergence of functions: the reference librarian as technician, author and consultant, *Reference Librarian*, **54**, 125–43.

Svengalis, K F (1991) Cost-effective acquisitions: an overview. In Mersky, R M and Leiter, R A, *The spirit of law librarianship: a reader*, Fred B. Rothman, 197–217.

Tedd, L A (1995) The changing face of CD-ROM, *Journal of Documentation*, **51** (2), 85–8.

Tennat, R (1998) The most important management decision: hiring staff for the new millennium, *Library Journal*, **123** (3), 102.

Ulrich's international periodicals directory, CD-ROM, Silver Platter Information Ltd.

UNISIST guidelines for the establishment and development of multilingual thesauri (1980) rev edn, Unesco.

UNISIST guidelines for the establishment and development of monolingual thesauri (1981), 2nd edn, Unesco.

Vickery, B and Vickery, A (1987) *Information science in theory and practice*, Butterworth.

Walker, G and Janes, J (1993) *Online retrieval: a dialogue of theory and practice*, Libraries Unlimited.

Walton, G and Edwards, C (1997) Strategic management of the electronic library in the UK higher education sector: implications of elib's IMPEL2 project at the University of Northumbria at Newcastle. In Raitt, D (ed) *Libraries for the new millennium: implications for managers*, Library Association Publishing, 169–98.

Waters, D J (1998) What are digital libraries?, *CLIR Issues*, 4, July/August, available at
http://www.clir.org/pubs/issues/issues04.html#dlf [visited 3.12.99].

Webber, S (1995) Online pricing: charging strategies in a changing world. In Raitt, D and Jeaps, B (eds) *Online Information 95: proceedings of the 19th International Online Information Meeting*, Learned Information Europe Ltd, 1–12.

Webber, S (1998) Pricing and marketing online information services, *Annual Review of Information Science and Technology*, **33**, 39–83.

Williams, M E (1998) The state of databases today: 1998. In Braun, E E (ed) *Gale directory of databases*, Vol 1, Online databases; Vol 2, CD-ROM, diskette, magnetic tape, handheld, and batch access databases products, Gale, xvii–xxix.

Williams, M E and Burgard, D E (1999) New database products: social science and humanities, news and general (issue14), *Online and CD-ROM Review*, **23** (5), 271–82.

Williams, M E and Gaylord, H A (1999) New database products: business and law (issue 14), *Online & CD-ROM Review*, **23** (6), 331–41.

Williams, M E and Smith, L C (1999) New database products: science, technology and medicine (issue 14), *Online & CD-ROM Review*, **23** (4), 215–24.

World of Learning (1947), Allen & Unwin, 1947–. Annual.

Wynar, B (1998) *American reference books annual*, Libraries Unlimited.

Index

Introduction to Modern Information Retrieval

G G CHOWDHURY

'a useful all-in-one overview of the various aspects of modern information retrieval.' LASIE

This text is one of the first to blend together traditional and new theory, techniques and tools to give the student of information studies a comprehensive view of information retrieval. Areas covered include:

- classification, cataloguing, subject indexing, abstracting and vocabulary control
- CD-ROM and online information retrieval, multimedia, hypertext and hypermedia
- expert systems and natural language processing techniques
- knowledge-based natural language text processing and user interface systems
- information retrieval in the context of the Internet, the world wide web and the digital library environment.

1999; 480pp; paperback; 1-85604-318-5; £39.95

A Guide to Finding Quality Information on the Internet
Selection and evaluation strategies
2nd edition

ALISON COOKE

About the first edition:
'Cooke has produced a valuable work which . . . gives plentiful advice for those undertaking literature searches or using the Internet as an information resource.'
Internet Resources Newsletter
'this book adds a lot of value by bringing together valuable insights, examples and checklists in a highly accessible format'
UKOLUG Newsletter

This book addresses the growing problem of how to sort the quality sites from the mass of junk available. Uniquely, it suggests a system of criteria and guidelines, developed through empirical research, for selecting and evaluating high-quality information resources. It also advises on devising checklists and rating schemes for numerically evaluating the quality of information.

This edition updates the user on the latest developments in Internet-based search tools for locating quality information including:

- search engines
- subject catalogues and directories
- rating and reviewing services
- subject-based gateway services
- virtual libraries.

Information and guidance about the new Resource Discovery Network, the potential role and usefulness of metadata in locating quality information, and using web 'citations' for retrieving quality material have also been added to this edition. Step-by-step examples have been included on how to evaluate particular types of resources available via the Internet.

2001; c176pp; paperback; 1-85604-379-7; c.£29.95

The Online Searcher's Companion

WILLIAM H FORRESTER AND JANE L ROWLANDS

'I would recommend this book as a tool with which to start the learning process.'
Online Information Review

This book is the first interactive learning text on the basics of online searching. Illustrated throughout with examples and exercises, it assumes no knowledge on the part of the reader and gives hands-on advice on the basics of online searching. Contents include:

- history of online searching
- how to physically access online hosts
- the pre-search process
- basic search techniques
- advanced search techniques
- full text searching
- basic Internet searching
- recall versus precision (quantity versus quality).

2000; 160pp; paperback; 1-85604-293-6; £19.95

The Student's Guide to the Internet
2000–2001 edition

IAN WINSHIP AND ALISON McNAB

'this book deserves to be the standard UK text . . . it is inexpensive, portable, relevant and usable.'

Managing Information

'The Student's Guide to the Internet sets out to describe every inch of cyberspace, and manages to do so in terrifying detail.'

The Guardian

'gets the balance just right . . . [and] works well as a springboard into the world of the Internet.'

Cultivate Interactive

For this revised edition URLs have been reviewed and updated. Many of the resources listed are new, and more sources are listed to help you with multimedia, student sites and searching the Internet. Topics include:

- electronic mail, discussion lists and newsgroups
- essential network etiquette
- techniques for browsing the WWW
- electronic journals and bibliographic databases
- help with overseas study, loans, jobs, counselling and support
- subject searching: resource guides and gateways
- what's new – keeping up with new resources
- producing your own web pages.

2000; 188pp; paperback; 1-85604-381-9; £8.50